Insolvency Practitioners' Handbook

Edition 5
England & Wales and Scotland
2017

Copyright Notice & Liability Disclaimer

INTRODUCTION

Welcome to the 2017 and 5th Edition of the IPA's Insolvency Practitioners Handbook.

The IPA started its life as a group of insolvency specialists back in 1961. The practitioners who came together then to form the origins of the Association shared a desire to see the profession recognised in its own right, and a common will to support each other. The IPA handbook continues that tradition, by bringing together in one useful volume most of the key guidance and codes that practitioners (and those studying for insolvency exams) need to have at their fingertips. We recognise that, increasingly, our members assist business and individuals across the UK. Therefore, for the first time in this edition, we are publishing a single edition to cover both England & Wales and Scotland.

We have a particular interest in supporting our students, who are of course potential future members of the Association. Our Certificates of Proficiency in Insolvency (CPI), Personal Insolvency (CPPI) and now Corporate Insolvency (CPCI) represent an enhanced suite of intermediate examinations, supported by training. The vast majority of those who sat one of these exams say it helped them in their careers, and feedback from members tells us that 99% of employers who funded a candidate considered it a worthwhile investment. The IPA can be rightly proud of its record of encouraging and supporting those who represent the future of the profession.

As well as being an examiner and membership body for those involved in insolvency and related professional activities, the IPA is of course a Recognised Professional Body (RPB) for the purposes of authorising IPs to act as such under the Insolvency Act 1986. As the only RPB solely involved in insolvency, we have been at the forefront in:

- creating insolvency qualifications;
- developing professional guidance;
- encouraging high standards in practice;
- widening access to insolvency knowledge;
- extending the regulatory reach into related activities; and
- leading debates on current issues such as regulation.

From 2017, our regulatory activities will cover ACCA-licensed IPs, and we welcome those practitioners to the IPA's 'better regulation' approach.

Maureen Leslie FIPA
IPA President 2016/17

CONTENTS

CONTENTS

IPA Events Calendar 2017

25 January	Evening	Annual Lecture	London
27 February	Afternoon	Insolvency Rules: Headline Issues for IPs	London
28 February	All Day	Insolvency Rules: Intensive Training Day	London
03 March	Afternoon	Insolvency Rules: Headline Issues for IPs	London
06 March	Afternoon	Insolvency Rules: Headline Issues for IPs	Manchester
07 March	All Day	Insolvency Rules: Intensive Training Day	Manchester
08 March	Morning	Insolvency Rules: Headline Issues for IPs	Manchester
13 March	Morning	Insolvency Rules: Headline Issues for IPs	London
13 March	Afternoon	Insolvency Rules: Headline Issues for IPs	London
15 March	Afternoon	Insolvency Rules: Headline Issues for IPs	Birmingham
16 March	All Day	Insolvency Rules: Intensive Training Day	Birmingham
22 March	All Day	Insolvency Rules: Intensive Training Day	London
23 March	Afternoon	Insolvency Rules: Headline Issues for IPs	Leeds
30 March	All Day	Annual Conference	London
25 September	Afternoon	Regional Roadshow	Edinburgh
28 September	Evening	Annual Dinner	London
02 October	Afternoon	Regional Roadshow	Bristol
03 October	Afternoon	Regional Roadshow	Birmingham
16 October	Afternoon	Regional Roadshow	Leeds
17 October	Afternoon	Regional Roadshow	Manchester
02 November	Afternoon	Regional Roadshow	London
30 November	All Day	Personal Insolvency Conference	Manchester

All dates are provisional as at the date of publication and may be subject to alternation.

Visit www.insolvency-practitioner.org,uk/events for further information and to book.

Section 1

The Ethics Code

SECTION 1 — THE ETHICS CODE

CONTENTS

1.1 INSOLVENCY CODE OF ETHICS BACKGROUND AND OVERVIEW

A. INTRODUCTION

1.   This document relates to the Insolvency Code of Ethics ("the Code"). This document has been prepared in order to assist the reader in understanding the Code and the background to it. This document is to be read in conjunction with the Code. This document does not form part of the Code. Its contents are not to be used for any interpretative purposes including during disciplinary proceedings. Neither are the contents of this document intended to be a comprehensive description of the Code. Accordingly where a section or part of the Code does not seem to require any comment, none is given.

B. BACKGROUND

2.   For some years the bodies recognised under the relevant legislation in England and Wales, Scotland and Ireland to grant licences to *insolvency practitioners* ("the RPBs") have agreed upon and produced a joint ethical code for *insolvency practitioners*, the most recent version being that adopted in January 2004 ("the Insolvency Ethical Guide"). In 2006, the professional accounting bodies in England and Wales, Scotland and Ireland altered their principal codes of ethics to align them to a model adopted by the International Federation of Accounting Bodies ("the IFAC Code"). It was subsequently agreed that the Insolvency Ethical Guide should be reviewed and redrafted to align it more closely to the IFAC Code.

3.   A draft of the Code was produced by the Joint Insolvency Committee[1] ("the JIC") in March 2007 for public consultation. The consultation period ended on 2 July 2007. Thereafter the JIC had regular meetings to discuss the responses to the consultation and produced a substantially revised draft of the Code.

4.   The revised version of the Code has now been adopted by each of the RPBs. Accordingly, all *insolvency practitioners* will continue to follow a standardised Code, regardless of their authorising body. It is recognised,

---

[1]   The JIC was formed in 1999 and aims to facilitate discussion between the RPBs in order to ensure that, as far as possible, there is a consistency of approach between them. Each of the RPBs is represented on the JIC.

however, that some of the RPBs may wish to adopt the Code with minor modifications in order that it is integrated with any additional guidance provided them.

5.   The Code is presented as a new document because the extent of the changes makes it impractical to issue a version highlighting the changes made to the earlier Insolvency Ethical Guide. However, it is not considered that the application of the Code in *practice* will be substantially different from the application of the Insolvency Ethical Guide.

C. OVERVIEW

Introduction

6.   The Code is intended to assist *insolvency practitioners* meet the obligations expected of them by providing professional and ethical guidance. The purpose of the Code is to provide a high standard of professional and ethical guidance amongst *insolvency practitioners*.

7.   Paragraphs 1 to 3 of the Code outline the purpose of the Code and its scope. The Code is to be applied to all professional work relating to an *insolvency appointment* including any professional work that may lead to such an appointment. An *Insolvency Practitioner* should ensure that the principles outlined in the Code are applied not only by himself but all members of the insolvency team.

8.   Paragraph 3 requires that *insolvency practitioners* should be guided not merely by the terms but also by the spirit of the Code. In this regard, it is important to note that the examples set out in the Code are intended to be illustrative only. It is impossible to define every situation to which the principles set out in the Code will be relevant.

Fundamental principles

9.   The earlier Insolvency Ethical Guide provided *insolvency practitioners* with five fundamental principles to which they must adhere, together with a list of common situations which *insolvency practitioners* may face.

10.   The Code also includes five fundamental principles which have been revised from the Insolvency Ethical Guide. Each of the fundamental principles set out in the Code is based upon and follows closely the fundamental principles contained in the IFAC Code.

November 2008

11. The JIC does not consider that the application of the fundamental principles of integrity, objectivity, professional competence and due care and professional behaviour will be materially different from the application of the fundamental principles contained in Insolvency Ethical Guide.

12. The fundamental principle of confidentiality did not appear in the Insolvency Ethical Guide. Some concern was expressed during the consultation period that the inclusion of this fundamental principle may be inconsistent with an *Insolvency Practitioner's* duty or obligation, in certain circumstances, to disclose confidential information. The JIC does not consider this to be the case. As drafted, the fundamental principle of confidentiality makes it clear that where an *Insolvency Practitioner* has a legal or professional right or duty to disclose he may do so.

13. Following comments received during the consultation period amendments were made to the drafting of the fundamental principle of professional behaviour. This principle now contains an additional requirement not explicitly set out in the IFAC Code that *insolvency practitioners* conduct themselves with courtesy and consideration towards all whom they come into contact with when performing their work. This requirement was contained in the Insolvency Ethical Guide. Following the comments received during the consultation period, it was considered important that this requirement remained explicitly set out in the description of the fundamental principle of professional behaviour.

Framework approach

14. The Code sets out a framework that *insolvency practitioners* can use to identify actual or potential threats to the fundamental principles and determine what safeguards, if any, may be available to meet such threats.

15. The framework approach requires *insolvency practitioners* to identify, evaluate and respond in an appropriate manner to any threats to compliance with the fundamental principles.

16. The Code also provides detail concerning the threats that *insolvency practitioners* may face in the conduct of their work. The earlier Insolvency Ethical Guide identified and discussed two main types of threat: self interest and self review. The Code also identifies and discusses advocacy, familiarity and intimidation threats.

17. Information is also included on potential safeguards. In particular examples are given of safeguards that may be introduced into the *practice* to create a work environment in which threats are identified and the introduction of appropriate safeguards is encouraged.

Insolvency appointments

18. Paragraphs 20 to 30 of the Code consider the particular application of the framework approach in relation to the decision by an *Insolvency Practitioner* to accept an *insolvency appointment*.

19. This part of the Code describes some of the safeguards that *insolvency practitioners* will need to consider implementing prior to accepting an appointment where there is a threat to the fundamental principles. The examples are not intended to be exhaustive. Neither will the examples given be applicable to all situations. As paragraph 28 makes clear, an *Insolvency Practitioner* may encounter situations where no safeguards can reduce a threat to an acceptable level. In such circumstances, an *Insolvency Practitioner* should conclude that it is not appropriate to accept an *insolvency appointment*.

20. Paragraphs 31 and 32 of the Code require an *Insolvency Practitioner* to take reasonable steps to identify any circumstances that pose a conflict of interest and give some examples of the types of situation in which such a conflict could arise.

21. Paragraphs 33 and 34 of the Code discuss some of the particular issues that can arise where two or more *practices* merge.

22. Paragraphs 37 to 39 of the Code expand upon the fundamental principle of professional competence and due care. An *Insolvency Practitioner* should only accept an *insolvency appointment* when the *Insolvency Practitioner* has sufficient expertise. This part of the Code also stresses the importance of maintaining professional competence by a continuing awareness of relevant technical and professional developments.

Professional and personal relationship

23. Paragraphs 40 to 48 of the Code discuss some of the particular threats to the fundamental principle of objectivity that can arise from certain professional and personal relationships.

24. This section requires an *Insolvency Practitioner* to identify any threats to the principle of objectivity that may arise from a professional and personal relationship, to evaluate the significance of the threat in relation to the conduct of the *insolvency appointment* being considered and consider whether any safeguards will be appropriate to reduce the threat to an acceptable level.

25. Where there are no or no reasonable safeguards that can be introduced to eliminate a threat arising from a professional or personal relationship, or to reduce it to an acceptable level the relationship in question will constitute a "significant professional relationship" or a "significant personal relationship". Where this is case the *Insolvency Practitioner* should conclude that it is not appropriate to take the *insolvency appointment*.

26. Some concern was expressed during the consultation period as to the use of the term "significant professional relationship". The term "material professional relationship" was used in the Insolvency Ethical November 2008 Guide. The JIC does not consider that there is any substantial difference between the two terms.

27. Some concern was also expressed during the consultation period that the requirement for safeguards to be adopted to identify relationships between *individuals* within the *practice* and third parties that may gives rise to a threat to the fundamental principles would be impractical in the case of large *practices*. Paragraph 43 now makes it clear that only such safeguards that are proportionate and reasonable in relation to the *insolvency appointment* being considered are necessary.

Paragraphs 49 to 73 of the Code

28. Paragraphs 49 to 73 of the Code discuss a number of areas in which an *Insolvency Practitioner* will commonly encounter threats to the fundamental principles. Each section gives some examples of the types of safeguard that may be available to reduce the particular threats to an acceptable level.

29. Paragraphs 49 to 52 of the Code discuss some of the particular threats that may arise where an *Insolvency Practitioner* realises assets. This section stresses the importance for an *Insolvency Practitioner* to take care

to ensure (where to do so does not conflict with any legal or professional obligation) that his decision making processes are transparent, understandable and readily identifiable to all third parties who may be affected by any sale or proposed sale.

30. Paragraphs 53 to 56 of the Code describe some of the threats to the fundamental principles that can arise when an *Insolvency Practitioner* intends to seek specialist advice and services. Such threats can arise where the *Insolvency Practitioner* obtains services from a regular source or where services are provided from within the *practice* or by a party with whom the *practice* or an *individual within the practice* has a business or personal relationship. This section describes some of the safeguards that may be available to reduce these threats to an acceptable level.

31. Paragraphs 57 to 62 of the Code concern the acceptance of fees and other types of remuneration (including referral fees and commissions) both prior to and after accepting an *insolvency appointment*.

32. Paragraph 63 of the Code prohibits the payment or offer of any commission for or the furnishing of any valuable consideration towards, the introduction of *insolvency appointments*. Paragraphs 64 to 69 discuss some of the particular threats that can arise where an *Insolvency Practitioner* seeks an appointment or work that may lead to an appointment through advertising or other forms of marketing. Paragraphs 70 to 73 concern the offer and acceptance of gifts and hospitality.

Record keeping

33. Paragraphs 74 to 75 of the Code stress the importance of record keeping in relation to the work carried out by an *Insolvency Practitioner*.

The application of the framework to specific circumstances

34. Paragraphs 76 to 88 of the Code contain specific circumstances and relationships that will create threats to the fundamental principles. The examples describe the threats and the safeguards that may in some circumstances be appropriate to eliminate the threats or reduce them to an acceptable level in each case. In other circumstances, the examples contain a complete prohibition on the acceptance of an *insolvency*

appointment. The examples are divided into three parts: examples which do not relate to a previous or existing *insolvency appointment*; examples that do relate to a previous or existing *insolvency appointment*; and some examples under Scots law.

1.2 ETHICS CODE FOR MEMBERS

1. As a professional membership body promoting high standards of practice in relation to work undertaken by its members, the Insolvency Practitioners Association ("IPA") requires its members to adhere to certain principles in all aspects of their professional work.

2. Furthermore, one of the bases for recognition (by the Secretary of State for Business, Innovation and Skills) of the IPA as a body entitled to authorise its members to act as insolvency practitioners, is that the IPA:

   • will arrange for appropriate ethical guidance to be made available to its members;

   • will ensure through its ethical code or guide that its members, when accepting appointments as office holders, are and are seen to be independent from influences which could affect their objectivity; and

   • will firmly but fairly apply its relevant professional and ethical codes or guides in relation to the activities of its members.

3. The Code of Ethics set out below ("the Code") was produced by the Joint Insolvency Committee and has been adopted in substantially similar terms by all of the bodies recognised under the relevant legislation in England and Wales, Scotland and Ireland to grant licences to insolvency practitioners. The Code is stated to apply to all Insolvency Practitioners. However, all members are required to adhere to the Code and in particular the spirit of the Code (with such modifications as are appropriate in all the circumstances) in all their professional and business activities and in other circumstances where to fail to do so might bring discredit upon themselves or the IPA.

4. The Code will replace all previous Codes of Ethics issued by the Council. For the purposes of Article 66 of the Articles of Association of the IPA misconduct shall include any breach by a member of the Code.

INSOLVENCY CODE OF ETHICS

LIST OF CONTENTS

Definitions

Authorising body	A body declared to be a recognised professional body or a competent authority under any legislation governing the administration of insolvency in the United Kingdom.
Close or immediate family	A spouse (or equivalent), dependant, parent, child or sibling.
Entity	Any natural or legal person or any group of such persons, including a partnership.
He/she	In this Code, he is to be read as including she.
Individual within the practice	The *Insolvency Practitioner*, any principals in the *practice* and any employees within the *practice*.
Insolvency appointment	A formal appointment:

(a) which, under the terms of legislation must be undertaken by an *Insolvency Practitioner*; or

(b) as a nominee or supervisor of a voluntary arrangement.

Insolvency Practitioner	An individual who is authorised or recognised to act as an *Insolvency Practitioner* in the United Kingdom by an *authorising body*. For the purpose of the application of this Code only, the term *Insolvency Practitioner* also includes an individual who acts as a nominee or supervisor of a voluntary arrangement.
Insolvency team	Any person under the control or direction of an *Insolvency Practitioner*.
Practice	The organisation in which the *Insolvency Practitioner* practises.
Principal	In respect of a *practice*:

(a) which is a company: a director;

(b) which is a partnership: a partner;

(c) which is a limited liability partnership: a member;

(d) which is comprised of a sole practitioner: that person;

Alternatively any person within the *practice* who is held out as being a director, partner or member.

GENERAL APPLICATION OF THE CODE

Introduction

1. This Code is intended to assist *Insolvency Practitioners* meet the obligations expected of them by providing professional and ethical guidance.

2. This Code applies to all *Insolvency Practitioners*. *Insolvency Practitioners* should take steps to ensure that the Code is applied in all professional work relating to an *insolvency appointment*, and to any professional work that may lead to such an *insolvency appointment*. Although, an *insolvency appointment* will be of the *Insolvency Practitioner* personally rather than his *practice* he should ensure that the standards set out in this Code are applied to all members of the *insolvency team*.

3. It is this Code, and the spirit that underlies it, that governs the conduct of *Insolvency Practitioners*.

Fundamental principles

4. An *Insolvency Practitioner* is required to comply with the following fundamental principles:

    #### (a) Integrity

    An *Insolvency Practitioner* should be straightforward and honest in all professional and business relationships.

    #### (b) Objectivity

    An *Insolvency Practitioner* should not allow bias, conflict of interest or undue influence of others to override professional or business judgements.

    #### (c) Professional competence and due care

    An *Insolvency Practitioner* has a continuing duty to maintain professional knowledge and skill at the level required to ensure that a client or employer receives competent professional service based on current developments in practice, legislation and techniques. An *Insolvency Practitioner* should act diligently and in accordance with applicable technical and professional standards when providing professional services.

(d) Confidentiality

An *Insolvency Practitioner* should respect the confidentiality of information acquired as a result of professional and business relationships and should not disclose any such information to third parties without proper and specific authority unless there is a legal or professional right or duty to disclose. Confidential information acquired as a result of professional and business relationships should not be used for the personal advantage of the *Insolvency Practitioner* or third parties.

(e) Professional behaviour

An *Insolvency Practitioner* should comply with relevant laws and regulations and should avoid any action that discredits the profession. *Insolvency Practitioners* should conduct themselves with courtesy and consideration towards all with whom they come into contact when performing their work.

Framework approach

5. The framework approach is a method which *Insolvency Practitioners* can use to identify actual or potential threats to the fundamental principles and determine whether there are any safeguards that might be available to offset them. The framework approach requires an *Insolvency Practitioner* to:

    (a) take reasonable steps to identify any threats to compliance with the fundamental principles;

    (b) evaluate any such threats; and

    (c) respond in an appropriate manner to those threats.

6. Throughout this Code there are examples of threats and possible safeguards. These examples are illustrative and should not be considered as exhaustive lists of all relevant threats or safeguards. It is impossible to define every situation that creates a threat to compliance with the fundamental principles or to specify the safeguards that may be available.

Identification of threats to the fundamental principles

7. An *Insolvency Practitioner* should take reasonable steps to identify the existence of any threats to compliance with the fundamental principles which arise during the course of his professional work.

8.   An *Insolvency Practitioner* should take particular care to identify the existence of threats which exist prior to or at the time of taking an *insolvency appointment* or which, at that stage, it may reasonably be expected might arise during the course of such an *insolvency appointment*. Paragraphs 20 to 48 below contain particular factors an *Insolvency Practitioner* should take into account when deciding whether to accept an *insolvency appointment*.

9.   In identifying the existence of any threats, an *Insolvency Practitioner* should have regard to relationships whereby the *practice* is held out as being part of a national or an international association.

10.   Many threats fall into one or more of five categories:

   (a) **Self-interest threats**: which may occur as a result of the financial or other interests of a *practice* or an *Insolvency Practitioner* or of a *close or immediate family* member of an *individual within the practice*;

   (b) **Self-review threats**: which may occur when a previous judgement made by an *individual within the practice* needs to be re-evaluated by the *Insolvency Practitioner*;

   (c) **Advocacy threats**: which may occur when an *individual within the practice* promotes a position or opinion to the point that subsequent objectivity may be compromised;

   (d) **Familiarity threats**: which may occur when, because of a close relationship, an *individual within the practice* becomes too sympathetic or antagonistic to the interests of others; and

   (e) **Intimidation threats**: which may occur when an *Insolvency Practitioner* may be deterred from acting objectively by threats, actual or perceived.

11.   The following paragraphs give examples of the possible threats that an *Insolvency Practitioner* may face.

12.   Examples of circumstances that may create self-interest threats for an *Insolvency Practitioner* include:

   (a) An *individual within the practice* having an interest in a creditor or potential creditor with a claim which requires subjective adjudication.

   (b) Concern about the possibility of damaging a business relationship.

(c) Concerns about potential future employment.

13. Examples of circumstances that may create self-review threats include:

(a) The acceptance of an *insolvency appointment* in respect of an *entity* where an *individual within the practice* has recently been employed by or seconded to that *entity*.

(b) An *Insolvency Practitioner* or the *practice* has carried out professional work of any description, including sequential *insolvency appointments*, for that *entity*.

Such self-review threats may diminish over the passage of time.

14. Examples of circumstances that may create advocacy threats include:

(a) Acting in an advisory capacity for a creditor of an *entity*.

(b) Acting as an advocate for a client in litigation or dispute with an *entity*.

15. Examples of circumstances that may create familiarity threats include:

(a) An *individual within the practice* having a close relationship with any individual having a financial interest in the insolvent *entity*.

(b) An *individual within the practice* having a close relationship with a potential purchaser of an insolvent's assets and/or business.

In this regard a close relationship includes both a close professional relationship and a close personal relationship.

16. Examples of circumstances that may create intimidation threats include:

(a) The threat of dismissal or replacement being used to:

(i) Apply pressure not to follow regulations, this Code, any other applicable code, technical or professional standards.

(ii) Exert influence over an *insolvency appointment* where the *Insolvency Practitioner* is an employee rather than a *principal* of the *practice*.

(b) Being threatened with litigation.

(c) The threat of a complaint being made to the *Insolvency Practitioner's authorising body*.

Evaluation of threats

17.   An *Insolvency Practitioner* should take reasonable steps to evaluate any threats to compliance with the fundamental principles that he has identified.

18.   In particular, an *Insolvency Practitioner* should consider what a reasonable and informed third party, having knowledge of all relevant information, including the significance of the threat, would conclude to be acceptable.

Possible safeguards

19.   Having identified and evaluated a threat to the fundamental principles an *Insolvency Practitioner* should consider whether there any safeguards that may be available to reduce the threat to an acceptable level. The relevant safeguards will vary depending on the circumstances. Generally safeguards fall into two broad categories. Firstly, safeguards created by the profession, legislation or regulation. Secondly, safeguards in the work environment. In the insolvency context safeguards in the work environment can include safeguards specific to an *insolvency appointment*. These are considered in paragraphs 20 to 39 below. In addition, safeguards can be introduced across the *practice*. These safeguards seek to create a work environment in which threats are identified and the introduction of appropriate safeguards is encouraged. Some examples include:

(a)   Leadership that stresses the importance of compliance with the fundamental principles.

(b)   Policies and procedures to implement and monitor quality control of engagements.

(c)   Documented policies regarding the identification of threats to compliance with the fundamental principles, the evaluation of the significance of these threats and the identification and the application of safeguards to eliminate or reduce the threats, other than those that are trivial, to an acceptable level.

(d)   Documented internal policies and procedures requiring compliance with the fundamental principles.

(e)   Policies and procedures to consider the fundamental principles of this Code before the acceptance of an *insolvency appointment*.

(f) Policies and procedures regarding the identification of interests or relationships between *individuals within the practice* and third parties.

(g) Policies and procedures to prohibit individuals who are not members of the *insolvency team* from inappropriately influencing the outcome of an *insolvency appointment*.

(h) Timely communication of a *practice's* policies and procedures, including any changes to them, to all *individuals within the practice*, and appropriate training and education on such policies and procedures.

(i) Designating a member of senior management to be responsible for overseeing the adequate functioning of the safeguarding system.

(j) A disciplinary mechanism to promote compliance with policies and procedures.

(k) Published policies and procedures to encourage and empower individuals within the *practice* to communicate to senior levels within the *practice* and/or the *Insolvency Practitioner* any issue relating to compliance with the fundamental principles that concerns them.

SPECIFIC APPLICATION OF THE CODE

Insolvency appointments

20. The practice of insolvency is principally governed by statute and secondary legislation and in many cases is subject ultimately to the control of the Court. Where circumstances are dealt with by statute or secondary legislation, an *Insolvency Practitioner* must comply with such provisions. An *Insolvency Practitioner* must also comply with any relevant judicial authority relating to his conduct and any directions given by the Court.

21. An *Insolvency Practitioner* should act in a manner appropriate to his position as an officer of the Court (where applicable) and in accordance with any quasi-judicial, fiduciary or other duties that he may be under.

22. Before agreeing to accept any *insolvency appointment* (including a joint appointment), an *Insolvency Practitioner* should consider whether acceptance would create any threats to compliance with the fundamental principles. Of particular importance will be any threats to the fundamental principle of objectivity created by conflicts of interest or by any significant professional or personal relationships. These are considered in more detail below.

23. In considering whether objectivity or integrity may be threatened, an *Insolvency Practitioner* should identify and evaluate any professional or personal relationship (see paragraphs 40 to 48 below) which may affect compliance with the fundamental principles. The appropriate response to the threats arising from any such relationships should then be considered, together with the introduction of any possible safeguards.

24. Generally, it will be inappropriate for an *Insolvency Practitioner* to accept an *insolvency appointment* where a threat to the fundamental principles exists or may reasonably be expected might arise during the course of the *insolvency appointment* unless:

    (a) disclosure is made, prior to the *insolvency appointment*, of the existence of such a threat to the Court or to the creditors on whose behalf the *Insolvency Practitioner* would be appointed to act and no objection is made to the *Insolvency Practitioner* being appointed; and

    (b) safeguards are or will be available to eliminate or reduce that threat to an acceptable level. If the threat is other than trivial, safeguards should be considered and applied as necessary to reduce them to an acceptable level, where possible.

25. The following safeguards may be considered:

    (a) Involving and/or consulting another *Insolvency Practitioner* from within the *practice* to review the work done.

    (b) Consulting an independent third party, such as a committee of creditors, an *authorising body* or another *Insolvency Practitioner*.

    (c) Involving another *Insolvency Practitioner* to perform part of the work, which may include another *Insolvency Practitioner* taking a joint appointment where the conflict arises during the course of the *insolvency appointment.*

    (d) Obtaining legal advice from a solicitor or barrister with appropriate experience and expertise.

    (e) Changing the members of the *insolvency team.*

    (f) The use of separate *Insolvency Practitioners* and/or staff.

    (g) Procedures to prevent access to information by the use of information barriers (e.g. strict physical separation of such teams, confidential and secure data filing).

(h) Clear guidelines for *individuals within the practice* on issues of security and confidentiality.

(i) The use of confidentiality agreements signed by *individuals within the practice*.

(j) Regular review of the application of safeguards by a senior *individual within the practice* not involved with the *insolvency appointment*.

(k) Terminating the financial or business relationship that gives rise to the threat.

(l) Seeking directions from the court.

26. As regards joint appointments, where an *Insolvency Practitioner* is specifically precluded by this Code from accepting an *insolvency appointment* as an individual, a joint appointment will not be an appropriate safeguard and will not make accepting the *insolvency appointment* appropriate.

27. In deciding whether to take an *insolvency appointment* in circumstances where a threat to the fundamental principles has been identified, the *Insolvency Practitioner* should consider whether the interests of those on whose behalf he would be appointed to act would best be served by the appointment of another *Insolvency Practitioner* who did not face the same threat and, if so, whether any such appropriately qualified and experienced other *Insolvency Practitioner* is likely to be available to be appointed.

28. *An Insolvency Practitioner* will encounter situations where no safeguards can reduce a threat to an acceptable level. Where this is the case, an *Insolvency Practitioner* should conclude that it is not appropriate to accept an *insolvency appointment*.

29. Following acceptance, any threats should continue to be kept under appropriate review and an *Insolvency Practitioner* should be mindful that other threats may come to light or arise. There may be occasions when the *Insolvency Practitioner* is no longer in compliance with this Code because of changed circumstances or something which has been inadvertently overlooked. This would generally not be an issue provided the *Insolvency Practitioner* has appropriate quality control policies and procedures in place to deal with such matters and, once discovered, the matter is corrected promptly and any necessary safeguards are applied. In deciding

whether to continue an *insolvency appointment* the *Insolvency Practitioner* may take into account the wishes of the creditors, who after full disclosure has been made have the right to retain or replace the *Insolvency Practitioner*.

30. In all cases an *Insolvency Practitioner* will need to exercise his judgment to determine how best to deal with an identified threat. In exercising his judgment, an *Insolvency Practitioner* should consider what a reasonable and informed third party, having knowledge of all relevant information, including the significance of the threat and the safeguards applied, would conclude to be acceptable. This consideration will be affected by matters such as the significance of the threat, the nature of the work and the structure of the *practice*.

Conflicts of interest

31. An *Insolvency Practitioner* should take reasonable steps to identify circumstances that could pose a conflict of interest. Such circumstances may give rise to threats to compliance with the fundamental principles. Examples of where a conflict of interest may arise are where:

    (a) An *Insolvency Practitioner* has to deal with claims between the separate and conflicting interests of entities over whom he is appointed.

    (b) There are a succession of or sequential *insolvency appointments* (see paragraphs 76 to 88 below).

    (c) A significant relationship has existed with the *entity* or someone connected with the *entity* (see paragraphs 40 to 48 below)

32. Some of the safeguards listed at paragraph 25 may be applied to reduce the threats created by a conflict of interest to an acceptable level. Where a conflict of interest arises, the preservation of confidentiality will be of paramount importance; therefore, the safeguards used should generally include the use of effective information barriers.

Practice mergers

33. Where *practices* merge, they should subsequently be treated as one for the purposes of assessing threats to the fundamental principles. At the time of the merger, existing *insolvency appointments* should be reviewed and any threats identified. *Principals* and employees of the merged *practice*

become subject to common ethical constraints in relation to accepting new *insolvency appointments* to clients of either of the former *practices*. However existing *insolvency appointments* which are rendered in apparent breach of the Code by such a merger need not be determined automatically, provided that a considered review of the situation by the *practice* discloses no obvious and immediate ethical conflict.

34. Where an *individual within the practice* has, in any former *practice*, undertaken work upon the affairs of an *entity* in a capacity that is incompatible with an *insolvency appointment* of the new *practice*, the individual should not work or be employed on that assignment.

Transparency

35. Both before and during an *insolvency appointment* an *Insolvency Practitioner* may acquire personal information that is not directly relevant to the insolvency or confidential commercial information relating to the affairs of third parties. The information may be such that others might expect that confidentiality would be maintained.

36. Nevertheless an *Insolvency Practitioner* in the role as office holder has a professional duty to report openly to those with an interest in the outcome of the insolvency. An *Insolvency Practitioner* should always report on his acts and dealings as fully as possible given the circumstances of the case, in a way that is transparent and understandable. An *Insolvency Practitioner* should bear in mind the expectations of others and what a reasonable and informed third party would consider appropriate.

Professional competence and due care

37. Prior to accepting an *insolvency appointment* the *Insolvency Practitioner* should ensure that he is satisfied that the following matters have been considered:

   (a) Obtaining knowledge and understanding of the *entity*, its owners, managers and those responsible for its governance and business activities.

   (b) Acquiring an appropriate understanding of the nature of the *entity's* business, the complexity of its operations, the specific requirements of the engagement and the purpose, nature and scope of the work to be performed.

(c)   Acquiring knowledge of relevant industries or subject matters.

(d)   Possessing or obtaining experience with relevant regulatory or reporting requirements.

(e)   Assigning sufficient staff with the necessary competencies.

(f)   Using experts where necessary.

(g)   Complying with quality control policies and procedures designed to provide reasonable assurance that specific engagements are accepted only when they can be performed competently.

38.   The fundamental principle of professional competence and due care requires that an *Insolvency Practitioner* should only accept an *insolvency appointment* when the *Insolvency Practitioner* has sufficient expertise. For example, a self interest threat to the fundamental principle of professional competence and due care is created if the *Insolvency Practitioner* or the *insolvency team* does not possess or cannot acquire the competencies necessary to carry out the *insolvency appointment*. Expertise will include appropriate training, technical knowledge, knowledge of the *entity* and the business with which the *entity* is concerned.

39.   Maintaining and acquiring professional competence requires a continuing awareness and understanding of relevant technical and professional developments, including:

(a)   Developments in insolvency legislation.

(b)   Statements of Insolvency Practice.

(c)   The regulations of their *authorising body*, including any continuing professional development requirements.

(d)   Guidance issued by their *authorising body* or the Insolvency Service.

(e)   Technical issues being discussed within the profession.

Professional and personal relationships

40.   The environment in which *Insolvency Practitioners* work and the relationships formed in their professional and personal lives can lead to threats to the fundamental principle of objectivity.

Identifying relationships

41. In particular, the principle of objectivity may be threatened if any *individual within the practice*, the *close or immediate family* of an *individual within the practice* or the *practice* itself, has or has had a professional or personal relationship which relates to the *insolvency appointment* being considered.

42. Professional or personal relationships may include (but are not restricted to) relationships with:-

    (a) the *entity*;

    (b) any director or shadow director or former director or shadow director of the *entity*;

    (c) shareholders of the *entity*;

    (d) any *principal* or employee of the *entity*;

    (e) business partners of the *entity*;

    (f) companies or entities controlled by the *entity*;

    (g) companies which are under common control;

    (h) creditors (including debenture holders) of the *entity*;

    (i) debtors of the *entity*;

    (j) *close or immediate family* of *the entity* (if an individual) or its officers (if a corporate body);

    (k) others with commercial relationships with the *practice*

43. Safeguards within the *practice* should include policies and procedures to identify relationships between *individuals within the practice* and third parties in a way that is proportionate and reasonable in relation to the *insolvency appointment* being considered.

Is the relationship significant to the conduct of the insolvency appointment?

44. Where a professional or personal relationship of the type described in paragraph 41 has been identified the *Insolvency Practitioner* should evaluate the impact of the relationship in the context of the *insolvency appointment* being sought or considered. Issues to consider in evaluating whether a relationship creates a threat to the fundamental principles may include the following:

(a) The nature of the previous duties undertaken by a *practice* during an earlier relationship with the *entity*.

(b) The impact of the work conducted by the *practice* on the financial state and/or the financial stability of the *entity* in respect of which the *insolvency appointment* is being considered.

(c) Whether the fee received for the work by the *practice* is or was significant to the *practice* itself or is or was substantial.

(d) How recently any professional work was carried out. It is likely that greater threats will arise (or may be seen to arise) where work has been carried out within the previous three years. However, there may still be instances where, in respect of non-audit work, any threat is at an acceptable level. Conversely, there may be situations whereby the nature of the work carried out was such that a considerably longer period should elapse before any threat can be reduced to an acceptable level.

(e) Whether the *insolvency appointment* being considered involves consideration of any work previously undertaken by the *practice* for that *entity*.

(f) The nature of any personal relationship and the proximity of the *Insolvency Practitioner* to the individual with whom the relationship exists and, where appropriate, the proximity of that individual to the *entity* in relation to which the *insolvency appointment* relates.

(g) Whether any reporting obligations will arise in respect of the relevant individual with whom the relationship exists (e.g. an obligation to report on the conduct of directors and shadow directors of a company to which the *insolvency appointment* relates).

(h) The nature of any previous duties undertaken by an *individual within the practice* during any earlier relationship with the *entity*.

(i) The extent of the *insolvency team's* familiarity with the individuals connected with the *entity*.

45. Having identified and evaluated a relationship that may create a threat to the fundamental principles, the *Insolvency Practitioner* should consider his response including the introduction of any possible safeguards to reduce the threat to an acceptable level.

46. Some of the safeguards which may be considered to reduce the threat created by a professional or personal relationship to an acceptable level are considered in paragraph 25. Other safeguards may include:

    (a) Withdrawing from the *insolvency team*.

    (b) Terminating (where possible) the financial or business relationship giving rise to the threat.

    (c) Disclosure of the relationship and any financial benefit received by the *practice* (whether directly or indirectly) to the *entity* or to those on whose behalf the *Insolvency Practitioner* would be appointed to act.

47. An *Insolvency Practitioner* may encounter situations in which no or no reasonable safeguards can be introduced to eliminate a threat arising from a professional or personal relationship, or to reduce it to an acceptable level. In such situations, the relationship in question will constitute a **significant** professional relationship ("Significant Professional Relationship") or a **significant** personal relationship ("Significant Personal Relationship"). Where this is case the *Insolvency Practitioner* should conclude that it is not appropriate to take the *insolvency appointment*.

48. Consideration should always be given to the perception of others when deciding whether to accept an *insolvency appointment*. Whilst an *Insolvency Practitioner* may regard a relationship as not being significant to the *insolvency appointment*, the perception of others may differ and this may in some circumstances be sufficient to make the relationship significant.

Dealing with the assets of an entity

49. Actual or perceived threats (for example self interest threats) to the fundamental principles may arise when during an *insolvency appointment*, an *Insolvency Practitioner* realises assets.

50. Save in circumstances which clearly do not impair the *Insolvency Practitioner*'s objectivity, *Insolvency Practitioners* appointed to any *insolvency appointment* in relation to an *entity*, should not themselves acquire, directly or indirectly, any of the assets of an *entity*, nor knowingly permit *any individual within the practice*, or any *close or immediate family member* of the *Insolvency Practitioner* or of an *individual within the practice*, directly or indirectly, to do so.

51. Where the assets and business of an insolvent company are sold by an *Insolvency Practitioner* shortly after appointment on pre-agreed terms, this could lead to an actual or perceived threat to objectivity. The sale may also be seen as a threat to objectivity by creditors or others not involved in the prior agreement. The threat to objectivity may be eliminated or reduced to an acceptable level by safeguards such as obtaining an independent valuation of the assets or business being sold, or the consideration of other potential purchasers.

52. It is also particularly important for an *Insolvency Practitioner* to take care to ensure (where to do so does not conflict with any legal or professional obligation) that his decision making processes are transparent, understandable and readily identifiable to all third parties who may be affected by the sale or proposed sale.

Obtaining specialist advice and services

53. When an *Insolvency Practitioner* intends to rely on the advice or work of another, the *Insolvency Practitioner* should evaluate whether such reliance is warranted. The *Insolvency Practitioner* should consider factors such as reputation, expertise, resources available and applicable professional and ethical standards. Any payment to the third party should reflect the value of the work undertaken.

54. Threats to the fundamental principles (for example familiarity threats and self interest threats) can arise if services are provided by a regular source independent of the *practice*.

55. Safeguards should be introduced to reduce such threats to an acceptable level. These safeguards should ensure that a proper business relationship is maintained between the parties and that such relationships are reviewed periodically to ensure that best value and service is being obtained in relation to each *insolvency appointment*. Additional safeguards may include clear guidelines and policies within the *practice* on such relationships. An *Insolvency Practitioner* should also consider disclosure of the existence of such business relationships to the general body of creditors or the creditor's committee if one exists.

56. Threats to the fundamental principles can also arise where services are provided from within the practice or by a party with whom the practice, or an individual within the practice, has a business or personal relationship. An Insolvency Practitioner should take particular care in such circumstances to ensure that the best value and service is being provided.

Fees and other types of remuneration

Prior to accepting an *insolvency appointment*

57. Where an engagement may lead to an *insolvency appointment*, an *Insolvency Practitioner* should make any party to the work aware of the terms of the work and, in particular, the basis on which any fees are charged and which services are covered by those fees.

58. Where an engagement may lead to an *insolvency appointment*, *Insolvency Practitioners* should not accept referral fees or commissions unless they have established safeguards to reduce the threats created by such fees or commissions to an acceptable level.

59. Safeguards may include disclosure in advance of any arrangements. If after receiving any such payments, an *Insolvency Practitioner* accepts an *insolvency appointment*, the amount and source of any fees or commissions received should be disclosed to creditors.

After accepting an *insolvency appointment*

60. During an *insolvency appointment*, accepting referral fees or commissions represents a significant threat to objectivity. Such fees or commissions should not therefore be accepted other than where to do so is for the benefit of the insolvent estate.

61. If such fees or commissions are accepted they should only be accepted for the benefit of the estate; not for the benefit of the *Insolvency Practitioner* or the *practice*.

62. Further, where such fees or commissions are accepted an *Insolvency Practitioner* should consider making disclosure to creditors.

Obtaining *insolvency appointments*

63. The special nature of *insolvency appointments* makes the payment or offer of any commission for or the furnishing of any valuable consideration towards, the introduction of *insolvency appointments* inappropriate. This

does not, however, preclude an arrangement between an *Insolvency Practitioner* and an employee whereby the employee's remuneration is based in whole or in part on introductions obtained for the *Insolvency Practitioner* through the efforts of the employee.

64. When an *Insolvency Practitioner* seeks an *insolvency appointment* or work that may lead to an *insolvency appointment* through advertising or other forms of marketing, there may be threats to compliance with the fundamental principles.

65. When considering whether to accept an *insolvency appointment* an *Insolvency Practitioner* should satisfy himself that any advertising or other form of marketing pursuant to which the *insolvency appointment* may have been obtained is or has been:

    (a) Fair and not misleading.

    (b) Avoids unsubstantiated or disparaging statements.

    (c) Complies with relevant codes of practice and guidance in relation to advertising.

66. Advertisements and other forms of marketing should be clearly distinguishable as such and be legal, decent, honest and truthful.

67. If reference is made in advertisements or other forms of marketing to fees or to the cost of the services to be provided, the basis of calculation and the range of services that the reference is intended to cover should be provided. Care should be taken to ensure that such references do not mislead as to the precise range of services and the time commitment that the reference is intended to cover.

68. An *Insolvency Practitioner* should never promote or seek to promote his services, or the services of another *Insolvency Practitioner*, in such a way, or to such an extent as to amount to harassment.

69. Where an *Insolvency Practitioner* or the *practice* advertises for work via a third party, the *Insolvency Practitioner* is responsible for ensuring that the third party follows the above guidance.

Gifts and hospitality

70. An *Insolvency Practitioner*, or *a close or immediate family* member, may be offered gifts and hospitality. In relation to an *insolvency appointment*, such an offer will give rise to threats to compliance with the fundamental principles. For example, self-interest threats may arise if a gift is accepted and intimidation threats may arise from the possibility of such offers being made public.

71. The significance of such threats will depend on the nature, value and intent behind the offer. In deciding whether to accept any offer of a gift or hospitality the *Insolvency Practitioner* should have regard to what a reasonable and informed third party having knowledge of all relevant information would consider to be appropriate. Where such a reasonable and informed third party would consider the gift to be made in the normal course of business without the specific intent to influence decision making or obtain information the *Insolvency Practitioner* may generally conclude that there is no significant threat to compliance with the fundamental principles.

72. Where appropriate, safeguards should be considered and applied as necessary to eliminate any threats to the fundamental principles or reduce them to an acceptable level. If an *Insolvency Practitioner* encounters a situation in which no or no reasonable safeguards can be introduced to reduce a threat arising from offers of gifts or hospitality to an acceptable level he should conclude that it is not appropriate to accept the offer.

73. An *Insolvency Practitioner* should also not offer or provide gifts or hospitality where this would give rise to an unacceptable threat to compliance with the fundamental principles.

Record keeping

74. It will always be for the *Insolvency Practitioner* to justify his actions. An *Insolvency Practitioner* will be expected to be able to demonstrate the steps that he took and the conclusions that he reached in identifying, evaluating and responding to any threats, both leading up to and during an *insolvency appointment*, by reference to written contemporaneous records.

75. The records an *Insolvency Practitioner* maintains, in relation to the steps that he took and the conclusions that he reached, should be sufficient to enable a reasonable and informed third party to reach a view on the appropriateness of his actions.

THE APPLICATION OF THE FRAMEWORK TO SPECIFIC SITUATIONS

Introduction

76. The following examples describe specific circumstances and relationships that will create threats to compliance with the fundamental principles. The examples may assist an *Insolvency Practitioner* and the members of the *insolvency team* to assess the implications of similar, but different, circumstances and relationships.

77. The examples are divided into three parts. Part 1 contains examples which do not relate to a previous or existing *insolvency appointment*. Part 2 contains examples that do relate to a previous or existing *insolvency appointment*. Part 3 contains some examples under Scottish law. The examples are not intended to be exhaustive.

Examples that do not relate to a previous or existing insolvency appointment

78. The following situations involve a professional relationship which does not consist of a previous *insolvency appointment*:

79. **Insolvency appointment following audit related work**

   Relationship: The *practice* or an *individual within the practice* has previously carried out audit related work within the previous 3 years.

   Response: A Significant Professional Relationship will arise: an *Insolvency Practitioner* should conclude that it is not appropriate to take the *insolvency appointment*.

   Where audit related work was carried out more than three years before the proposed date of the appointment of the *Insolvency Practitioner* a threat to compliance with the fundamental principles may still arise. The *Insolvency Practitioner* should evaluate any such threat and consider whether the threat can be eliminated or reduced to an acceptable level by the existence or introduction of safeguards.

This restriction does not apply where the *insolvency appointment* is in a members' voluntary liquidation; an *Insolvency Practitioner* may normally take an appointment as liquidator. However, the *Insolvency Practitioner* should consider whether there are any other circumstances that give rise to an unacceptable threat to compliance with the fundamental principles. Further, the *Insolvency Practitioner* should satisfy himself that the directors' declaration of solvency is likely to be substantiated by events.

80. **Appointment as investigating accountant at the instigation of a creditor**

    Previous relationship: The *practice* or an *individual within the practice* was instructed by, or at the instigation of, a creditor or other party having a financial interest in an entity, to investigate, monitor or advise on its affairs.

    Response: A Significant Professional Relationship would <u>not</u> normally arise in these circumstances provided that:-

    (a) there has not been a direct involvement by *an individual within the practice* in the management of the entity; and

    (b) the *practice* had its principal client relationship with the creditor or other party, rather than with the company or proprietor of the business; and

    (c) the entity was aware of this.

    An *Insolvency Practitioner* should however consider all the circumstances before accepting an *insolvency appointment*, including the effect of any discussions or lack of discussions about the financial affairs of the company with its directors, and whether such circumstances give rise to an unacceptable threat to compliance with the fundamental principles.

    Where such an investigation was conducted at the request of, or at the instigation of, a secured creditor who then requests an *Insolvency Practitioner* to accept an *insolvency appointment* as an administrator or administrative receiver, the *Insolvency Practitioner* should satisfy himself that the company, acting by its board of directors, does not object to him taking such an *insolvency appointment*. If the secured creditor does not give prior warning of the *insolvency appointment* to the company or if such warning is given and the company objects but the secured creditor still wishes to appoint the *Insolvency Practitioner*, he should consider whether the circumstances give rise to an unacceptable threat to compliance with the fundamental principles.

Examples relating to previous or existing *insolvency appointments*

81. The following situations involve a prior professional relationship that involves a previous or existing *insolvency appointment*:-

82. **Insolvency appointment following an appointment as Administrative or other Receiver**

    Previous appointment: An *individual within the practice* has been administrative or other receiver.

    Proposed appointment: Any insolvency appointment.

    Response: An *Insolvency Practitioner* should not accept any insolvency appointment.

    This restriction does not, however, apply where the *individual within the practice* was appointed a receiver by the Court. In such circumstances, the *Insolvency Practitioner* should however consider whether any other circumstances which give rise to an unacceptable threat to compliance with the fundamental principles.

83. **Administration or liquidation following appointment as Supervisor of a Voluntary Arrangement**

    Previous appointment: An *individual within the practice* has been supervisor of a company voluntary arrangement.

    Proposed appointment: Administrator or liquidator.

    Response: An *Insolvency Practitioner* may normally accept an appointment as administrator or liquidator. However the *Insolvency Practitioner* should consider whether there are any circumstances that give rise to an unacceptable threat to compliance with the fundamental principles.

84. **Liquidation following appointment as Administrator**

    Previous Appointment: An *individual within the practice* has been administrator.

    Proposed Appointment: Liquidator.

Response: An *Insolvency Practitioner* may normally accept an appointment as liquidator provided he has complied with the relevant legislative requirements. However, the *Insolvency Practitioner* should also consider whether there are any circumstances that give rise to an unacceptable threat to compliance with the fundamental principles.

85. **Conversion of Members' Voluntary Liquation into Creditors' Voluntary Liquidation**

    Previous appointment: An *individual within the practice* has been the liquidator of a company in a members' voluntary liquidation.

    Proposed appointment: Liquidator in a creditors' voluntary liquidation, where it has been necessary to convene a creditors' meeting.

    Response: Where there has been a Significant Professional Relationship, an *Insolvency Practitioner* may continue or accept an appointment (subject to creditors' approval) only if he concludes that the company will eventually be able to pay its debts in full, together with interest.

    However, the *Insolvency Practitioner* should consider whether there are any other circumstances that give rise to an unacceptable threat to compliance with the fundamental principles.

86. **Bankruptcy following appointment as Supervisor of an Individual Voluntary Arrangement**

    Previous appointment: An *individual within the practice* has been supervisor of an individual voluntary arrangement.

    Proposed Appointment: Trustee in bankruptcy.

    Response: An *Insolvency Practitioner* may normally accept an appointment as trustee in bankruptcy. However, the *Insolvency Practitioner* should consider whether there are any circumstances that give rise to an unacceptable threat to compliance with the fundamental principles.

Examples in respect of cases conducted under Scottish Law

87. **Sequestration following appointment as Trustee under a Trust Deed for creditors**

    Previous appointment: An *individual within the practice* has been trustee under a trust deed for creditors.

Proposed appointment: Interim trustee or trustee in sequestration.

Response An *Insolvency Practitioner* may normally accept an appointment as an interim trustee or trustee in sequestration. However, the *Insolvency Practitioner* should consider whether there are any circumstances that give rise to an unacceptable threat to compliance with the fundamental principles.

88. **Sequestration where the Accountant in Bankruptcy is Trustee following appointment as Trustee under a Trust Deed for creditors**

    Previous appointment: An *individual within the practice* has been trustee under a trust deed for creditors.

    Proposed appointment: Agent for the Accountant in Bankruptcy in sequestration.

    Response: An *Insolvency Practitioner* may normally accept an appointment as agent for the Accountant in Bankruptcy. However, the *Insolvency Practitioner* should consider whether there are any circumstances that give rise to an unacceptable threat to compliance with the fundamental principles.

1.3 INSOLVENCY CODE OF ETHICS TRANSPARENCY AND CONFIDENTIALITY: A GUIDANCE NOTE

A. INTRODUCTION

1. This document relates to the Insolvency Code of Ethics ("the Code"). This document is to be read in conjunction with the Code.

2. This document has been prepared in order to supplement the principles contained within the Code. To the extent that there is any conflict between the contents of this document and the provisions of the Code, the provisions of the Code will take precedence.

3. The purpose of this document is to:

   (1) Emphasise the importance of the requirement that members should take care to ensure, where to do so does not conflict with any legal or professional obligation, that their acts, dealings and decision making processes are transparent, understandable and readily identifiable (as to which see Section B below); and

   (2) Offer some further guidance in relation to the fundamental principle of confidentiality (as to which see Section C below).

B. THE IMPORTANCE OF TRANSPARENCY

4. Paragraph 36 of the Code provides that an *Insolvency Practitioner* in his role as an office holder:

   " . . . has a professional duty to report openly to those with an interest in the outcome of the insolvency. An *Insolvency Practitioner* should always report on his acts and dealings as fully as possible given the circumstances of the case, in a way that is transparent and understandable. An Insolvency Practitioner should bear in mind the expectations of others and what a reasonable and informed third party would consider appropriate."

5. The Council regards this provision of the Code to be of fundamental importance. It is imperative that all members ensure that, except where to do so would conflict with any legal or professional obligation, their acts, dealings and decision making processes are transparent, understandable and readily identifiable. All members should endeavour to deal with third parties fairly in relation to the provision of information.

6. In particular, members in their capacity as office holders should maintain appropriate communication with creditors and such other persons who may be interested in the outcome of the insolvency in order to keep them informed of progress.

7. In this regard, office holders should take care to ensure that any reports prepared for creditors or other persons interested in the outcome of the insolvency are clear and understandable. Where appropriate, a full explanation should be given of any significant decisions or material events that have taken place in the insolvency and the reasons for them.

8. Where a report or information is provided in relation to the approval of any matter (for example the office holder's fees) the office holder should be particularly mindful to provide sufficient supporting information to enable those responsible for the approval to form a judgement as to whether approval is appropriate having regard to all the circumstances of the case.

9. The requirement for members to act transparently is particularly important where the assets and business of an insolvent company are sold shortly after appointment on pre-agreed terms. It is in the nature of such sales that creditors at large are not given the opportunity to consider the sale of the business or assets before it takes place. It is therefore particularly important that creditors are provided with a detailed explanation and justification of why a pre-agreed sale was undertaken, so that they can be satisfied that the office holder has acted with due regard to the interests of those affected.

10. Similar principles to those described above apply in relation to correspondence by members with third parties. Such correspondence should be clear, and understandable. Where the correspondence relates to a decision taken by the member in his capacity as an office holder or otherwise it should normally provide a full explanation of the relevant decision together with the reasons for it.

11. There may be circumstances in which it is not possible for a member to provide information relating to a particular matter because of a conflicting legal or professional obligation. Examples of such situations include where the relevant information is commercially sensitive or where there is a legal obligation not to disclose. In such circumstances, the member should still consider whether some details of the relevant matter can be

provided that do not conflict with the legal or professional obligation. This is particularly so where the relevant matter may be of significance to creditors or other persons interested in the outcome of the insolvency. Where the member is in doubt as to whether disclosure is appropriate in all the circumstances it may be appropriate for him to seek legal advice.

C. CONFIDENTIALITY

12. Paragraph 4 of the Code sets out five fundamental principles which an *Insolvency Practitioner* is required to comply with. The fundamental principle of confidentiality requires that:

    "An *Insolvency Practitioner* should respect the confidentiality of information acquired as a result of professional and business relationships and should not disclose any such information to third parties without proper and specific authority unless there is a legal or professional right or duty to disclose. Confidential information acquired as a result of professional and business relationships should not be used for the personal advantage of the *Insolvency Practitioner* or third parties."

13. In order for a party to be held liable for breach of confidence it must be usually be shown that: (1) the material communicated to him had the necessary quality of confidence; (2) it was communicated or became known to him in circumstances entailing an obligation of confidence; and (3) there was an unauthorised use of that material. For material to be protected as confidential its availability to the public must be restricted.

14. A member may acquire information which he is obliged to keep confidential. In particular, a member should be alert to the possibility of inadvertent disclosure of such confidential information, particularly in relation to any person with whom the member has had a long or close professional or personal relationship. Confidential information acquired by a member in the course of an assignment must not be used otherwise than for the proper performance of his professional duties.

15. The fundamental principle of confidentiality did not appear in the previous Insolvency Ethical Guide. Some concern was expressed during the consultation period that the inclusion of this fundamental principle may be inconsistent with an insolvency practitioner's duty or obligation, in certain circumstances, to disclose confidential information. This is not considered to be the case.

As drafted, the fundamental principle of confidentiality makes it clear that where an insolvency practitioner has a legal or professional right or duty to disclose he may do so.

16. When considering the application of the principle of confidentiality it is also important that members recognise that the circumstances in which obligations of confidence will arise are likely to be different where they have been appointed as an office holder to those where the member acts as an adviser. Where a member has been appointed as an office holder a client/professional relationship will not arise between the office holder and the entity in respect of which he has been appointed. Indeed, following the appointment of an office holder the rights of confidentiality formerly held by the entity will often vest in or fall under the control of the office holder (at least in the insolvency of a corporate body).

17. As emphasised in Section B above, where obligations of confidentiality do not exist and where to do so does not conflict with any other legal or professional obligation members will be required to ensure that their acts, dealings and decision making processes are transparent.

18. Members should be especially careful not to enter into new obligations of confidence that might have an impact on transparent communication with interested parties, other than for proper commercial reasons. A particular risk of this arises with non-disclosure agreements included in contracts for the sale of the business or assets of an entity in the circumstances outlined in paragraph 9 above.

Section 2

Statements of Insolvency
Practice — UK

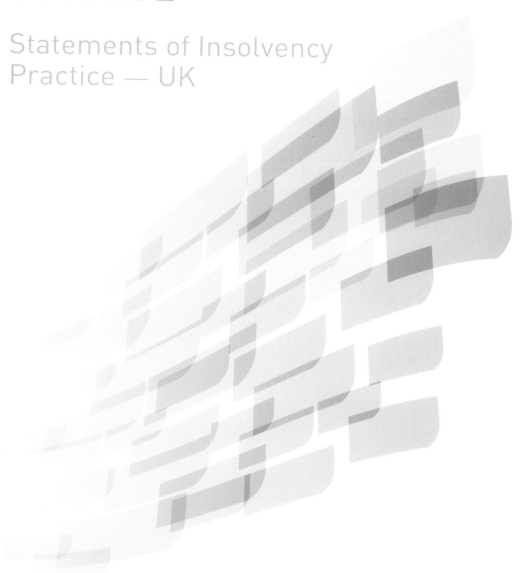

CONTENTS

2.1 STATEMENT OF INSOLVENCY PRACTICE 1
AN INTRODUCTION TO STATEMENTS OF INSOLVENCY PRACTICE

PURPOSE AND PRINCIPLES

1. The purpose of Statements of Insolvency Practice (SIPs) is to promote and maintain high standards by setting out required practice and harmonising the approach of insolvency practitioners to particular aspects of insolvency practice. They apply in parallel to the prevailing statutory framework.

2. SIPs should be read in conjunction with the wider fundamental principles embodied in the Insolvency Code of Ethics and should be applied in accordance with the spirit of that Code. A literal interpretation of a SIP may not be appropriate where it would be contrary to the fundamental principles of the Code.

3. The fundamental principles are:

Integrity

An insolvency practitioner should be straightforward and honest in all professional and business relationships.

Objectivity

An Insolvency Practitioner should not allow bias, conflict of interest or undue influence of others to override professional or business judgements.

Professional competence and due care

An insolvency practitioner has a continuing duty to maintain professional knowledge and skill at the level required to ensure that a client or employer receives competent professional service based on current developments in practice, legislation and techniques. An insolvency practitioner should act diligently and in accordance with applicable technical and professional standards when providing professional services.

Confidentiality

An insolvency practitioner should respect the confidentiality of information acquired as a result of professional and business relationships and should not disclose any such information to third parties without proper and specific authority unless there is a legal or professional right or duty to disclose. Confidential information acquired as a result of professional and business relationships should not be used for the personal advantage of the insolvency practitioner or third parties.

Professional behaviour

An insolvency practitioner should comply with relevant laws and regulations and should avoid any action that discredits the profession. Insolvency practitioners should conduct themselves with courtesy and consideration towards all with whom they come into contact when performing their work.

4. An insolvency practitioner who becomes aware of any insolvency practitioner who they consider is not complying or who has not complied with the relevant laws and regulations and whose actions discredit the profession, should report that insolvency practitioner to the complaints gateway operated by the Insolvency Service or to that insolvency practitioner's recognised professional body.

5. In addition, insolvency practitioners should ensure that their acts, dealings and decision making processes are transparent, understandable and readily identifiable, where to do so does not conflict with any legal or professional obligation. An insolvency practitioner should inform creditors at the earliest opportunity that they are bound by the Insolvency Code of Ethics when carrying out all professional work relating to an insolvency appointment. The insolvency practitioner should, if requested, provide details of any threats identified to compliance with the fundamental principles and the safeguards applied. If it is not appropriate to provide such details, the insolvency practitioner should provide an explanation why.

Regulatory status

6. SIPs set principles and key compliance standards with which insolvency practitioners are **required** to comply. Failure to observe the principles and/or maintain the standards set out in a SIP is a matter that may be

considered by a practitioner's regulatory authority for the purposes of disciplinary or regulatory action in accordance with that authority's membership and disciplinary rules.

7. Insolvency practitioners should evidence their compliance with SIPs and should, therefore, document their strategies and decision making processes appropriately.

8. SIPs set out required practice, but they are not statements of the law or the obligations imposed by insolvency legislation itself. Where an insolvency practitioner is in doubt about any obligation imposed upon them by a SIP, they should obtain appropriate guidance.

9. SIPs are issued to insolvency practitioners under procedures agreed between the insolvency regulatory authorities, acting through the Joint Insolvency Committee. They apply to practitioners authorised by each of the bodies listed below:

Recognised Professional Bodies:
- The Association of Chartered Certified Accountants
- The Insolvency Practitioners Association
- The Institute of Chartered Accountants in England and Wales
- The Institute of Chartered Accountants in Ireland
- The Institute of Chartered Accountants of Scotland
- The Law Society
- The Law Society of Northern Ireland
- The Law Society of Scotland

Competent Authorities:
- The Insolvency Service for the Secretary of State
- The Insolvency Service, Department of Enterprise, Trade & Investment

10. No liability attaches to any body or person that prepares, issues or distributes SIPs. The obligation to comply with SIPs rests solely upon the insolvency practitioner, as does any liability arising from any failure to do so.

Effective Date: 1 October 2015

2.2 STATEMENT OF INSOLVENCY PRACTICE 2 INVESTIGATIONS BY OFFICE HOLDERS IN ADMINISTRATIONS AND INSOLVENT LIQUIDATIONS AND THE SUBMISSION OF CONDUCT REPORTS BY OFFICE HOLDERS

INTRODUCTION

1. In any corporate insolvency there may be concerns regarding the way in which the business was conducted, how trading was controlled, whether proper decisions were made at the time, and whether assets have been sold at an under-value or otherwise dissipated. The way in which directors have acted may also be criticised by third parties.

2. Both an administrator and a liquidator of an insolvent entity have a duty to investigate what assets there are (including potential claims against third parties including the directors) and what recoveries can be made. Each of the above matters gives rise to the need for an office holder to carry out appropriate investigations, in order to satisfy the specific duties of the office holder and to allay, if possible, the legitimate concerns of creditors and other interested parties. This statement deals specifically with the investigations of an office holder in administration or insolvent liquidation.

3. Additionally, an administrator, liquidator, administrative receiver or receiver in Scotland may have a duty to report to the Secretary of State, or in Northern Ireland the Department of Enterprise, Trade and Investment (DETI), on the conduct of those that formerly controlled the company. This statement also deals with these obligations.

PRINCIPLES

4. This statement has been produced in recognition of the principles that:

    An office holder should carry out investigations that are proportionate to the circumstances of each case.

    An office holder should report clearly on the steps taken in relation to investigations, and the outcomes.

    Conduct reports and any subsequent new information should be submitted in a timely manner, noting the expectation that extensions to the statutorily prescribed period will only be considered in exceptional circumstances.

KEY COMPLIANCE STANDARDS

Seeking information

5.   The information available to an office holder upon appointment will vary from case to case depending on the extent of the office holder's prior involvement with the company, the publicity surrounding the insolvency, the quality and completeness of the company's books and records, and whether there has been a meeting of creditors. The office holder should locate the company's books and records (in whatever form), and ensure that they are secured, and listed as appropriate.

6.   In every case, the office holder should invite creditors to provide information on any concerns regarding the way in which the company's business has been conducted, and on potential recoveries for the estate, both:

at any meeting of creditors at which the office holder's appointment is made or confirmed, or, in other cases, at any later meeting convened by the office holder; and

in the first communication sent to creditors by the office holder.

7.   A similar invitation should also be extended to the members of any creditors' committee, upon or soon after the formation of the committee, and to any predecessor in office.

8.   An office holder should always have in mind the need to ascertain, and if necessary investigate, what assets can be realised. Enquiries should encompass whether prior transactions by the company, or the conduct of any person involved with the company, could give rise to an action for recovery under the relevant legislation.

Initial assessment

9.   Notwithstanding any shortage of funds, an office holder should consider the information acquired in the course of appraising and realising the business and assets of a company, together with any information provided by creditors or gained from other sources, and decide whether any further information is required or appropriate. The office holder should make enquiries of the directors and senior employees, by sending questionnaires and/or interviewing them, as appropriate.

10. In every case, an office holder should make an initial assessment as to whether there could be any matters that might lead to recoveries for the estate and what further investigations may be appropriate.

11. An office holder should determine the extent of the investigations in the circumstances of each case, taking account of the public interest, potential recoveries, the funds likely to be available, either from within the estate and/or from other sources, to fund an investigation, and the costs involved.

Further steps to be taken

12. An office holder may conclude that there are matters (for example, the conduct of management, prior transactions susceptible to challenge, or the consequences of possible criminal offences) that require early investigation, either as a matter of public policy or because there are real prospects of recoveries for the estate. It is for the office holder to decide whether investigation and subsequent legal action should proceed as quickly as possible, without consultation with, or sanction by, creditors or a creditors' committee (but subject to any statutory requirement to obtain sanction).

13. In other cases, the office holder may decide that further investigation and legal action should be carried out only after consultation or with sanction, in particular where the office holder concludes that the outcome is uncertain and the costs that would be incurred would materially affect the funds available for distribution. In such cases, the office holder may consult with major creditors (if that is appropriate) or convene a meeting of the creditors' committee or the creditors to discuss any proposals for investigation and/or action. Alternatively, consultation and approval can be carried out/sought by written resolution.

14. Any proposals should include sufficient information (subject to considerations of privilege and confidentiality) to enable an informed decision to be made by those consulted, and are likely to include the costs that could be incurred and the possible range of returns to creditors.

15. There may be circumstances where there are clearly insufficient funds to carry out a detailed investigation or to take action for recovery of assets, and an office holder should consider whether it is appropriate to seek funding from creditors or others.

Reporting to creditors

16. Creditors should be given information regarding investigations, any action being taken, and whether funding is being provided by third parties; disclosure would be subject to considerations of privilege and confidentiality and whether investigations and litigation might be compromised.

17. The times at which information is provided to creditors will vary from case to case, but as a minimum an office holder should:

    include within the first progress report a statement dealing with the office holder's initial assessment, whether any further investigations or action were considered, and the outcome; and

    include within subsequent reports a statement dealing with investigations and actions concluded during the period, and those that are continuing.

Record keeping

18. An office holder should document, at the time, initial assessments, investigations and conclusions, including any conclusion that further investigation or action is not required or feasible, and also any decision to restrict the content of reports to creditors.

Conduct reporting requirements

19. The office holder should base any conduct report on information coming to light in the ordinary course of their enquiries and is not required to carry out investigations specifically for the purpose of fulfilling their statutory reporting obligations. The submission of conduct reports is one of the statutory duties that automatically fall upon the office holder and, as such, must be complied with notwithstanding any shortage of funds.

20. If the office holder has not already interviewed the subject of the conduct report, the office holder may consider seeking a meeting with the subject, with a view to confirming the office holder's understanding of the facts.

21. An office holder should be mindful that the content of conduct reports are prepared for the purpose of the Secretary of State and DETI discharging their statutory functions and should not be disclosed to third parties.

22. Notwithstanding the confidential nature of conduct reports, office holders should be mindful that there may be circumstances in which the content of a conduct report is made available to the subject, or potentially others. Should the subject of a conduct report request disclosure, an office holder should contact the Secretary of State or DETI (as appropriate) as soon as a request is received in order to consider whether any factors apply that may result in an exemption from disclosure being applicable. Office holders should be aware that the subject may make a disclosure request directly to the Secretary of State or DETI (as appropriate), which will usually result, (after appropriate redactions) in a copy being provided to them. Additionally, conduct reports may be disclosed by Secretary of State or DETI to other Regulatory Authorities, where disclosure is considered to be in the public interest. An office holder should also bear in mind that, if disqualification proceedings are brought, the conduct report will usually be made available to the subject during the disclosure process.

23. When reporting on conduct or providing new information, the office holder should highlight whether recovery proceedings have or may be commenced against the subject of the report, as this may have an impact upon any decision taken by the Secretary of State or DETI (as appropriate) to seek a compensation order or undertaking.

Other reporting requirements

24. An office holder should report possible offences disclosed during the course of their investigations to the relevant authorities.

Effective Date: 06 April 2016

2.3 STATEMENT OF INSOLVENCY PRACTICE 3.2
COMPANY VOLUNTARY ARRANGEMENTS

INTRODUCTION

1. A Company Voluntary Arrangement (CVA) is a statutory contract between a company and its creditors under which an insolvency practitioner will have powers and duties. An insolvency practitioner will be central to the preparation and agreement of the proposal, and the implementation of the arrangement, whether acting as adviser, nominee or supervisor. The particular nature of an insolvency practitioner's position renders transparency and fairness in all dealings of primary importance. The company's directors, shareholders and creditors should be confident that an insolvency practitioner will act professionally and with objectivity in each role associated with the arrangement. Failure to do so may prejudice the interests of both the company and creditors, and is likely to bring the practitioner and the profession into disrepute.

2. An insolvency practitioner may be asked to assist a company's directors when a CVA may be the solution to the company's financial difficulties; or an insolvency practitioner may propose a CVA as administrator or liquidator. Where the principles and key compliance standards in this statement of insolvency practice are relevant only to a CVA proposed by a company's directors these are identified as such.

PRINCIPLES

3. An insolvency practitioner should differentiate clearly between the stages and roles that are associated with a CVA (these being, the provision of initial advice, assisting in the preparation of the proposal, acting as the nominee, and acting as the supervisor) and ensure that they are explained to the company's directors (where they are making the proposal), shareholders and creditors.

4. (*Directors' proposal*) An insolvency practitioner should ensure that information and explanations about all the options available are provided to the directors, so that they can make an informed judgement as to whether a CVA is an appropriate solution for the company.

5. An insolvency practitioner should explain to the directors, their responsibilities and role, and the consequences of a CVA.

6. Where a CVA is to be proposed, an insolvency practitioner should be satisfied that it is achievable and that a fair balance is struck between the interests of the company and the creditors.

7. An insolvency practitioner's reports should provide sufficient information to enable the company's shareholders and creditors to make informed decisions in relation to the proposal and the CVA, and report accurately in a manner that aims to be clear and useful.

KEY COMPLIANCE STANDARDS

8. Certain key compliance standards are of general application, but others will depend on whether the insolvency practitioner is acting as adviser, nominee, supervisor, administrator or liquidator.

STANDARDS OF GENERAL APPLICATION

Advice (directors' proposal)

9. The insolvency practitioner should have procedures in place to ensure that the information and explanations provided to the company and/or the directors at each stage of the process, as appropriate (that is, assessing the options available, and then preparing and implementing a CVA), are designed to set out clearly:

    (a) the advantages and disadvantages of each available option;

    (b) the key stages and the roles of the adviser, the nominee and the supervisor, any potential delays or complications, and the likely duration of the CVA;

    (c) what is required of the company and its directors;

    (d) the consequences of proposing and entering into a CVA, including the rights of challenge to the CVA and the potential consequences of those challenges; and

    (e) what may happen if the CVA is not approved or not successfully completed.

Meeting the directors (directors' proposal)

10. In view of the complex nature of CVAs the initial meeting with the directors should always be face to face.

Assessment

11. The insolvency practitioner needs to be satisfied, at each stage of the process, that there are procedures in place to ensure that an assessment is made of:

(a) the solutions available and their viability;

(b) whether the directors are being sufficiently cooperative (*directors' proposal*);

(c) where the directors' compliance is required for the implementation of the CVA, the directors' understanding of the process, and commitment to it;

(d) the likely attitude of any key creditors and the general body of creditors, in particular as to the fairness and balance of the proposals;

(e) whether a CVA would have a reasonable prospect of being approved and implemented; and

(f) whether a moratorium is required or available

Documentation

12. The insolvency practitioner should be able to demonstrate that proper steps have been taken at all stages of the CVA, by maintaining records of:

(a) (*Directors' proposal*) discussions with the directors, including the information and explanations provided, the options outlined, and the advantages and disadvantages of each. All advice provided to the directors should be confirmed in writing;

(b) (*Directors' proposal*) comments made by the directors, and their preferred option;

(c) any discussions with creditors (or their representatives) and the company's shareholders;

(d) where the proposal is made by an administrator or liquidator, a detailed note of the strategy, outlining the advantages and disadvantages of each option.

STANDARDS OF SPECIFIC APPLICATION

Preparing for a CVA

13. When preparing for a CVA, the insolvency practitioner should have procedures in place to ensure, taking account of the company's circumstances and the nature of the company's finances, that:

    (a) (*Directors' proposal*) the directors have had, or receive, the appropriate advice in relation to a CVA; this should be confirmed in writing if the insolvency practitioner or their firm has not done so before;

    (b) sufficient information is obtained to make an assessment of a CVA as a solution, and to enable a nominee to prepare a report, including;

        (i) the measures taken by the directors or others to avoid recurrence of the company's financial difficulties, if any;

        (ii) the likely expectations of any key creditors;

        (iii) the effect of the CVA on third parties where their view may have an effect on the viability of the CVA; and

        (iv) proportionate investigations into, and verification of, income and expenditure and assets and liabilities.

The proposal

14. Whether the insolvency practitioner has been asked to assist the directors to prepare a proposal or a proposal is being prepared by an administrator or liquidator, the insolvency practitioner should have procedures in place to ensure that the proposal contains the following:

    (a) sufficient information for creditors to understand the company's financial and trading history, including:

    (b) the roles of the directors and key employees and their future involvement in the company;

        (i) the background and financial history of the directors where relevant;

        (ii) if the company has become, or is about to become, insolvent, why it has become insolvent; and,

(iii) any other attempts that have been made to solve the company's financial difficulties, if there are any such difficulties.

(c) a comparison of the estimated outcomes of the CVA and the outcome if the CVA is not approved, including disclosure of the estimated costs of the CVA and the bases for those estimates;

(d) the identity of the source of any referral of the company, the relationship or connection of the referrer to the company and, where any payment has been made or is proposed to the referrer, the amount and reason for that payment;

(e) details of the amounts and source of any payments made, or proposed to be made, to the nominee and the supervisor or their firms in connection, or otherwise, with the proposed CVA, directly or indirectly and the reason(s) for the payment(s); and

(f) where relevant, sufficient information to support any profit and cash projections, subject to any commercial sensitivity.

The nominee

15. Where the nominee is not the administrator or liquidator, it is the responsibility of the nominee to report in relation to the proposed CVA. When acting as nominee, the insolvency practitioner should have procedures in place to ensure that:

(a) The nominee is able to report whether or not, in the nominee's judgement:

(i) the company's financial position is materially different from that contained in the proposal, explaining the extent to which the information has been verified;

(ii) the CVA is manifestly unfair;

(iii) the CVA has a reasonable prospect of being approved and implemented.

(b) The proposer's consent is sought on any modifications to the proposal put forward by creditors, and the proposer understands the impact of the modifications on the implementation of the CVA and its viability.

(c) Where a modification is adopted, the insolvency practitioner must ensure that consent is obtained from the proposer of the CVA and, if appropriate, the creditors. In the absence of consent, the CVA cannot proceed. The proposer's consent must be recorded.

16. Where the nominee is the administrator, and the directors' compliance will be required, their consent is sought.

The supervisor

17. When acting as supervisor, the insolvency practitioner should have procedures in place to ensure that:

    (a) where a proposal is modified, creditors have been made aware of the final form of the accepted CVA;

    (b) the CVA is supervised in accordance with its terms;

    (c) the progress of the CVA is monitored;

    (d) any departures from the terms of the CVA are identified at an early stage and appropriate action is taken promptly by the supervisor;

    (e) any discretions conferred on the supervisor are exercised where necessary, on a timely basis and that exercise is reported at the next available opportunity;

    (f) any variation to the terms of the CVA has been appropriately approved before it is implemented;

    (g) enquiries by creditors and shareholders are dealt with promptly;

    (h) full disclosure is made of the costs of the CVA and of any other sources of income of the insolvency practitioner or the practice, in relation to the case, in reports;

    (i) if the costs of the CVA have increased beyond previously reported estimates, this increase should be reported at the next available opportunity; and

    (j) the CVA is closed promptly on completion or termination.

Effective date: This SIP applies to all cases where the nominee is appointed on or after **1 July 2014**

2.4 STATEMENT OF INSOLVENCY PRACTICE 7 PRESENTATION OF FINANCIAL INFORMATION IN INSOLVENCY PROCEEDINGS

INTRODUCTION

An office holder is required to report regularly to creditors and other interested parties[1], and those reports should be clear and informative. Reports should be produced with the interests of the reader in mind and the office holder should consider what the reader might reasonably regard as appropriate or significant in the circumstances of each case.

Because payments made by an office holder should be appropriate and reasonable in all the circumstances of the case, an office holder should report in a way that will assist creditors and other interested parties properly to exercise their rights under the insolvency legislation.

PRINCIPLES

1. Information provided by an office holder, including information about receipts and payments, should be presented in a manner which is transparent, consistent and useful to creditors and other interested parties, whilst being proportionate to the circumstances of the case.

2. The information provided within receipts and payments accounts and any accompanying documents should be sufficient to enable creditors and other interested parties to understand the nature and amounts of the receipts and payments.

3. Requests for additional information, including on expenses, should be viewed upon their individual merits and treated by an office holder in a fair and reasonable way. The provision of additional information should be proportionate to the circumstances of the case.

---

[1] "other interested parties" means those parties with rights pursuant to the prevailing insolvency legislation to information about the office holders' receipts and payments. This may include the creditors' committee, the members (shareholders) of a company, or in personal insolvency, the debtor.

KEY COMPLIANCE STANDARDS

Form and general presentation of accounts

4. In addition to any statutory requirement to provide an account in a specified form, receipts and payments accounts should provide figures both for the period under review and on a cumulative basis.

5. Information provided in accordance with this statement may be in a separate document issued with the receipts and payments account or given by way of note.

6. Receipts and payments accounts should show categories of items under headings appropriate for the case, where practicable following headings used in any prior statements of affairs or estimated outcome statements. Alternatively, an analysis should be provided to enable comparison with the "estimated to realise" figures in any prior document.

7. A "statement of expenses incurred" should adopt, as far as possible, the principles of this statement but need only provide information for the period under review.

Further information on the form and presentation of receipts and payments accounts is set out below.

Payments to Insolvency office holders and their associates

8. The following should be disclosed, either separately in the receipts and payments account or by way of note:

    (a) Office holder's remuneration, showing the amounts paid on each basis;

    (b) Amounts paid to the office holder out of the estate in respect of pre-appointment costs;

    (c) Sums paid to the office holder in respect of the supervision of trading;

    (d) All other amounts required to be approved in the same manner as remuneration;

    (e) Amounts paid to sub-contractors for work that would otherwise have to be carried out by the office holders or their staff;

(f) Any remuneration or disbursements paid to the office holder other than out of the estate, giving the amounts paid, the name of the payor, its relationship to the insolvent estate and the nature of the payment.

9. These disclosures should always be made whenever reporting on remuneration and/or expenses, whether incurred, accrued or paid.

Reports to creditors and other interested parties

10. Where expenditure has been incurred that is significant in the context of the case, the office holder should report and explain why the expenditure was incurred.

11. Unless there is statutory provision to the contrary, this SIP does not require the repetition of information previously provided.

Requests for additional information

12. Creditors and other interested parties may have the statutory right to seek further information about payments made by the office holder. Such rights extend to the general expenses of administering the estate as well as the office holder's remuneration and disbursements. They may also have the right to apply to the court if they consider these costs to be excessive in all the circumstances. The office holder should provide creditors and other interested parties with sufficient information to enable them to consider whether to exercise those rights.

13. Adequate steps should be taken to bring the rights of creditors and other interested parties to their attention. Information on how to access a suitable explanatory note setting out the rights of creditors should be given, when appropriate in reports that present financial information.

Other presentational matters

14. **Receipts**

   (a) Realisations by or on behalf of the office holder should be shown gross, with the costs of realisation shown separately as payments.

   (b) Realisations by or on behalf of the office holder of assets subject to charges should be shown as above with the amounts accounted for to the charge holder shown separately as payments.

(c) When assets subject to charges are sold by or on the instructions of the charge holder (or other person with a legal right to do so), the net amount received should be shown in the account (even if "nil") with the gross realisation(s), costs of realisation and the amount retained by the charge holder shown separately by way of note.

15. **Payments**

Payments should be stated by category, distinguishing payments made under duress, in settlement of reservation of title claims, to secured creditors, and to preferential creditors and unsecured creditors as dividends. The dates and amounts of dividends (pence in the £) should also be stated.

16. **Trading under office holder's control**

A separate trading receipts and payments account should be provided, and the balance should be shown as a single item in the main receipts and payments account. The office holder should also provide, by way of note or in the accompanying report, details of:

(a) The assets in existence upon appointment (e.g. stock and work in progress) that have been used in trading.

(b) Any uncollected debts and unpaid liabilities in respect of trading.

(c) Trading assets (e.g. stock and work in progress) still to be realised.

17. **Hive-downs**

(a) Funds received from a hive-down company as consideration for the sale of the business or its assets should be shown in the account classified according to the categories of assets transferred and apportioned as provided for in the hive-down agreement. The proceeds of sale of the shares in the hive-down company should be shown separately. Funds received in respect of the hive-down company should not be shown simply as the proceeds of sale of the hive-down company.

(b) A trading account for a hive-down company should be prepared adopting the same principles as set out in paragraph 16 above.

18. **Third party funds**

   Where any monies are held which do not form part of the estate and are due to be paid to third parties, the amount should be noted. Any agreed fee charged to the person entitled to the monies should be disclosed.

19. **Statement of funds held**

   Disclosure should be made of where the balance of the funds is held, distinguishing between funds held on non-interest bearing accounts and interest bearing accounts in the office holder's or the insolvent estate's name, amounts held in the Insolvency Services Account and in Treasury Bills, and other forms of investments.

   An office holder may present multiple receipts and payments accounts in more than one currency where bank accounts are maintained in those currencies (with details of the transfers between each currency), but should explain:

   (a) Why funds have been held in currencies other then sterling;

   (b) The impact of currency holdings on the estate;

   (c) An indication of the sterling value as at the date of the account.

20. **Value added tax (VAT)**

   The treatment of VAT adopted within an account should be consistent and the implications of that treatment made clear.

Effective Date: 2 May 2011

2.5 STATEMENT OF INSOLVENCY PRACTICE 13 DISPOSAL OF ASSETS TO CONNECTED PARTIES IN AN INSOLVENCY PROCESS

Introduction

1. The disposal of assets in an insolvency process to connected parties may give rise to concerns that assets or groups of assets may have been disposed of at less than market value and/or on more favorable terms than would have been available to a third party.

2. It is recognised that connected party transactions may be in the best interests of creditors but require adequate disclosure to creditors and other interested parties[1] as soon as reasonably practicable. Transparency in all dealings is of primary importance.

3. It is equally important that the insolvency practitioner acts and is seen to be acting in the interests of the creditors as a whole and is able to demonstrate this.

4. This statement of insolvency practice applies to both personal and corporate insolvency appointments, with the exception of members' voluntary liquidations.

Principles

5. An insolvency practitioner should be clear about the nature and extent of the role of advisor in the pre-appointment period. The roles are to be explained to the debtor, the company directors and the creditors. For the purposes of this Statement of Insolvency Practice only, the role of "insolvency practitioner" is to be read as relating to the advisory engagement that an insolvency practitioner or their firm and or/any associates may have in the period prior to commencement of the insolvency process. The role of "office holder" is to be read as the formal appointment as an office holder. An insolvency practitioner should recognise that a different insolvency practitioner may be the eventual office holder. When instructed to advise a debtor, a company or companies

---

[1] "other interested parties" means those parties with rights pursuant to the prevailing insolvency legislation to information about insolvency proceedings. This may include a creditors' committee, the members (shareholders) of a company, or in personal insolvency, the debtor.

in a group, the insolvency practitioner should make it clear that the role is not to advise any parties connected with the purchaser, who should be encouraged to take independent advice. This is particularly important when there is a possibility that a connected party may acquire an interest in the business or assets.

6. The office holder should provide creditors and other interested parties with sufficient information such that a reasonable and informed third party would conclude that the transaction was appropriate and that the office holder has acted with due regard for the creditors' interests. As this is a connected party transaction the level of detail needs to be greater than in the reporting of a third party transaction.

Key compliance standards

7. An insolvency practitioner should exercise professional judgement in advising the client whether a formal valuation of any or all of the assets is necessary. Where a valuation is relied on, other than one undertaken by an appropriate independent valuer and/or advisor with adequate professional indemnity, this should be disclosed. The rationale for doing so and an explanation of why the officer holder was satisfied with the valuation should also be disclosed.

8. An office holder should keep a detailed record of the reasoning behind both the decision to make a sale to a connected party and all alternatives considered. When considering the manner of disposal of the business or assets the office holder should be able to demonstrate that their duties under the legislation have been met.

Disclosure

9. The office holder should demonstrate that they have acted with due regard to creditors' interests by providing creditors with a proportionate and sufficiently detailed justification of why a sale to a connected party was undertaken, including the alternatives considered. Such disclosure should be made in the next report to creditors after the transaction has been concluded.

10. Where legislation permits an office holder not to disclose information in certain limited circumstances, this Statement of Insolvency Practice will not restrict the effect of those statutory provisions.

Connected parties

11. In this context, a connected party includes the debtor or a party connected to the debtor or company as defined in section 249 and 435 (as an associate) of the Insolvency Act 1986 , Article 7 and Article 4 of the Insolvency (NI) Order 1989, or section 229 of the Bankruptcy (Scotland) Act 2016 (as appropriate) provided that in determining whether any person or company has control under section 435(10) and Article 4(10), sales to secured lenders who hold security for the granting of the loan (with related voting rights) as part of the secured lender's normal business activities, over one third or more of the shares in the insolvent company, are not included.

Effective date: 1 December 2016

2.6 STATEMENT OF INSOLVENCY PRACTICE 15 REPORTING AND PROVIDING INFORMATION ON THEIR FUNCTIONS TO COMMITTEES AND COMMISSIONERS

INTRODUCTION

1. The interests of creditors are of significant importance to office holders in fulfilling their duties. Legislation provides for creditors to assist office holders in the performance of their duties through representatives elected by creditors.

2. Legislation refers to such representatives using different terms: creditors' committee (administration, administrative receivership, receivership and bankruptcy), liquidation committee (company winding up), and commissioners (sequestration in Scotland). For the purposes of this statement the term "committee" is used to refer to the appropriate body in respect of each relevant insolvency procedures.

3. This SIP also applies where a committee is proposed or formed (as appropriate) in an individual, partnership or company voluntary arrangement or trust deed (in Scotland).

4. For the purposes only of this SIP the term "office holder" includes an insolvency practitioner providing advice or assistance to directors in connection with the appointment of a liquidator in a creditors voluntary liquidation.

PRINCIPLES

5. Office holders should ensure that those considering nomination to committees and those who are elected to committees are provided with sufficient information for them to consider nomination and be able to carry out their duties and functions.

6. Information provided by an office holder should be presented in a manner which is transparent and useful to the committee, whilst being proportionate to the case. Requests for additional information should be treated by an office holder in a fair and reasonable way.

7. Office holders should exercise professional judgement according to the circumstances of the case whilst having regard to the views of the committee. Office holders should ensure that such views do not fetter their decision making.

KEY COMPLIANCE STANDARDS

8. Creditors should be able to make an informed decision on whether they wish to be nominated to serve on a committee. Office holders should advise creditors (or in relation to a creditors voluntary liquidation, ensure that creditors are advised) in writing how they may access suitable information on the rights, duties and the functions of the committee prior to inviting nomination of committee members.

9. At the committee's first meeting, office holders should discuss with committee members how frequently they wish to receive reports and obtain their directions. These directions are likely to depend on the circumstances of the case. Office holders should also discuss with committee members the type of matters which they wish to have reported to them so that matters of particular concern to them are identified. The first meeting of the committee should be held as early as practical after the committee is established.

10. Office holders should on each occasion they report, identify what matters (in addition to those already identified) should be included in the report, exercising professional judgement as to which aspects of the proceedings may be of concern to the committee.

11. Office holders should ensure that any arrangements which are made for reporting to a committee are properly documented and adhered to.

12. The frequency of reporting and directions obtained at the outset of the case may not be appropriate throughout the course of the proceedings. The office holder should therefore consider throughout the lifetime of the case whether circumstances have altered which may change the committee's requirements for reporting frequency or their directions. Where circumstances have altered, the office holder should when next reporting to the committee set out the change of circumstances and obtain new agreement on reporting frequency and any new directions necessary.

13. Where an office holder considers their professional judgement should override the views of a committee, the office holder should clearly document why it is inappropriate to follow the views of the committee and provide an explanation to the committee. The office holder should also consider whether it is appropriate, in matters of contention to seek the views of creditors more widely or to seek the direction of the court or the Accountant in Bankruptcy (in Scotland).

Effective date: This SIP applies to insolvency appointments starting on or after **1 March 2017**

2.7 STATEMENT OF INSOLVENCY PRACTICE 16 PRE-PACKAGED SALES IN ADMINISTRATIONS

INTRODUCTION

1. The term 'pre-packaged sale' refers to an arrangement under which the sale of all or part of a company's business or assets is negotiated with a purchaser prior to the appointment of an administrator and the administrator effects the sale immediately on, or shortly after, appointment.

2. The particular nature of an insolvency practitioner's position in these circumstances renders transparency in all dealings of primary importance. Administration is a collective insolvency proceeding - creditors and other interested parties should be confident that the insolvency practitioner has acted professionally and with objectivity; failure to demonstrate this clearly may bring the insolvency practitioner and the profession into disrepute.

3. An insolvency practitioner should recognise the high level interest the public and the business community have in pre-packaged sales in administration. The insolvency practitioner should assume, and plan for, greater interest in and possible scrutiny of such sales where the directors and/or shareholders of the purchasing entity are the same as, or are connected parties of, the insolvent entity.

4. It is equally important that the insolvency practitioner acts and is seen to be acting in the interests of the company's creditors as a whole and is able to demonstrate this.

PRINCIPLES

5. An insolvency practitioner should differentiate clearly the roles that are associated with an administration that involves a pre-packaged sale, that is, the provision of advice to the company before any formal appointment and the functions and responsibilities of the administrator following appointment. The roles are to be explained to the directors and the creditors. For the purposes of this Statement of Insolvency Practice only, the role of "insolvency practitioner" is to be read as relating to the advisory engagement that an insolvency practitioner or their firm and or/any associates may have with a company in the period prior to the company

entering administration. The role of "administrator" is to be read as the formal appointment as administrator after the company has entered administration. An insolvency practitioner should recognise that a different insolvency practitioner may be the eventual administrator.

6. The administrator should provide creditors with sufficient information ("the SIP 16 statement") such that a reasonable and informed third party would conclude that the pre-packaged sale was appropriate and that the administrator has acted with due regard for the creditors' interests. In a connected party transaction the level of detail may need to be greater.

KEY COMPLIANCE STANDARDS

Preparatory work

7. An insolvency practitioner should be clear about the nature and extent of the role of advisor in the pre-appointment period. When instructed to advise the company or companies in a group, the insolvency practitioner should make it clear that the role is not to advise the directors or any parties connected with the purchaser, who should be encouraged to take independent advice. This is particularly important if there is a possibility that the directors may acquire an interest in the business or assets in a pre-packaged sale.

8. An insolvency practitioner should bear in mind the duties and obligations which are owed to creditors in the pre-appointment period. The insolvency practitioner should recognise the potential liability which may attach to any person who is party to a decision that causes a company to incur credit and who knows that there is no good reason to believe it will be repaid. Such liability is not restricted to the directors.

9. The insolvency practitioner should ensure that any connected party considering a pre - packaged purchase is aware of their ability to approach the pre-pack pool (see appendix) and the potential for enhanced stakeholder confidence from the connected party approaching the pre-pack pool and preparing a viability statement for the purchasing entity.

10. An insolvency practitioner should keep a detailed record of the reasoning behind both the decision to undertake a pre-packaged sale and all alternatives considered.

11. The insolvency practitioner should advise the company that any valuations obtained should be carried out by appropriate independent valuers and/or advisors, carrying adequate professional indemnity insurance for the valuation performed.

12. If the administrator relies on a valuation or advice other than by an appropriate independent valuer and/or advisor with adequate professional indemnity insurance this should be disclosed and with the reason for doing so and the reasons that the administrator was satisfied with the valuation, explained.

Marketing

13. Marketing a business is an important element in ensuring that the best available consideration is obtained for it in the interests of the company's creditors as a whole, and will be a key factor in providing reassurance to creditors. The insolvency practitioner should advise the company that any marketing should conform to the marketing essentials as set out in the appendix to this Statement of Insolvency Practice.

14. Where there has been deviation from any of the marketing essentials, the administrator is to explain how a different strategy has delivered the best available outcome.

After appointment

15. When considering the manner of disposal of the business or assets the administrator should be able to demonstrate that the duties of an administrator under the legislation have been met.

Disclosure

16. An administrator should provide creditors with a detailed narrative explanation and justification (the SIP 16 statement) of why a pre-packaged sale was undertaken and all alternatives considered, to demonstrate that the administrator has acted with due regard for their interests. The information disclosure requirements in the appendix should be included in the SIP 16 statement unless there are exceptional circumstances, in which case the administrator should explain why the information has not been provided. In any sale involving a connected party, it is very unlikely that commercial confidentiality alone would outweigh the need for creditors to be provided with this information.

17. The explanation of the pre-packaged sale in the SIP 16 Statement should be provided with the first notification to creditors and in any event within seven calendar days of the transaction. If the administrator has been unable to meet this requirement, the administrator will provide a reasonable explanation for the delay. The SIP 16 statement should be included in the administrator's statement of proposals filed at Companies House.

18. The administrator should recognise that, if creditors have had to wait until, or near, the statutory deadline for the proposals to be issued there may be some confusion on the part of creditors when they do receive them, the sale having been completed some time before. Accordingly, when a pre-packaged sale has been undertaken, the administrator should seek any requisite approval of the proposals as soon as practicable after appointment and, ideally, the proposals should be sent with the notification of the sale. If the administrator has been unable to meet this requirement the proposals should include an explanation for the delay.

19. The Insolvency Act 1986 and the Insolvency (Northern Ireland) Order 1989 permits an administrator not to disclose information in certain limited circumstances. This Statement of Insolvency Practice will not restrict the effect of those statutory provisions.

Effective date: This SIP applies to insolvency appointments starting on or after 1 November 2015

Appendix

Marketing essentials

Marketing a business is an important element in ensuring that the best available consideration is obtained for it in the interests of creditors, and will be a key factor in providing reassurance to creditors. Any marketing should conform to the following:

- **Broadcast** – the business should be marketed as widely as possible proportionate to the nature and size of the business – the purpose of the marketing is to make the business's availability known to the widest group of potential purchasers in the time available, using whatever media or other sources are likely to achieve this outcome.

- **Justify the marketing strategy** – the statement to creditors should not simply be a list of what marketing has been undertaken. It should explain the reasons underpinning the marketing and media strategy used.

- **Independence** – where the business has been marketed by the company prior to the insolvency practitioner being instructed, this should not be used as a justification in itself to avoid further marketing. The administrator should be satisfied as to the adequacy and independence of the marketing undertaken.

- **Publicise rather than simply publish** – marketing should have been undertaken for an appropriate length of time to satisfy the administrator that the best available outcome for creditors as a whole in all the circumstances has been achieved. Creditors should be informed of the reason for the length of time settled upon.

- **Connectivity** – include online communication alongside other media by default. The internet offers one of the widest populations of any medium. If the business is not marketed via the internet, this should be justified.

- **Comply or explain** – particularly with sales to connected parties where the level of interest is at its highest, the administrator needs to explain how the marketing strategy has achieved the best available outcome for creditors as a whole in all the circumstances.

Information disclosure requirements in the SIP 16 statement

The administrator should include a statement explaining the statutory purpose pursued, confirming that the transaction enables the statutory purpose to be achieved and that the outcome achieved was the best available outcome for creditors as a whole in all the circumstances.

The following information should be included in the administrator's explanation of a pre-packaged sale, as far as the administrator is aware after making appropriate enquiries:

Initial introductions

The source (to be named) of the initial introduction to the insolvency practitioner and the date of the administrator's initial introduction.

Pre-appointment matters

The extent of the administrator's (and that of their firm, and/or any associates) involvement prior to appointment.

The alternative options considered, both prior to and within formal insolvency by the insolvency practitioner and the company, and on appointment the administrator with an explanation of the possible outcomes.

Whether efforts were made to consult with major or representative creditors and the upshot of any consultations. If no consultation took place, the administrator should explain the reasons.

Why it was not appropriate to trade the business and offer it for sale as a going concern during the administration.

Details of requests made to potential funders to fund working capital requirements. If no such requests were made, explain why.

Details of registered charges with dates of creation.

If the business or business assets have been acquired from an insolvency process within the previous 24 months, or longer if the administrator deems that relevant to creditors' understanding, the administrator should disclose both the details of that transaction and whether the administrator, administrator's firm or associates were involved.

Marketing of the business and assets

The marketing activities conducted by the company and/or the administrator and the effect of those activities. Reference should be made to the marketing essentials above. Any divergence from these essentials is to be drawn to creditor's attention, with the reasons for such divergence, together with an explanation as to why the administrator relied upon the marketing conducted.

Valuation of the business and assets

The names and professional qualifications of any valuers and /or advisors and confirmation that they have confirmed their independence and that they carry adequate professional indemnity insurance. In the unlikely event that valuers and /or advisors who do not meet these criteria have been employed, the reasons for doing so should be explained.

The valuations obtained for the business or its underlying assets. Where goodwill has been valued, an explanation and basis for the value given.

A summary of the basis of valuation adopted by the administrator or the valuers and/or advisors.

The rationale for the basis of the valuations obtained and an explanation of the value achieved of the assets compared to those valuations.

If no valuation has been obtained, the reason for not having done so and how the administrator was satisfied as to the value of the assets.

The transaction

The date of the transaction.

Purchaser and related parties

- The identity of the purchaser.
- Any connection between the purchaser and the directors, shareholders or secured creditors of the company or their associates.
- The names of any directors, or former directors (or their associates), of the company who are involved in the management, financing, or ownership of the purchasing entity, or of any other entity into which any of the assets are transferred.
- In transactions impacting on more than one related company (e.g. a group transaction) the administrator should ensure that the disclosure is sufficient to enable a transparent explanation (for instance, allocation of consideration paid).

- Whether any directors had given guarantees for amounts due from the company to a prior financier and whether that financier is financing the new business.

Assets

- Details of the assets involved and the nature of the transaction.

Sale consideration

- The consideration for the transaction, terms of payment and any condition of the contract that could materially affect the consideration.
- The consideration disclosed under broad asset valuation categories and split between fixed and floating charge realisations (where applicable) and the method by which this allocation of consideration was applied.
- Any options, buy-back agreements, deferred consideration or other conditions attached to the transaction.
- Details of any security taken by the administrator in respect of any deferred consideration. Where no such security has been taken, the administrator's reasons for this and the basis for the decision that none was required.
- If the sale is part of a wider transaction, a description of the other aspects of the transaction.

Connected Party transactions only

Where the sale has been undertaken to a connected party the additional details should be included in the SIP 16 statement.

In this context only, a connected party is as defined in section 249 and 435 of the Insolvency Act 1986 and Article 7 and Article 4 of the Insolvency (NI) Order 1989, provided that in determining whether any person or company has control under section 435(10) and Article 4(10), sales to secured lenders who hold security for the granting of the loan (with related voting rights) as part of the secured lender's normal business activities, over one third or more of the shares in the insolvent company, are not included.

Pre-pack pool

The administrator should include one of the following in the SIP 16 statement –

- a statement that the pre-pack pool has been approached by the connected party, or not;
- a statement that the administrator has requested a copy of the opinion given by the pool member.

If an opinion is made by the pre –pack pool and is provided by the connected party to the administrator, a copy of that opinion is to be included within the SIP 16 statement, clearly stating the date of that opinion.

Viability statement

A viability review can be drawn up by a connected party wishing to make a pre-packaged purchase, stating how the purchasing entity will survive for at least 12 months from the date of the proposed purchase. The connected party should consider providing a short narrative detailing what the purchasing entity will do differently in order that the business will not fail ("the viability statement).

The administrator should request that the connected party considering a pre-packaged purchase provide a copy of their viability statement.

- If provided, it should be attached to the SIP 16 statement.
- If the viability statement has been requested but not provided, the administrator should notify creditors of this in the SIP 16 statement.

Section 3

Statements of Insolvency Practice — England & Wales

SECTION 3 — STATEMENTS OF INSOLVENCY PRACTICE — E&W

CONTENTS

3.1 STATEMENT OF INSOLVENCY PRACTICE 3.1 (E&W) INDIVIDUAL VOLUNTARY ARRANGEMENTS

INTRODUCTION

1. An Individual Voluntary Arrangement (IVA) is a statutory contract between a debtor and his or her creditors under which an insolvency practitioner will have powers and duties. An insolvency practitioner will be central to the preparation and agreement of the proposal, and the implementation of the arrangement, whether acting as adviser, nominee or supervisor. The particular nature of an insolvency practitioner's position renders transparency and fairness in all dealings of primary importance. The debtor and creditors should be confident that an insolvency practitioner will act professionally and with objectivity in each role associated with the arrangement. Failure to do so may prejudice the interests of both the debtor and creditors, and is likely to bring the practitioner and the profession into disrepute.

PRINCIPLES

2. An insolvency practitioner should differentiate clearly between the stages and roles that are associated with an IVA (these being, the provision of initial advice, assisting in the preparation of the proposal, acting as the nominee, and acting as the supervisor) and ensure that they are explained to the debtor and the creditors.

3. An insolvency practitioner should ensure that the information and explanations provided to a debtor about all the options available are such that the debtor can make an informed judgement as to whether an IVA is an appropriate solution.

4. An insolvency practitioner should explain to the debtor, the debtor's responsibilities and the consequences of an IVA.

5. Where an IVA is to be proposed, an insolvency practitioner should be satisfied that it is achievable and that a fair balance is struck between the interests of the debtor and the creditors.

6. An insolvency practitioner's reports should provide sufficient information to enable creditors to make informed decisions in relation to the proposal and the IVA, and report accurately in a manner that aims to be clear and useful.

KEY COMPLIANCE STANDARDS

7. Certain key compliance standards are of general application, but others will depend on whether the insolvency practitioner is acting as adviser nominee, or supervisor.

STANDARDS OF GENERAL APPLICATION

Advice to the debtor

8. The insolvency practitioner should have procedures in place to ensure that the information and explanations provided to the debtor at each stage of the process (that is, assessing the options available, and then preparing and implementing an IVA), are designed to set out clearly:

   (a) the advantages and disadvantages of each available option;

   (b) the key stages and the roles of the adviser, the nominee and the supervisor, any potential delays or complications, and the likely duration of the IVA;

   (c) what is required of the debtor;

   (d) the consequences of proposing and entering into an IVA, including the rights of challenge to the IVA and the potential consequences of those challenges; and

   (e) what may happen if the IVA is not approved or not successfully completed.

Meeting the debtor

9. A meeting should always be offered to the debtor. At each stage of the process, an assessment should be made as to whether a face-to-face meeting with the debtor is required, depending on the debtor's attitude and the circumstances and complexity of the case.

Assessment

10. The insolvency practitioner needs to be satisfied, at each stage of the process, that there are procedures in place to ensure that an assessment is made of:

    (a) the solutions available and their viability;

(b) whether the debtor is being sufficiently cooperative;

(c) the debtor's understanding of the process, and commitment to it;

(d) the likely attitude of any key creditors and the general body of creditors, in particular as to the fairness and balance of the proposals;

(e) whether an IVA would have a reasonable prospect of being approved and implemented; and

(f) whether an interim order is needed or available.

Documentation

11. The insolvency practitioner should be able to demonstrate that proper steps have been taken at all stages of the IVA, by maintaining records of:

(a) discussions with the debtor, including the information and explanations provided, the options outlined, and the advantages and disadvantages of each;

(b) comments made by the debtor, and the debtor's preferred option;

(c) any discussions with creditors or their representatives;

If the insolvency practitioner considers it appropriate in the circumstances, summaries of these discussions should be sent to the debtor.

STANDARDS OF SPECIFIC APPLICATION

Initial advice

12. An insolvency practitioner may be asked to give advice on a debtor's financial difficulties, and the way in which those difficulties might be resolved. The insolvency practitioner should have procedures in place to ensure, taking account of the personal circumstances of the debtor, that:

(a) the role of adviser is explained to the debtor, at this stage advising the debtor (in the debtor's interests) but in the context of needing to find a workable solution to the debtor's financial difficulties;

(b) sufficient information is obtained to make a preliminary assessment of the solutions available and their viability;

(c) the obligations of the debtor to cooperate and provide full disclosure are explained. The insolvency practitioner should be able to form a view of whether the debtor has a sufficient understanding of the situation and the consequences, and whether there will be full cooperation in seeking a solution;

(d) when considering possible solutions, account is taken of the impact of each solution on the debtor and the debtor's assets, in particular the family home, and on any third parties that may be affected;

(e) the debtor is provided with an explanation of all the options available, the advantages and disadvantages of each, and the likely costs of each so that the solution best suited to the debtor's circumstances can be identified. This explanation should be confirmed to the debtor in writing.

Preparing for an IVA

13. When preparing for an IVA, the insolvency practitioner should have procedures in place to ensure, taking account of the personal circumstances of the debtor and the nature of the debtor's finances, that:

(a) the debtor has had, or receives, the appropriate advice in relation to an IVA. This should be confirmed in writing if the insolvency practitioner or their firm has not done so before;

(b) the obligations of the debtor to cooperate and provide full and accurate disclosure, are explained and the consequences of not doing so if the insolvency practitioner has not done so before. The insolvency practitioner should be able to form a view of whether the debtor has a sufficient understanding of the process of an IVA, its likely duration and the consequences, and whether there will be full cooperation and commitment from the debtor;

(c) sufficient information is obtained to make an assessment of an IVA as a solution, and to enable a nominee to prepare a report, including;

(i) the measures taken by the debtor to avoid recurrence of their financial difficulties, if any;

(ii) the likely expectations of any key creditors;

(iii) the effect of the IVA on third parties where their view may have an effect on the viability of the IVA; and

(d) proportionate investigations into, and verification of, income and expenditure and assets and liabilities.

The proposal

14. Where the insolvency practitioner has been asked to assist the debtor to prepare a proposal, the insolvency practitioner should have procedures in place to ensure that the proposal contains the following:

(a) sufficient information for creditors to understand the debtor's financial and trading history (where appropriate), including:

(i) the background and financial history of the debtor;

(ii) why the debtor has become insolvent;

(iii) any other attempts that have been made to solve the debtor's financial difficulties, if there are any such difficulties;

(b) a comparison of the estimated outcomes of the IVA and the outcome if the IVA is not approved, including disclosure of the estimated costs of the IVA and the bases for those estimates;

(c) the identity of the source of any referral of the debtor, the relationship or connection of the referrer to the debtor and, where any payment has been made or is proposed to the referrer, the amount and reason for that payment;

(d) details of the amounts and source of any payments made, or proposed to be made, to the nominee and the supervisor or their firms in connection, or otherwise, with the proposed IVA, directly or indirectly and the reason(s) for the payment(s); and;

(e) where relevant, sufficient information to support any profit and cash projections, subject to any commercial sensitivity.

The nominee

15. It is the responsibility of the nominee to report in relation to the proposed IVA. When acting as nominee, the insolvency practitioner should have procedures in place to ensure that:

    (a) the debtor has had, or receives, the appropriate advice in relation to an IVA. This should be confirmed in writing if the insolvency practitioner or his firm has not done so before;

    (b) the nominee is able to report whether or not:

        (i) the debtor's financial position is materially different from that contained in the proposal, explaining the extent to which the information has been verified;

        (ii) the IVA is manifestly unfair;

        (iii) the IVA has a reasonable prospect of being approved and implemented.

    (c) the debtor's consent is sought on any modifications to the proposal put forward by creditors, and the debtor understands the impact of the modifications on the implementation of the IVA and its viability;

    (d) where a modification is adopted, the insolvency practitioner must ensure that consent is obtained from the debtor and, if appropriate, the creditors.

    (e) in the absence of consent, the IVA cannot proceed. The debtor's consent must be recorded.

The supervisor

16. When acting as supervisor, the insolvency practitioner should have procedures in place to ensure that:

    (a) where a proposal is modified, creditors have been made aware of the final form of the accepted IVA;

    (b) the IVA is supervised in accordance with its terms;

    (c) the progress of the IVA is monitored;

    (d) any departures from the terms of the IVA are identified at an early stage and appropriate action is then taken promptly by the supervisor;

    (e) any discretion(s) conferred on the supervisor are exercised where necessary, on a timely basis and that exercise is reported at the next available opportunity;

    (f) any variation to the terms of the IVA has been appropriately approved before it is implemented;

    (g) enquiries by the debtor and creditors are dealt with promptly;

    (h) full disclosure is made of the costs of the IVA and of any other sources of income of the insolvency practitioner or the practice, in relation to the case, in reports;

    (i) if the costs of the IVA have increased beyond previously reported estimates, this increase should be reported at the next available opportunity; and

    (j) the IVA is closed promptly on completion or termination.

Effective date: This SIP applies to all cases where the nominee is appointed on or after **1 July 2014**

3.2 STATEMENT OF INSOLVENCY PRACTICE 8 (E&W) SUMMONING AND HOLDING MEETINGS OF CREDITORS CONVENED PURSUANT TO SECTION 98 OF THE INSOLVENCY ACT 1986

INTRODUCTION

1. *[Not reproduced. Superseded by SIP 1 with effect from 02 May 2011.]*

2. This statement has been prepared for the sole use of members in connection with liquidations of companies registered in England and Wales. The statement concentrates on creditors' meetings held under section 98 of the Insolvency Act 1986 (IA 1986), and does not purport to cover the practice to be adopted in respect of all creditors' meetings. Throughout this statement the member who has received instructions from the company's directors to advise in relation to the convening of the creditors' meeting will be referred to as the 'advising member'. An advising member is reminded that he must have regard to the relevant primary and secondary legislation; and that if he intends seeking nomination as liquidator he must be qualified to act as an insolvency practitioner in relation to the company.

3. All members and their staff should conduct themselves in a professional manner at all meetings of creditors.

INSTRUCTIONS TO CONVENE MEETING

4. It is the responsibility of the company's directors to convene the creditors' meeting and to ensure that arrangements are made for the meeting to be held in accordance with current legislation. The advising member must therefore satisfy himself that the directors are aware of their responsibilities. He should also obtain written instructions from the board of directors which clearly define the matters on which he is to advise.

5. If the advising member receives instructions which would require him to act in a manner materially contrary to the Statements of Insolvency Practice, he should only accept those instructions after careful consideration of the implications of acceptance in that particular case. Where the directors act contrary to the guidance contained in this

statement the advising member may be called upon to show that the directors' actions were undertaken either without his knowledge or against his advice.

6. A member who is unable to accept an appointment as liquidator of a company because he or his firm has had a material professional relationship with the company during the preceding three years may act as an advising member. However, he should only do so after careful consideration of the implications of so acting in the light of his professional body's most recent guide to professional ethics.

7. A member who is asked to act as advising member in relation to any company should not agree to act unless he is satisfied that he is competent to provide the level of advice needed by the company in question, or is able to recommend where to obtain the appropriate level of advice if he himself is not able to provide it.

8. It is most undesirable that shareholders should pass a resolution for the winding up of a company unless a liquidator is also appointed and accordingly no member should accept instructions to act as advising member unless he has good grounds for believing that such appointment will be made. If, having accepted instructions, the advising member concludes that although a winding up is desirable, a voluntary winding up is inappropriate, he should advise the directors and shareholders that steps leading to a compulsory winding up should be taken. Such a situation could arise where a liquidator is unlikely to be appointed under the voluntary winding up, or where there is a strong case in favour of the liquidation commencing before a meeting of shareholders can be held.

VENUE AND TIME OF MEETING

9. When choosing the venue for the meeting, the advising member should not only fulfil the legal requirement to choose a place which is convenient for persons who are invited to attend, but he should also ensure that the accommodation is adequate for the number of persons likely to attend. Subject thereto, there is no objection to an advising member arranging for the meeting to be held at his own offices, provided that the requirements of Rule 4.60(1) are satisfied. He may make a reasonable charge for the use of the room.

10. The date and time of the meeting must be fixed with the convenience of creditors in mind and having regard to their geographical location. As an example, notices of a meeting should not normally be despatched shortly before the commencement of a known holiday period with the meeting taking place immediately after the holiday.

11. It is for the advising member to advise the directors whether, in all the circumstances of a particular case, it would be preferable for the members' and creditors' meetings to be held on the same or different days.

NOTICE OF THE MEETING

12. The notice convening the meeting should, where possible, be sent simultaneously to all classes of known creditors (including employees and secured creditors). The advising member should take all reasonable steps to ensure that the list of creditors provided by the directors is complete. Thus, for example, he should advise the company to identify and send notices to such creditors as hire purchase companies, lessors and former lessors and public utilities.

13. Although the legal requirement is that notices of the meeting must be sent not less than seven days before the day on which the meeting is to be held, this is often insufficient time to enable creditors to arrange representation. For the convenience of creditors, the advising member should ensure that notices of the meeting are despatched as early as possible having regard to the circumstances of the case. This should be no later than the date when the notices are despatched to shareholders. Note that the reference to seven days means seven clear days, i.e. it excludes the day on which the notices are sent and the day on which the meeting is held.

14. The notice advertised in the Gazette and local newspapers should appear as soon as possible and should not be deferred until shortly before the meeting. The advertised notice should meet the requirements of section 98(2) IA 1986.

15. Copies of the notice convening the shareholders' meeting should not be circulated to creditors. However, in order to reflect the provisions of section 183(2)(a) IA 1986, the notice of the creditors' meeting may contain a note of the convening of the shareholders' meeting.

16. A copy of the notice of the shareholders' meeting should be sent to all Under Sheriffs, Sheriff's Officers and County Courts known by the advising member to be interested in the company's affairs. In addition, notice of the creditors' meeting should be sent where practicable to solicitors or debt collection agencies acting for creditors.

17. When dealing with the issue of notices of the meeting, members should have regard to the provisions of Statement of Insolvency Practice 9 (E & W) by ensuring that creditors are notified of the possibility that resolutions may be passed at the meeting to determine the amount of fees payable from the company's assets and, where relevant, by providing creditors with explanatory notes setting out the manner in which the remuneration of liquidators is fixed.

18. Where the name of the company has been changed sufficiently recently for there to be any risk that creditors might not be aware of the new name, it is advisable to include reference to the former name or names both in the notices sent to creditors and in those inserted in the Gazette and local newspapers.

19. Section 98 IA 1986 requires that at least seven days' notice of the creditors' meeting shall be given. Occasions may arise when for the general benefit of creditors, a liquidator can be appointed before the day fixed for the creditors' meeting. Where the company is to be placed in liquidation and the creditors' meeting is held later, the advising member should, if possible, ensure that the secretary or a director of the company signs the notices of the creditors' meeting before the resolution to wind up is passed by the shareholders.

PROVISION OF INFORMATION PRIOR TO CREDITORS' MEETING

20. Where the directors have decided to arrange for an authorised insolvency practitioner to provide information to creditors under section 98(2)(a) IA 1986, the creditors are to be given 'such information concerning the company's affairs as they may reasonably require'. The information which it is reasonable to request will normally include information contained in the statement of affairs and the list of creditors, when available. Requests for information need not be made in writing. However, oral requests should be treated with caution and information should not be supplied

unless the caller can show that he is a creditor or a representative of a creditor. The advising member may decline to comply with a particular request for information if:

(a) it is unreasonable to expect him to be in a position to supply such information within the time remaining before the meeting; or

(b) the information requested ought to remain confidential on the grounds that its release would be prejudicial to the company or its creditors.

21. If the directors have decided to make a list of creditors available for inspection under section 98(2)(b) IA 1986, the advising member should take steps to ensure that:

(a) the list provides details of the names and addresses of all known creditors but not necessarily the amounts due to them;

(b) the names are arranged in alphabetical order;

(c) it is available at least between the hours of 10 a.m. and 4 p.m. on the two business days before the date of the meeting;

(d) sufficient copies are available for inspection to avoid undue delays to creditors' representatives; and

(e) the place where the list is to be made available is, in all the circumstances, reasonably convenient for creditors.

PROXIES AND OTHER REPRESENTATION

22. The forms of proxy accompanying the notice should conform to the Rules and should incorporate the name of the company and the date of the meeting before despatch in order to reduce the possibility of errors by creditors in completing the forms. The proxy must not be sent out with the name or description of any other person inserted on it.

23. Proxies to be used at the meeting are valid only if they are lodged by the time stated in the notice convening the meeting to the place specified in the notice. Faxed proxies should not be treated as invalid solely on the basis that they have been transmitted by fax.

24. Proxies which are lodged out of time should be treated as invalid. Proxies which are incorrectly completed in a material way will be invalid. There is a requirement for proxies to be signed by the principal or by a person

authorised by him, in which case the nature of the authority must be stated. Proxies which are unsigned or which do not explain the authority under which they are signed will, therefore, be invalid. However, proxies should not be rejected simply because of a minor error in their completion provided:

(a) the form of proxy sent with the notice of the meeting (or a substantially similar form) has been used;

(b) the identity of the creditor and the proxy holder, the nature of the proxy holder's authority and any instructions given to the proxy holder are clear.

25. When advising the chairman of the meeting on the validity of proxies, a member should bear in mind that he has a personal interest if he has been appointed liquidator at the shareholders' meeting and seeks to retain office following the creditors' meeting or intends to seek appointment as liquidator at that meeting. Where circumstances so demand, he should suggest prior to the meeting that the chairman takes advice on the validity of proxies from an independent source, for example the company's solicitors.

26. There is no requirement for proxies which are considered invalid to be returned to the creditors who have lodged them.

27. A person may be authorised to represent a creditor which is a body corporate under section 375 of the Companies Act 1985. Where a person is so authorised he must produce to the Chairman a copy of the resolution from which he derives his authority. The copy must be under the seal of the corporation or certified by the secretary or a director of the corporation to be a true copy. Where Customs and Excise is represented at a meeting by a Customs officer attending in person, the officer's commission constitutes sufficient authority for him to act on Customs' behalf without the need for the submission of a proxy.

PROOFS OF DEBT

28. Creditors may submit proofs at any time before voting, even during the course of the meeting itself. The admission or rejection of proofs for voting purposes is the responsibility of the chairman of the meeting. A proof should be accepted as valid for voting purposes, provided it identifies both

the creditor and the amount claimed by him with sufficient clarity. The amount for which the chairman should be advised to admit the proof for voting purposes should normally be the lower of:

(a) the amount stated in the proof; and

(b) the amount considered by the company to be due to the creditor.

The advising member may assist the chairman to decide the amounts for which claims should be admitted but if he intends to seek appointment as liquidator he should bear in mind that his own personal interests might create a conflict, in which case the chairman should be advised independently.

The amount for which the proof is admitted for voting purposes should be set out in writing and signed by the chairman. In most instances it is expected that the chairman will do this prior to the meeting.

AVAILABILITY OF PROXIES AND PROOFS FOR INSPECTION

29. Any person entitled to attend the meeting may inspect the proxies and proofs, either immediately before or during the meeting. Notwithstanding that a form of proxy submitted is ruled by the chairman to be invalid or a proof is rejected in whole or in part these documents should be made available for inspection.

ATTENDANCE AT THE CREDITORS' MEETING

30. A liquidator appointed by the shareholders before the creditors' meeting takes place is required to attend the meeting of creditors personally. He must report to the meeting on any exercise of his powers under sections 112, 165 or 166 IA 1986. Such attendance is required even if the shareholders' appointment was made only shortly before the creditors' meeting. He must also attend any adjourned meeting. He is liable to a fine if he fails to comply without reasonable excuse. He should in such a case document at the time the reason for non-attendance and ensure that a suitably experienced colleague attends in his place.

31. One of the directors of the company will have been nominated to act as chairman of the meeting and he must attend. In addition, the advising member should consider whether any other director or employee of the

company will be able to provide information which is relevant to the meeting and if so, he should advise that that person be invited to attend the meeting.

32.   Creditors and their authorised representatives are entitled to attend. In addition, a person who holds himself out as representing a creditor should, in the absence of evidence to the contrary, be allowed admittance and to raise questions, but he may be unable to vote.

33.   The chairman of the meeting should be advised that he must decide whether to allow any third parties, such as shareholders, the press or the police, to attend, after taking into account the views of the creditors present.

INFORMATION TO BE PROVIDED TO THE MEETING

34.   The advising member should ensure that a summary or a copy of the directors' sworn statement of affairs is handed to all those attending the meeting. This summary will normally be expected to include a list of the names of the major creditors and of the amounts owing to them. Sufficient copies of the full list of creditors should be available to facilitate its inspection by those attending the meeting. The meeting should be told that the sworn statement of affairs is available for inspection at the meeting.

35.   Information to be given to the meeting should include:

(a)   details of any prior involvement with the company or its directors by the advising member or, if a different person, the proposed liquidator;

(b)   a report of the previously held shareholders' meeting, stating the date the notice of the meeting was issued, the date and time that the meeting was held and, if it was held at short notice, the reasons therefore and the fact that the required consents were received. The resolutions passed at the meeting should be reported and if the liquidator has not yet consented to act, that fact should be stated. If the shareholders' meeting was adjourned without a resolution for voluntary winding up being passed, there should be reported:

(i)   the date and time to which the meeting had been adjourned; and

(ii)   the fact that any resolutions passed at the section 98 meeting will come into effect if and when the winding-up resolution is passed;

(c) the date on which the directors gave instructions for the meeting of creditors to be convened and the date on which the notices were despatched;

(d) the details of the costs paid by the company or on its behalf in connection with:

(i) the preparation of the statement of affairs;

(ii) the arrangements for the creditors' meeting; and

(iii) advice to the company or its directors in the period from the time the advising members was first consulted by or on behalf of the company or its directors;

the details for each category should include the name of the recipient, the amount, the source of the payment; and, in the case of (iii), the nature of the advice given.

If no payments have been made in respect of these costs prior to the meeting, the estimated amount of the costs should be stated. If any of the costs have been or are proposed to be paid to someone other than the advising member, the nature of the relationship of the company or its directors to that person (e.g. auditor, solicitor, financial adviser) should be stated.

(e) a report on the company's relevant trading history which should include:

(i) date of incorporation and registered number;

(ii) names of all persons who have acted as directors of the company or as its company secretary at any time during the three years preceding the meeting;

(iii) names of major shareholders together with the details of their shareholdings;

(iv) details of all classes of shares issued;

(v) nature of the business conducted by the company;

(vi) location of the business and the address of the registered office;

(vii) details of parent, subsidiary and associated companies;

(viii) the directors' reasons for the failure of the company;

March 2002

(ix) extracts from any formal or, if none, draft accounts produced for periods covering the previous three years or for any earlier period which is relevant to the failure of the company. The extracts should include details of turnover, net result, directors' remuneration, shareholders' funds, dividends paid, reserves carried forward at year end and the date of the auditors' report. Creditors should also be advised if the accounts have been qualified by the auditors;

(x) a deficiency account reconciling the position shown by the most recent balance sheet to the deficiency in the statement of affairs;

(xi) the names and professional qualifications of any valuers whose valuations have been relied upon for the purpose of the statement of affairs, together with the basis or bases of valuation;

(xii) such other information as the advising member considers necessary to give the creditors a proper appreciation of the company's affairs;

(f) if a receiver has been appointed over any assets of the company, the meeting should be provided with a report on the conduct of the receivership to date, including a summary of the receiver's receipts and payments, unless disclosure would be in breach of the receiver's duty to his appointor, for example where market sensitive information was involved. In such circumstances, a receipts and payments account only should be provided, together with an explanation of the circumstances which prevent further information being given. Where any member is an authorised practitioner and is a receiver of a company whose shareholders pass a resolution for voluntary winding up, that member should assist the advising member by providing this information;

(g) an explanation of the contents of the statement of affairs.

36. There should also be provided to the meeting details of any transactions (other than in the ordinary course of business) between the company, any of its subsidiaries or any other company in which it has or had an interest (together 'the company') and any one or more of its directors or any other associate of him or them (as defined in section 435 of the Insolvency Act 1986) during the period of one year prior to the resolution of the directors that the company be wound up specifying -

- the assets acquired and the consideration therefor together with the date(s) of the acquisition(s) and the date(s) the consideration for their acquisition was paid
- the names and qualifications of any person who advised independently on the value of any assets the subject of such transactions
- the dates on which any resolutions of the company authorising any such transactions were passed

There should also be reported to the creditors whether (or not) the advising member or the proposed liquidator or any partner or employee of either of them acted in any capacity either for the company (as defined above) or any other party to any transaction subject to the disclosure requirements set out above.

37. The advising member should take all practicable steps to ensure that there are available to hand to those attending the meeting a written summary of the more important financial information which is contained in a report given orally to the meeting.

38. In assisting in the preparation of a report to be presented to the meeting, the advising member may rely upon information contained in the company's accounts and records and also upon information provided by directors and employees. He is not expected to conduct an investigation to ensure that the information is accurate, but should provide the creditors with any material conflicting information of which he is aware.

CONDUCT OF THE MEETING

39. Although the chairman of the meeting must be a director of the company and his identity must be made clear at the outset, there is no reason why the meeting should not be conducted by the advising member or some other professional adviser. It should be explained to the meeting that, although this is being done on behalf of the directors, the report is their responsibility and is based upon information supplied by them. The chairman is the arbiter on all procedural matters but may seek advice from the advising member.

40. Creditors and their representatives attending the meeting are required to sign an attendance list. This list should be made available for inspection to anyone attending the meeting. In addition, any creditor or creditor's representative wishing to speak, ask questions, or make a nomination, should be asked to identify himself and the creditor he represents.

41. Creditors and their representatives should be given the opportunity to ask questions. Whilst every effort should be made to give a reasonable answer to such questions within the context of the meeting, the chairman may be advised to refuse a question to be put if, for example:

    - the questioner refuses to give the name of the creditor he represents and his own name or that of his firm;
    - the questioner does not claim to be or to represent a creditor;

    or may decline to answer it if, for example:

    - the answer could prejudice the successful outcome of the liquidation or creditors' interests;
    - the answer could be construed as slanderous if subsequently proved incorrect.

    The chairman should be advised to state the grounds on which he refuses to allow a question. Creditors are entitled to information on the causes of the company's failure but it is not appropriate for a detailed investigation of the company's affairs to be undertaken at a meeting of creditors.

42. Nominations for the appointment of a liquidator should be requested before any vote is taken. The holder of a proxy requiring him to vote for the appointment of a particular liquidator is required to nominate that person, and it is therefore possible that the chairman or any other holder of such proxies may need to make more than one nomination.

43. The chairman must accept all nominations and put them to the meeting, unless he has good grounds for supposing that the person nominated is not qualified or is unwilling to act as an insolvency practitioner in relation to the company.

44. The procedure to be followed when voting for the appointment of a liquidator should be explained to the meeting. It is acceptable in the first instance for a vote to be taken on an informal show of hands and if the

result is accepted by all interested parties, the chairman of the meeting may conclude that a resolution has been passed. If a formal vote becomes necessary it should be conducted by stating the names of all those nominated and by the issue of voting papers on which those wishing to vote will be required to show their name, the name of the creditor they are representing, the amount of the creditor's claim and the name of the nominated person for whom they wish to vote. It is the advising member's responsibility to ensure that voting papers are available.

45. When all votes have been counted, the chairman should announce the result to the meeting, giving details of the total value of votes cast in favour of each nomination. He should also give details of votes which have been rejected, either in whole or in part, and should also state which nomination those creditors supported and the reasons for the rejection.

46. An absolute majority is required and if the first poll is not conclusive, the nominee receiving the least value of votes is excluded on the next poll where no other nominee has withdrawn. In the event of the withdrawal of at least one nominee, then the nominee with the least value of votes remains in the next poll. The same procedure should be followed in all successive polls.

47. If a proxy-holder has been instructed to vote for a particular person as liquidator and that person is eliminated or withdraws, then, if the second set of words in square brackets on the proxy form (Form 8.5) allowing him to vote or abstain at his discretion has not been deleted, the proxy-holder will be able to vote for such other person as he thinks fit. If the second set of words in square brackets has been deleted, the proxy-holder will have to abstain on any further ballot.

48. The meeting should be told of its right to appoint a liquidation committee and of the nature of the committee's functions, including its rights in relation to the liquidator's remuneration. The committee must consist of not less than three and not more than five creditors (not being fully secured) who have lodged proofs which have not been wholly disallowed for voting purposes or rejected. The meeting should be advised of any shareholders' nominations to the committee and of the creditors' right to veto them (subject to court order) and the voting procedure should be explained. When the constitution of the committee is not contentious, a resolution may be passed on a show of hands and may also appoint a

committee en bloc. If there are more than five nominations for appointment to the liquidation committee, it is recommended that voting papers should be issued on which each person voting should enter his own name, the name of the creditor he represents and the amount of the claim. Each such person should be allowed to vote for up to five members of the committee and in doing so may vote for his own appointment (if he is a creditor) or that of the creditor he represents. The provision of voting papers is the responsibility of the advising member.

49. When declaring the result the chairman should follow the same procedures as those outlined in paragraph 46 above. The five creditors receiving the greatest value of votes will form the committee, together with any shareholders' nominations which have not been vetoed.

50. Voting papers should be made available for inspection by any creditor or creditor's representative whose claim has been admitted for voting purposes at any time during the meeting or during normal business hours on the business day following the meeting.

51. Apart from the appointment of a liquidator and the establishment of a liquidation committee, the only other resolutions which may be taken by the meeting are:

- (unless it has been resolved to establish a liquidation committee) a resolution specifying the terms on which the liquidator is to be remunerated, or to defer consideration of that matter;

- in the event of two or more persons being appointed to act jointly as liquidators, a resolution specifying whether acts are to be done by both or all of them, or by only one;

- a resolution to adjourn the meeting for not more than three weeks;

- any other resolution which the chairman thinks it right to allow for special reasons.

52. A record of the meeting should be prepared in accordance with Statement of Insolvency Practice 12 (E&W).

PROVISION OF INFORMATION TO LIQUIDATOR

53. In instances where the advising member has not been appointed to be the liquidator of the company, he must provide reasonable assistance to the liquidator. This will include handing over such of the company's books and papers as are held by him, together with documents he has received in relation to the meeting of creditors (e.g. proofs, proxies, statement of affairs, shareholders' resolutions, attendance lists and record of the creditors' meeting). It is expected that this information will be handed over as quickly as possible and, in any event, within seven days of the conclusion of the creditors' meeting. Likewise, all sums received by the advising member from the company or on its behalf, less any proper disbursements which he has made, duly vouched, should also be handed over.

REPORT TO CREDITORS FOLLOWING THE MEETING

54. The liquidator shall send to creditors and contributories a report of the proceedings at the meeting, together with a copy or summary of the statement of affairs. If a list of creditors is not supplied, the liquidator should undertake to supply or make available a copy to any creditor on request. The report to creditors should include the name and address of the liquidator and of the creditors appointed to the liquidation committee. Details of other resolutions passed at the meeting should also be supplied. It is not necessary to supply a detailed report on all that transpired at the meeting, but matters of particular relevance should be mentioned. Creditors should be asked to bring the liquidator's attention to any matter of which they consider he should be aware.

SOLICITATION TO OBTAIN NOMINATION

55. Members are reminded of the provisions of section 164 IA 1986 (corrupt inducement), Rule 4.150 of the Insolvency Rules 1986 (solicitation) and their professional body's most recent guide to professional ethics.

Issued January 2002 Version 3 (E&W)

This Statement of Insolvency Practice is currently being revised and is likely to be withdrawn and re-issued during 2017 within a new combined SIP 8 / 10 / 12. Please check www.insolvency-practitioners.org.uk for further details.

3.3 STATEMENT OF INSOLVENCY PRACTICE 9 (E&W) PAYMENTS TO INSOLVENCY OFFICE HOLDERS AND THEIR ASSOCIATES

INTRODUCTION

1. The particular nature of an insolvency office holder's position renders transparency and fairness of primary importance in all their dealings. Creditors and other interested parties[1] with a financial interest in the level of payments from an insolvent estate should be confident that the rules relating to approval and disclosure of fees and expenses have been properly complied with.

2. This statement applies to all forms of proceedings under the Insolvency Act 1986. Nothing within this SIP obligates a practitioner to provide a fee estimate where one is not required by statute.

PRINCIPLES

3. Payments to an office holder or their associates, and expenses incurred by an office holder, should be fair and reasonable reflections of the work necessarily and properly undertaken.

4. Those responsible for approving payments to an office holder or their associates should be provided with sufficient information to make an informed judgement about the reasonableness of the office holder's requests.

5. Information provided by an office holder should be presented in a manner which is transparent, consistent throughout the life of the case and useful to creditors and other interested parties, whilst being proportionate to the circumstances of the case.

---

[1] "other interested parties" means those parties with rights pursuant to the prevailing insolvency legislation to information about the office holder's receipts and payments. This may include a creditors' committee, the members (shareholders) of a company, or in personal insolvency, the debtor.

KEY COMPLIANCE STANDARDS

PROVISIONS OF GENERAL APPLICATION

6. An office holder should disclose:

    (a) payments, remuneration and expenses arising from an insolvency appointment to the office holder or his or her associates;

    (b) any business or personal relationships with parties responsible for approving his or her remuneration or who provide services to the office holder in respect of the insolvency appointment where the relationship could give rise to a conflict of interest.

7. An office holder should inform creditors and other interested parties of their rights under insolvency legislation. Creditors should be advised how they may access suitable information setting out their rights within the first communication with them and in each subsequent report. An insolvency practitioner is not precluded from providing information, including a fee estimate, within pre-appointment communications (such as when assisting directors in commencing an insolvency process).

8. Where an office holder sub-contracts out work that could otherwise be carried out by the office holder or his or her staff, this should be drawn to the attention of creditors with an explanation of why it is being done.

9. The key issues of concern to those who have a financial interest in the level of payments from the insolvency estate will commonly be:

    (a) the work the office holder anticipates will be done and why that work is necessary;

    (b) the anticipated cost of that work, including any expenses expected to be incurred in connection with it;

    (c) whether it is anticipated that the work will provide a financial benefit to creditors, and if so what anticipated benefit (or if the work provides no direct financial benefit, but is required by statute);

    (d) the work actually done and why that work was necessary;

    (e) the actual costs of the work, including any expenses incurred in connection with it, as against any estimate provided;

(f)   whether the work has provided a financial benefit to creditors, and if so what benefit (or if the work provided no direct financial benefit, but was required by statute);

When providing information about payments, fees and expenses to those with a financial interest in the level of payments from an insolvent estate, the office holder should do so in a way which facilitates clarity of understanding of these key issues. Narrative explanations should be provided to support any numerical information supplied. Such an approach allows creditors and other interested parties to better recognise the nature of an office holder's role and the work they intend to undertake, or have undertaken, in accordance with the key issues. Where it is practical to do so, the office holder should provide an indication of the likely return to creditors when seeking approval for the basis of their remuneration.

10.   When approval for a fixed amount or a percentage basis is sought, the office holder should explain why the basis requested is expected to produce a fair and reasonable reflection of the work that the office holder anticipates will be undertaken.

11.   When providing a fee estimate the office holder should supply that information in sufficient time to facilitate that body making an informed judgement about the reasonableness of the office holder's requests. Fee estimates should be based on all of the information available to the office holder at the time that the estimate is provided and may not be presented on the basis of alternative scenarios and/or provide a range of estimated charges.

12.   Each part of an office holder's activities will require different levels of expertise, and therefore related cost. It will generally assist the understanding of creditors and other interested parties to divide the office holder's narrative explanations and any fee estimate provided into areas such as:

(a)   Administration (including statutory reporting);

(b)   Realisation of assets;

(c)   Creditors (claims and distribution);

(d)   Investigations;

(e)   Trading (where applicable);

(f) Case specific matters (where applicable)

13. These are examples of common activities and not an exhaustive list. Alternative or further sub-divisions may be appropriate, depending on the nature and complexity of the case and the bases of remuneration sought and/or approved. It is unlikely that the same divisions will be appropriate in all cases and an office holder should consider what divisions are likely to be appropriate and proportionate in the circumstances of each case.

14. When providing a fee estimate of time to be spent, creditors and other interested parties may find a blended rate (or rates) and total hours anticipated to be spent on each part of the anticipated work more easily understandable and comparable than detail covering each grade or person working on the case. The estimate should also clearly describe what activities are anticipated to be conducted in respect of the estimated fee. When subsequently reporting to creditors, the actual hours and average rate (or rates) of the costs charged for each part should be provided for comparison purposes.

15. Where remuneration is sought on more than one basis, it should be clearly stated to which part of the office holder's activities the basis relates. In all cases, an office holder should endeavour to use consistent divisions throughout the duration of the case. The use of additional categories or further division may become necessary where a task was not foreseen at the commencement of the appointment.

REPORTS TO CREDITORS AND OTHER INTERESTED PARTIES

16. Any disclosure by an office holder of payments, remuneration and expenses should be of assistance to those who have a financial interest in the level of payments from an insolvent estate in understanding what was done, why it was done, and how much it costs.

17. Irrespective of the basis or bases of remuneration approved, reports to creditors and interested parties should include a narrative update in respect of the office holder's activity during the period being reported upon, using consistent divisions for each part of the work reported upon, as far as possible.

18. When reporting the amount of remuneration charged or expenses incurred during a period, the office holder should use a consistent format throughout the life of the case and provide figures for both the period being reported upon and on a cumulative basis.

19. Requests for additional information about payments to an office holder or their associates, or about expenses incurred by an office holder, should be treated by an office holder in a fair and reasonable way. The provision of additional information should be proportionate to the circumstances of the case.

EXPENSES

20. Expenses are amounts properly payable by the office holder from the estate which are not otherwise categorised as the office holder's remuneration or as a distribution to a creditor or creditors. These may include, but are not limited to, legal and agents' fees, trading expenses and tax liabilities. When providing details of the expenses an office holder anticipates will, or are likely to be, incurred it is acceptable to provide a range, or repeat a range quoted by a third party (for instance for legal costs in litigation).

DISBURSEMENTS

21. Disbursements are expenses met by and reimbursed to an office holder in connection with an insolvency appointment and will fall into two categories; Category 1 and Category 2.

22. **Category 1 disbursements**: These are payments to independent third parties where there is specific expenditure directly referable to the appointment in question. Category 1 disbursements can be drawn without prior approval, although an office holder should be prepared to disclose information about them in the same way as any other expenses.

23. **Category 2 disbursements**: These are expenses that are directly referable to the appointment in question but not to a payment to an independent third party. They may include shared or allocated costs that may be incurred by the office holder or their firm, and that can be allocated to the appointment on a proper and reasonable basis. Category 2 disbursements require approval in the same manner as an office holder's remuneration.

When seeking approval, an office holder should explain, for each category of cost, the basis on which the charge is being made. If an office holder has obtained approval for the basis of Category 2 disbursements, that basis may continue to be used in a sequential appointment where further approval of the basis of remuneration is not required, or where the office holder is replaced.

24. The following are not permissible as disbursements:

    (a) a charge calculated as a percentage of remuneration;

    (b) an administration fee or charge additional to an office holder's remuneration;

    (c) recovery of basic overhead costs such as office and equipment rental, depreciation and finance charges.

PRE-APPOINTMENT COSTS

25. Where recovery of pre-appointment cost is expressly permitted and approval is sought for the payment of outstanding costs from the estate, disclosure should follow the principles and standards contained in this statement. Disclosure should also be made of amounts already paid to the office holder in respect of pre-appointment costs, giving the amounts paid, the name of the payor and its relationship to the estate and the nature of the payment.

PAYMENTS TO ASSOCIATES

26. Where services are provided from within the practice or by a party with whom the practice, or an individual within the practice, has a business or personal relationship, an office holder should take particular care to ensure that the best value and service is being provided. An office holder should also have regard to relationships where the practice is held out to be part of a national or international network.

27. Payments that could reasonably be perceived as presenting a threat to the office holder's objectivity by virtue of a professional or personal relationship should not be made unless disclosed and approved in the same manner as an office holder's remuneration or category 2 disbursements.

PROVISION OF INFORMATION TO SUCCESSIVE OFFICE HOLDERS

28. When an office holder's appointment is followed by the appointment of another insolvency practitioner, whether or not in the same proceedings, the prior office holder should provide the successor with information in accordance with the principles and standards contained in this statement.

PROVISION OF INFORMATION

29. In order to facilitate information requests under statute or to support the reporting of remuneration, time recording systems used by insolvency practitioners should record time units of not greater than 6 minutes for each grade of staff used.

30. Where realisations are sufficient for payment of creditors in full with interest, the creditors will not have the principal financial interest in the level of remuneration. An office holder should provide the beneficiaries of the anticipated surplus, on request, with information in accordance with the principles and standards contained in this statement.

Effective Date: 01 December 2015

3.4 STATEMENT OF INSOLVENCY PRACTICE 10 (E&W) PROXY FORMS

1.   *[Not reproduced. Superseded by SIP 1 with effect from 02 May 2011.]*

2.   This statement applies to England and Wales only.

3.   Rule 8.2 of the Insolvency Rules 1986 stipulates that, when notice is given of a meeting to be held in insolvency proceedings and forms of proxy are sent out with the notice, no form so sent out shall have inserted in it the name or description of any person. No proxy form, therefore, should have inserted in it the name or description of any person for appointment as an insolvency office holder, either solely or jointly, or for appointment as a member of a committee, or as proxy-holder.

4.   Members who send out proxy forms should ensure that no part of the form is pre-completed with the name or description of any person (except for the title of the proceedings, which may be inserted for the convenience of the person completing the form).

5.   When a member advises on the sending out of proxy forms he is required to take all reasonable steps to ensure that no part of the form is pre-completed with the name or description of any person. If the person whom a member is advising refuses to accept the member's advice in this regard the member should ensure that he has put his advice in writing so that he can demonstrate that he has given advice consistent with the law.

Issued: August 1996

This Statement of Insolvency Practice is currently being revised and is likely to be withdrawn and re-issued during 2017 within a new combined SIP 8 / 10 / 12. Please check www.insolvency-practitioners.org.uk for further details.

3.5 STATEMENT OF INSOLVENCY PRACTICE 11 (E&W) THE HANDLING OF FUNDS IN FORMAL INSOLVENCY APPOINTMENTS

1. INTRODUCTION

1.1   *[Not reproduced. Superseded by SIP 1 with effect from 02 May 2011.]*

2. STATEMENT OF INSOLVENCY PRACTICE

2.1   This statement of insolvency practice concerns the handling of funds by insolvency office holders in the administration of insolvency cases. It applies to England and Wales only.

2.2   Members should ensure that records are maintained to identify the funds (including any interest earned thereon) and other assets of each case for which they have responsibility as insolvency office holder. Such funds and assets must be maintained separately from those of the office holder or his firm. Subject to the rules relating to the payment of monies into the Insolvency Services Account, case funds should be held in a bank account(s) which meet the following criteria to ensure that these principles are adhered to:

- all money standing to the credit of the account(s) is held by the office holder as case money and the bank is not entitled to combine the account with any other account (including any global, omnibus, master, hub, nominee, sub accounts or similar) or exercise any right to set off or counterclaim against money in that account in respect of any money owed to it on any other account (including any global, omnibus, master, hub, nominee, sub accounts or similar) of the office holder or his firm;

- interest payable on the money in the account(s) must be credited to that account(s);

- the bank must describe the account(s) in its records to make it clear that the money in the account does not belong to office holder or his firm;

- no individual case funds/account(s) can be set off against any overdrawn case funds/accounts (including any global, omnibus, master, hub, nominee, sub accounts or similar).

2.3 Where funds relating to a case are received by cheque payable to the office holder or his firm which cannot be endorsed to the insolvent estate, such cheques may be cleared through an account maintained in the name of the office holder or his firm. Such accounts should be operated on a trust basis and should be maintained separately from the practitioner's office accounts. Funds paid into such accounts should be paid out to the case to which they relate as soon as possible.

2.4 Monies coming into the hands of practitioners which are the property of individuals or companies for which they are acting otherwise than in the capacity of insolvency office holder must be held in an account operated on trust principles and subject to any applicable client money rules.

Effective date: 1 June 2007

This Statement of Insolvency Practice is currently being revised and is likely to be withdrawn and re-issued during 2017 within a new combined SIP 8 / 10 / 12. Please check www.insolvency-practitioners.org.uk for further details.

3.6 STATEMENT OF INSOLVENCY PRACTICE 12 (E&W) RECORDS OF MEETINGS IN FORMAL INSOLVENCY PROCEEDINGS

1. INTRODUCTION

1.1   *[Not reproduced. Superseded by SIP 1 with effect from 02 May 2011.]*

1.2   This statement of insolvency practice concerns the keeping of records of meetings of creditors, committees of creditors, and members or contributories of companies in formal insolvency proceedings. The statement is in two parts. The first summarises the statutory provisions regarding the keeping of such records in the various types of insolvency appointment. The second sets out the minimum standards which should be observed with regard to such records in all cases as a matter of best practice.

1.3   The statement applies to England and Wales only. References to the Act are to the Insolvency Act 1986, and references to the Rules are to the Insolvency Rules 1986.

2. THE STATUTORY PROVISIONS

2.1   Meetings of creditors - administration

The chairman of the meeting shall cause minutes of its proceedings to be entered in the company's minute book. The minutes shall include a list of the creditors who attended (personally or by proxy) and, if a creditors' committee has been established, the names and addresses of those elected to be members of the committee. (Rule 2.28)

2.2   Meetings of creditors - administrative receivership

The chairman of the meeting shall cause a record to be made of the proceedings and kept as part of the records of the receivership. The record shall include a list of the creditors who attended (personally or by proxy) and, if a creditors' committee has been established, the names and addresses of those elected to be members of the committee. (Rule 3.15)

2.3 Meetings of creditors and contributories - liquidation

At any meeting of creditors or contributories the chairman shall cause minutes of the proceedings to be kept. The minutes shall be signed by him and retained as part of the records of the liquidation. The chairman shall also cause to be made up and kept a list of all the creditors or, as the case may be, contributories who attended the meeting. The minutes of the meeting shall include a record of every resolution passed. In the case of compulsory liquidations, it is the chairman's duty to see to it that particulars of all such resolutions, certified by him, are filed in court not more than 21 days after the date of the meeting. (Rule 4.71)

2.4 Meetings of creditors - bankruptcy

The chairman at any creditors' meeting shall cause minutes of the proceedings at the meeting, signed by him, to be retained by him as part of the records of the bankruptcy. He shall also cause to be made up and kept a list of all the creditors who attended the meeting. The minutes of the meeting shall include a record of every resolution passed. It is the chairman's duty to see to it that the particulars of all such resolutions, certified by him, are filed in court not more than 21 days after the date of the meeting. (Rule 6.95)

2.5 Meetings of creditors and members - voluntary arrangements

Where, in the case of a company, meetings of the company and its creditors are held under section 3 of the Act, or, in the case of an individual, a meeting of creditors is held under Section 257 of the Act, a report of the meeting or meetings shall be prepared by the chairman. The report shall -

- state whether the proposal for a voluntary arrangement was approved or rejected, and, if approved with what (if any) modifications;
- set out the resolutions which were taken at the meetings, and the decision on each one;
- list the creditors and, in the case of a company, the members of the company, (with their respective values) who were present or represented at the meetings, and how they voted on each resolution; and
- include such further information (if any) as the chairman thinks it appropriate to make known to the court.

2.6 Meetings of committees of creditors

2.6.1 At all meetings of committees of creditors established under the Act every resolution passed shall be recorded in writing, either separately or as part of the minutes of the meeting. A record of each resolution shall be signed by the chairman and kept with the records of the proceedings (or, in the case of administrations, placed in the company's minute book). (Rules 2.42 (administration); 3.26 (administrative receivership); 4.165 (compulsory liquidation); 4.166 (creditors' voluntary liquidation); 6.161 (bankruptcy))

2.6.2 Where resolutions of the committee are taken by post, a copy of every resolution passed, and a note that the committee's concurrence was obtained, shall be kept with the records of the proceedings (or, in the case of administrations, placed in the company's minute book). (Rules 2.43 (administration); 3.27 (administrative receivership); 4.167 (liquidation); 6.162 (bankruptcy))

2.6.3 The Act contains no provisions for the establishment of committees in voluntary arrangements, but the terms of a proposal may provide for the establishment of a committee and may lay down procedures for keeping a record of its proceedings.

2.7 Minutes as evidence of proceedings

A minute of proceedings at a meeting of creditors, or the members or contributories of a company, held under the Act or Rules, signed by a person describing himself as or appearing to be the chairman of the meeting, is admissible in insolvency proceedings without further proof. The minute is prima facie evidence that -

- the meeting was duly convened and held,
- all resolutions passed at the meeting were duly passed, and
- all proceedings at the meeting duly took place (Rule 12.5)

3. BEST PRACTICE

3.1 Records should be kept of all meetings of creditors, committees of creditors, or members or contributories of companies, held under the Act or Rules or under provisions contained in a voluntary arrangement approved by the creditors. The record should include, as a minimum, the following information:

- The title of the proceedings
- The date, time and venue of the meeting
- The name and description of the chairman and any other person involved in the conduct of the meeting
- A list, either incorporated into the report or appended to it, of the creditors, members or contributories attending or represented at the meeting
- The name of any officer or former officer of the company attending the meeting if not attending in one of the above capacities
- The exercise of any discretion by the chairman in relation to the admissibility or value of any claim for voting purposes
- The resolutions taken and the decision on each one and, in the event of a poll being taken, the value or number (as appropriate) of votes for and against each resolution
- Where a committee is established, the names and addresses of the members
- Such other matters as are required by the statutory provisions applicable to the relevant insolvency procedure as set out in section 2 above or, in the case of a voluntary arrangement, by the terms of the proposal

Where a meeting has been asked to approve an office holder's remuneration, the information provided to the meeting in support of that request should form part of, or be retained with, the record of the proceedings.

3.2   The record should be signed by the chairman and be either

- retained with the record of the proceedings, or

- entered in the company's minute book, with a copy retained with the record of the proceedings, whichever is appropriate. In the case of committee meetings a copy of the record should be sent to every person who attended, or was entitled to attend, the meeting.

3.3   Forms of proxy retained under Rule 8.4 and, where a poll is taken, the poll cards, should be kept with the record of the proceedings.

3.4   Where a member is the office holder or is appointed office holder as a result of the proceedings at the meeting and has not himself acted as chairman of the meeting, he should endeavour to ensure that the record is signed by the chairman and complies with the above principles. If the member is not satisfied that the record signed by the chairman is an accurate record of the proceedings, he should either prepare his own record for his files or prepare a note for his files explaining in what respects he disagrees with the chairman's record.

Issued August 1996

This Statement of Insolvency Practice is currently being revised and is likely to be withdrawn and re-issued during 2017 within a new combined SIP 8 / 10 / 12. Please check www.insolvency-practitioners.org.uk for further details.

3.7 STATEMENT OF INSOLVENCY PRACTICE 14 (E&W)
A RECEIVER'S RESPONSIBILITY TO PREFERENTIAL CREDITORS

1. INTRODUCTION

1.1 *[Not reproduced. Superseded by SIP 1 with effect from 02 May 2011.]*

1.2 This statement has been prepared to summarise what is considered to be the best practice to be adopted by receivers of the assets of companies where any of those assets are subject to a floating charge so that the office holder has legal obligations to creditors whose debts are preferential. Its purpose is to:

- ensure that members are familiar with the statutory provisions;
- set out best practice with regard to the application of the statutory provisions;
- set out best practice with regard to the provision of information to creditors whose debts are preferential and to responses to enquiries by such creditors.

Whilst this statement does not specifically address the treatment of preferential claims in liquidations, members acting as liquidators (or in any other relevant capacity) should have due regard to the principles which it contains.

1.3 The statement has been produced in recognition of the likelihood that creditors whose debts are preferential may be concerned about the categorisation of assets as between fixed and floating charges and the manner in which costs incurred during a receivership are charged against the different categories of assets.

1.4 The statement is divided into the following sections:

- the statutory provisions
- the categorisation of assets and allocation of proceeds as between fixed and floating charges
- the apportionment of costs incurred in the course of the receivership
- the determination of claims for preferential debts
- the payment of preferential debts

- disclosure of information and responses to queries raised by creditors whose debts are preferential
- other matters

2. THE STATUTORY PROVISIONS

2.1 The rights of creditors whose debts are preferential in a receivership derive from section 40 of the Insolvency Act 1986 ('the Act').

Where a receiver is appointed on behalf of the holders of any debentures of a company secured by a charge which, as created, was a floating charge and the company is not at the time in the course of being wound up, its preferential debts shall be paid out of the assets coming into the hands of the receiver in priority to any claims for principal or interest in respect of the debentures. Where the receiver is appointed under both fixed and floating charges, this requirement does not extend to assets coming into the receiver's hands pursuant to the fixed charge(s).

Preferential debts are defined in section 386 of the Act and are set out in Schedule 6 to the Act (as amended from time to time), which is to be read in conjunction with Schedule 4 to the Pensions Schemes Act 1993. The date at which they are to be ascertained is the date of the appointment of the receiver (section 387(4) of the Act).

2.2 Members should note that the statutory provisions give a right to creditors whose debts are preferential to be paid those debts in priority to the claims of floating charge holders, and the corollary of this right is the obligation of the receiver to pay them. Failure by a receiver to pay preferential debts out of available assets is a breach of statutory duty. However it is recognised that circumstances may arise when it is administratively convenient or cost-effective to cooperate with a company's liquidator and arrange for him to pay the receivership preferential debts, and guidance on such arrangements is given in paragraph 6.2 below. It should be noted that such arrangements do not exonerate the receiver from his obligations.

2.3 There are no statutory provisions requiring creditors with preferential debts in a receivership to prove those debts in any formal manner and no statutory obligation is imposed on a receiver to advertise for claims.

3. CATEGORISATION OF ASSETS AND ALLOCATION OF PROCEEDS

3.1 In order to ascertain what assets are subject to the statutory rights of creditors whose debts are preferential, it is necessary to distinguish, on a proper interpretation of the charging document(s), which assets are subject to a fixed charge and which are subject to a floating charge. In this statement this process is referred to as 'categorisation'.

3.2 The overriding principle, as laid down by the courts, is that it is not of itself sufficient for the charging document to state that an asset is subject to a fixed charge for it to be subject to such a charge. There have been cases where the courts have struck down charges that purported to be fixed and held that they were floating.

3.3 It is the duty of a receiver to effect the right categorisation and legal advice should be taken in cases of doubt. In some instances where there is doubt as to the correct categorisation it may be possible to consult preferential creditors and reach agreement with them and the chargeholder. However, if this is not possible and the receiver, in conjunction with his legal advisers, cannot determine the correct categorisation, it may be necessary to apply to the court for directions.

3.4 Members are reminded that:

- it is the type of charge at the time of its creation which determines whether the assets are available to meet preferential debts. Crystallisation of a floating charge into a fixed charge prior to or upon the appointment of a receiver does not affect the rights of creditors with preferential debts to be paid out of assets subject to a crystallised floating charge;

- the conversion, during receivership, of assets (for example, stock) subject at the date of appointment of the receiver to a floating charge into assets (for example, book debts) subject to a fixed charge, will not remove them from the pool of assets which is available to pay preferential debts.

3.5 Section 40 of the Act requires that the preferential debts 'shall be paid out of the [floating charge] assets coming to the hands of the receiver in priority to the debenture holder. The effect is that a receiver is under a liability in tort to the preferential creditors if, having had available assets in hand, he fails to apply them in payment of the preferential debts. Where any action which he proposes to take could result in a diminution in the amount available to meet preferential debts the receiver should give the most serious consideration to the risks of such action.

3.6 When assets are sold as part of a going concern (or otherwise in parcels comprising both fixed and floating charge assets) the apportionment of the total consideration suggested by the purchaser (for example for his own financial reasons) may not properly reflect the financial interests of the different classes of creditors in the individual assets or categories of assets. In these circumstances the receiver should ensure that he will be able properly to discharge his obligations to account to holders of fixed charges on the one hand and creditors interested in assets subject to floating charges on the other.

4. APPORTIONMENT OF COSTS

4.1 The amount available to meet preferential debts is the funds realised from the disposal of assets subject to a floating charge net of the costs of realisation. It is dependent, therefore, not only on the correct categorisation of the assets but also on the appropriate allocation of costs incurred in effecting realisations.

4.2 These costs will normally fall into one of three categories:
- liabilities incurred by the company (the receiver being its agent until winding up supervenes) and costs incurred by the receiver and recoverable by him out of the company's assets under his statutory indemnity (other than those referred to below);
- the costs of the receiver in discharging his statutory duties;
- the remuneration and disbursements of the receiver.

4.3 Liabilities incurred by the company and the receiver's reasonable costs are sometimes readily identifiable as applicable to either the fixed charge or floating charge assets, but in other cases may not be so easily allocated between the two categories of assets.

Where costs are clearly identifiable as having been incurred in the realisation or collecting in of one or other of the two categories they should be recorded as such in the receiver's records so that they can be deducted from realisation proceeds in ascertaining the amount available for each class of creditors.

4.4 It is in the nature of receiverships, and particularly receiverships where trading is continued, that there will be continuation of employment of the company's directors and staff, ongoing occupation of its premises, purchase of supplies for manufacturing and other purposes and much of the other expenditure normally associated with a company's operations. In these circumstances it may be difficult to arrive at an appropriate allocation of costs. Many of the activities in a trading receivership will enhance the realisations of assets in both of the categories identified above. They may of necessity be incurred before full categorisation has been completed.

These factors do not affect the duty of a receiver to allocate costs appropriately but that allocation will involve the exercise of professional judgement undertaken with a full appreciation that it must be made with independence of mind and with integrity.

4.5 The key principles for a receiver in his consideration of the allocation of costs (including any trading losses) are:

- the statutory rights of preferential creditors as set out in the Insolvency Act 1986 and the decisions of the courts in cases under that Act and predecessor legislation;
- the provisions of the charging document(s);
- the maintenance of a proper balance as between the classes of creditors with whose interests he is required to deal in the light of their legal rights.

In order to enable a receiver to allocate costs on an appropriate basis, contemporaneous records of the dominant reasons for incurring costs should be maintained. These will also assist him in providing explanations as to how he arrived at what he considers to be an appropriate allocation and provide evidence should that allocation be challenged by any of the parties involved.

4.6 In allocating costs a receiver should have regard to:

- the objectives for which costs were incurred, it being recognised that certain types of costs may, properly, be allocated to the fixed charge assets in one case and to the floating charge assets in another.[1] In another case such costs may enhance realisations in both categories.

- the benefits actually obtained for those financially interested in one or other category of asset in terms of protection of those assets or their value and any augmentation of that value.

- whether the benefits to those interested in assets subject to a fixed charge has been enhanced by action which proves to be detrimental to those interested in floating charge assets (for example where trading losses are incurred to protect or enhance the value of property or book debts subject to a fixed charge).

- whether the realisation of the undertaking and assets by means of a going concern sale has resulted in a reduction in the quantum of debts which are preferential due to the transfer of employment contracts.

4.7 A receiver will incur costs in complying with his statutory duties. The extent of those duties depends upon the nature of his appointment and they are more onerous in the case of administrative receivers.

An administrative receivership arises only when there is a floating charge and the charges under which the receiver is appointed are over the whole or substantially the whole of the company's assets. There are no decided cases as to how the additional costs incurred by an administrative receiver (as opposed to a receiver not so designated) should be allocated.

In apportioning the costs of fulfilling their statutory duties and in the absence of any guidance from the courts, members should have regard to the general principle referred to in paragraph 4.5 above of maintaining a proper balance.

4.8 The allocation of a receiver's remuneration and disbursements should be undertaken adopting the same principles as those applicable to costs and he should ensure that he maintains contemporaneous records which will enable him to make an appropriate division of his remuneration and disbursements between the different categories of assets.

---

[1] For example the payment of rent on a leasehold property may be to preserve the value of the lease or to enable manufacturing to continue and work in progress to be completed.

5. DETERMINATION OF PREFERENTIAL DEBTS

5.1 As stated in paragraphs 2.2 and 2.3 of this statement it is a receiver's obligation to pay preferential debts out of assets available for that purpose and no proof of debt or advertisement for creditors is required.

5.2 Following initial notification to potential preferential creditors of his appointment and before beginning the process of determining preferential debts, a receiver should assess whether there are likely to be sufficient floating charge realisations to pay a distribution. Where no payment will be made, it is not necessary to agree preferential claims. However, in such circumstances the receiver should write to creditors whose claims are preferential explaining why he is unable to make a payment to them.

5.3 Where there will be a distribution to preferential creditors, the receiver should assist those creditors, where possible, by providing adequate information to enable them to calculate their claims. In the case of all preferential creditors other than employees, the receiver is entitled to assume they have full knowledge of their legal entitlements under the Insolvency Act and should invite them to submit their claims. The receiver should then check those claims, and accept or reject them as appropriate.

5.4 In determining the preferential claims of employees, the receiver is not entitled to regard an individual employee as having full knowledge of his rights and entitlements. Accordingly, the receiver should obtain information from either the company's records or from the employee before calculating the claim (other than one which is payable to the Secretary of State by way of subrogation). The employee should be provided with details of the calculation of his claim and any further explanation that he may reasonably require.

5.5 Members are reminded that Schedule 6 (paragraph 11) of the Act provides that anyone who has advanced money for the purpose of paying wages, salaries or accrued holiday remuneration of any employee is a preferential creditor to the extent that the preferential claim of the employee is reduced by such advance.

5.6 When an employee's preferential debt has been paid out of the National Insurance Fund under the provisions of the Employment Rights Act 1996, the Secretary of State is entitled, by virtue of section 189 of that Act to the benefit of the employee's preferential debt, in priority to any residual claim of the employee himself. Members are reminded that a receiver is not obliged to accept the preferential claim of the Secretary of State without satisfying himself that it is correct. If a member is not able to accept the Secretary of State's claim he should contact the Redundancy Payments Service to explain why and attempt to reach agreement on the amount to be admitted.

6. PAYMENT OF PREFERENTIAL DEBTS

6.1 As soon as practicable after funds become available and the amount of the preferential debts has been ascertained, members should take steps to pay them. Under the statutory provisions preferential debts do not attract interest and payments to creditors should not be unnecessarily delayed. A receiver who does not comply timeously with his obligations under section 40 and against whom judgment is obtained may find himself ordered to pay interest by the court. While members cannot be expected to bear any financial risk by paying some preferential debts before all such debts are agreed, there are often circumstances when it is possible to make payment either in full or on account before all claims have been agreed and this course of action should be adopted whenever it is practicable to do so.

6.2 Situations may arise where, notwithstanding a receiver's statutory duty to pay preferential debts, it may (exceptionally) be administratively convenient or cost- effective for a receiver to make arrangements for the liquidator to make payment of the preferential debts arising in the receivership. Such arrangements are made at the receiver's risk, and should not be on any basis which could result in payment of an amount less than that which would have been available to meet those debts if the receiver had himself paid them, or which would cause delay in paying them.

6.3 The receiver should provide preferential creditors with details of any such arrangements and the reason for making them.

7. DISCLOSURE TO CREDITORS WITH PREFERENTIAL DEBTS

7.1 When the funds realised from assets subject to a floating charge are inadequate to pay the preferential debts in full, the receiver should (unless he has already written to them as suggested in paragraph 5.2) send those creditors a statement setting out:

- the assets which have, in accordance with the charging document, been categorised as subject to the floating charge;
- the costs charged against the proceeds of the realisation of those assets.

7.2 Any further information which a creditor with a preferential debt reasonably requires should be provided promptly.

8. OTHER MATTERS

8.1 Difficulties may arise in determining the rights of creditors to have debts paid preferentially in priority to a prior floating charge holder when the receiver has been appointed under a second or subsequent charge. The law in this area is complex and members should seek legal advice (and if necessary apply to the court for directions) when appointed under such a charge.

8.2 Situations will arise where payments sent out are not encashed and the payee cannot readily be located. The insolvency legislation does not make provision for this eventuality and there have been no reported cases where the courts have decided the matter. Where a receiver decides to account to the next person entitled to such monies he should bear in mind his overriding obligation to pay preferential debts. He should make such arrangements as he considers appropriate to enable him to recover the funds from the party to whom he has paid them so that he will be able to discharge his obligation to any preferential creditor who subsequently asserts his claim to payment.

Issued June 1999

3.8 STATEMENT OF INSOLVENCY PRACTICE 17 (E&W) AN ADMINISTRATIVE RECEIVER'S RESPONSIBILITY FOR THE COMPANY'S RECORDS

INTRODUCTION

This document was issued as SIP 1 (Version 2 England and Wales) in August 1997. It was re-numbered as SIP 17 (without updating of the text) with effect from 2 May 2011.

1. *[Not reproduced. Superseded by SIP 1 with effect from 02 May 2011.]*

2. This statement has been prepared to summarise what is considered to be the best practice in circumstances where administrative receivers are approached by liquidators or directors seeking access to or custody of a company's books and records. The best practice is considered below both with regard to company records maintained prior to the appointment of an administrative receiver and with regard to those records prepared after the administrative receiver's appointment.

COMPANY RECORDS MAINTAINED PRIOR TO APPOINTMENT OF AN ADMINISTRATIVE RECEIVER

3. The records which a company maintains prior to the appointment of an administrative receiver may be classified under two main headings.

4. The first comprises the non-accounting records which the directors are required to maintain by the Companies Act 1985 (as amended) (the statutory records). These consist of various registers (e.g. of members) and minute books (e.g. of directors' meetings).

5. The second category of records maintained by a company prior to the appointment of an administrative receiver includes accounting records required by statute and all other non-statutory records of the company (statutory accounting and other non-statutory records). Taking each in turn:

Statutory records

6. The company's statutory records should be kept at its registered office (see paragraph 11 below) having regard to the provisions of the Companies Act 1985, sections 288, 353, 383 and 407 (registers of directors, members, minute books and charges).

7. Directors' powers to cause entries to be made in these statutory records do not cease on the appointment of an administrative receiver. Indeed, the directors' statutory duties to maintain them are unaffected by his appointment.

8. An administrative receiver would have the power to inspect the statutory records as part of his right to take possession of, collect and get in the property of the company (cf paragraph 1 of Schedule 1 to the Insolvency Act 1986). He is not, however, placed under an obligation to maintain those records after his appointment and should not normally do so.

9. The abolition by section 130 of the Companies Act 1989 of the requirement for a company formed under the Companies Acts to have a common seal means that in many cases the company in receivership will have no common seal. Provided that an appropriately worded attestation clause is used, deeds can be executed without the use of the common seal. Given that the common seal may still be used for the execution of deeds by the company, however, it is considered best practice for the administrative receiver to take possession of it.

10. On appointment, an administrative receiver has two possible options:

    i. To leave the statutory records in the custody of the directors so that they are in a position to continue to carry out their statutory duties to maintain them.

    ii. To take possession of the statutory records for safe keeping. In such circumstances, the administrative receiver should remind the directors of their statutory responsibilities to maintain the records and allow them free access for this purpose. It would also be advisable for the administrative receiver to prepare a detailed receipt for all the records taken into his possession. This should be signed by a director or other responsible official of the company in receivership.

11. The administrative receiver may change the company's registered office to that of his own firm, in which case, the statutory records should also be transferred to the new registered office and the procedure outlined in paragraph 10 (ii) above followed.

12. Any statutory records (and if applicable any seals) taken into an administrative receiver's possession (see paragraphs 8 and 9) should be returned to the directors (or liquidator) on the receiver's ceasing to act.

Statutory accounting and non-statutory records

13. All such records as are necessary for the purposes of the receivership and for the discharge of the administrative receiver's statutory duties should be taken into the administrative receiver's possession and/or control and any which he will definitely not require may be left with the directors. If the administrative receiver encounters difficulty in obtaining possession of the records, the provisions of sections 234-236 of the Insolvency Act 1986 may be of assistance. These are the provisions allowing an administrative receiver to apply to the court for an order for property in the control of any party to be handed to him, placing officers and others under a statutory obligation to co-operate with the administrative receiver and allowing him to apply to the court for an order summoning officers of the company in receivership and others before it for questioning.

14. An administrative receiver is under no statutory duty to bring these records up to date to the date of his appointment although for practical purposes (such as to give prospective purchasers some indication of the financial state of the business) it may be necessary for him to do so.

15. If an administrative receiver does not take possession of all the records it would be advisable for him to make a list of all those not taken into his custody with a note of their whereabouts.

16. When making sales of certain assets (e.g. book debts or plant and machinery) it may be necessary for the administrative receiver to hand over to the purchaser company records (eg debtors' ledgers or plant registers) relating to those assets. In such circumstances, the administrative receiver should ensure that the relevant asset sale agreement specifies the need for these records to be made available to the company on request. Although this will invariably be a matter of negotiation between the administrative receiver and his purchaser, it would be preferable for him to retain the originals of such records. He may make copies available to the purchaser or allow the purchaser to retain them for a short time for the purpose of making copies. Once again, appropriate provision should be made in the asset sale agreement as to the particular circumstances and as to whom is to bear the costs.

17. If an administrative receiver transfers the business of the company to a third party as a going concern, section 49 and paragraph 6 of Schedule 11 to the Value Added Tax Act 1994 place the obligation of preserving any records relating to the business upon the transferee. This applies unless the Commissioners of Customs & Excise, at the request of the transferor, otherwise direct.

18. This is a wide-ranging obligation. It applies regardless of whether the VAT registration is itself transferred or whether the transfer is treated as a supply of neither goods nor services.

19. The categories of records covered by Schedule 11 paragraph 6 are wide-ranging. They include orders and delivery notes, purchase and sales records, annual accounts, VAT accounts and credit and debit notes.

Entitlement of liquidator to records

20. The case of *Engel v South Metropolitan Brewing & Bottling Company* ([1892] 1 Ch 442) is authority to the effect that a liquidator becomes entitled to possession of all books and records relating to the "management and business" of the company which are not necessary to support the title of the chargeholder as against a court-appointed receiver. The court held that a court-appointed receiver can be compelled to deliver such documents to the liquidator against the liquidator's undertaking to produce them to the receiver on request. While there is no equivalent authority with respect to an administrative receiver, general practice supports the proposition that delivery up of records in return for an undertaking and subsequent production on request should occur (Lightman & Moss, *Law of Receivers of Companies*, 2nd Edition, paragraph 11-17).

21. An administrative receiver has no statutory authority to destroy pre-appointment records and in due course these must be returned to the company's directors or, if the company is in liquidation, to its liquidator.

POST APPOINTMENT RECORDS

Statutory accounting records

(i) Relating to the period prior to the appointment of a liquidator

22. The administrative receiver should establish appropriate accounting records as from the date of his appointment. The case of *Smiths Limited v Middleton* ([1979] 3 A11 ER 842) shows that he has a duty to render full and proper records to the company in order that the company (and its directors) may comply with the duties imposed by sections 221, 226, 227 and 241 Companies Act 1985 (preparation and approval of accounts).

23. An administrative receiver is also under obligation to make returns of his receipts and payments pursuant to Rule 3.32 of the Insolvency Rules 1986. The statutory requirements and the best practice to be followed in the preparation of insolvency office holders' receipts and payments accounts are summarised in the statement of insolvency practice entitled "Preparation of Insolvency Office Holders' Receipts and Payments Accounts", to which members are referred for further information.

24. When a liquidator is appointed, the *Engel* case would seem to apply so that the liquidator becomes entitled to possession of records (see paragraph 20 above).

25. Administrative receivers have no statutory authority to destroy such records and on ceasing to act must hand these over to the company's directors or, if it is in liquidation, to the liquidator.

(ii) Relating to the period after the appointment of a liquidator

26. As from the commencement of liquidation, the administrative receiver loses his status as agent of the company (section 44(1)(a) Insolvency Act 1986). The administrative receiver's obligation to make returns of receipts and payments and to maintain accounting records (paragraph 23 above) remains in force.

27. Section 41 Insolvency Act 1986 allows any member, creditor, the Registrar of Companies or the liquidator to enforce these duties.

Other records

28.   The remaining records, books and papers relating to a receivership may be subdivided between "company records", "receiver's personal records" and "chargeholder's records".

(i) Company records

Company records will include as a minimum all those records which exist as a result of carrying on the company's business and dealing with the assets. These records fall in the same category as the non-statutory records mentioned in paragraphs 13 to 21 above. They should be treated in the same way, being returned to the company's directors or if it is in liquidation, to its liquidator when the receiver ceases to act. In the case of *Gomba Holdings UK Limited v Minories Finance Limited*, ((1989) 5BCC 27) consideration was given to precisely which records fall within the definition of "company records". It was held that an administrative receiver acts in several capacities during the course of a receivership. In addition to being agent of the company, he owes fiduciary obligations to his appointor and to the company. It is only documents generated or received pursuant to his duty to manage the company's business or dispose of its assets which belong to the company.

(ii) Chargeholder's records

As explained above, in the *Gomba* case quoted in paragraph 28(i) above it was held that documents containing advice and information to the appointor and "notes, calculations and memoranda" prepared to enable the administrative receiver to discharge his professional duty to his appointor or to the company belong either to the appointor (if he wishes to claim them) or to the administrative receiver. They do not belong to the company.

(iii) Administrative receiver's personal records

An administrative receiver's personal records are those prepared by him for the purpose of better enabling him to discharge his professional duties. They will include, for instance, his statutory record which he is required to maintain by Regulation 17 of the Insolvency Practitioners' Regulations 1990 ("the Regulations"). The record must take the form set out in Schedule 3 to the Regulations.

BEST PRACTICE

29. It is considered best practice that all records mentioned above, with the exception of a receiver's personal records (paragraph 28 (iii) above) and the appointor's records (paragraph 28 (ii) above) should be made available on request to the company acting by its directors or if it is in liquidation, its liquidator unless the administrative receiver is of the opinion that disclosure at that time would be contrary to the interests of the appointor, for instance because of current negotiations for the sale of assets (*Gomba Holdings UK Limited v Homan*, [1986] 3 All ER 94). Subject to the interests of the appointor, it appears from this case that directors are entitled to such information as they need to enable them to exercise their residual powers and to perform their residual statutory duties considered above.

30. Disclosure of the administrative receiver's personal records is a matter for his discretion, although in any legal action brought against him it could be that if such records have not been disclosed they may be held to be discoverable.

31. Where there is no liquidator and the directors cannot be traced (or the administrative receiver has reason to suppose that they are not reliable) he will need to consider whether he feels it necessary to present a petition for the company to be wound up using his powers under Schedule 1 to the Insolvency Act 1986. Whether or not a liquidator is appointed, the administrative receiver has no statutory power to destroy a company's records even after the expiry of the statutory period for which the company would need to retain them (usually six years). Thus, if he does so without the authority of the company or the liquidator, he does so at his peril. Note also that the record an administrative receiver is required to keep by the Regulations must be preserved for a period of ten years from the later of the date upon which the administrative receiver ceases to hold office or any security or caution maintained in respect of the company ceases to have effect (Regulation 20).

Issued August 1997

Re-issued 2 May 2011

Section 4

Statements of Insolvency
Practice — Scotland

SECTION 4 — STATEMENTS OF INSOLVENCY PRACTICE — SCOTLAND

CONTENTS

4.1 STATEMENT OF INSOLVENCY PRACTICE 3.3 (SCOTLAND) TRUST DEEDS

Introduction

1. A Trust Deed is a voluntary deed granted by a debtor whereby the debtor conveys all or part of his estate to a named Trustee to be administered for the benefit of creditors and to effect the settlement of debts in whole or in part. The Trustee may seek to make the Trust Deed protected by following the relevant statutory procedures. A Trust Deed will not satisfy the requirements for protection unless it complies with the definition of "trust deed" in section 228(1) of the Bankruptcy (Scotland) Act 2016 ("the Act") and satisfies the requirements in section 167 of the Act).[1]

2. Creditors may agree or be deemed to agree to the Trust Deed. If the Trust Deed becomes protected, all creditors are bound by the terms laid down in the statutory provisions. However, if objections reach the prescribed levels the Trust Deed will not become protected. Even if objections do not reach the prescribed levels, protection may be refused by the Accountant in Bankruptcy in prescribed circumstances.

3. The advice provided by an insolvency practitioner will be central to the decision taken by the debtor. Where the decision is to grant a Trust Deed and seek its protection the insolvency practitioner will take the necessary steps. The particular nature of an insolvency practitioner's position renders transparency and fairness in all dealings of primary importance. The debtor and the creditors should be confident that an insolvency practitioner acts professionally and with objectivity. Failure to do so may prejudice the interests of both the debtor and creditors and is likely to bring the practitioner and the profession into disrepute.

4. It is not competent in terms of the Act to have a conjoined Trust Deed signed by more than one party, and purporting to deal with the combined estates of more than one person. Individual Trust Deeds are required for each separate legal person or entity.

---

[1] The legislative references in this SIP have been updated to reflect the fact that the Bankruptcy (Scotland) Act 2016 came into effect on 30 November 2016 and the Bankruptcy (Scotland) Act 1985 was repealed for the purposes of all new sequestrations and trust deeds on or after 30 November 2016. The 2016 Act is a consolidation of existing legislation and therefore the requirements of this SIP remain unchanged notwithstanding the changes to the legislative references.

5. The insolvency practitioner should exercise his judgement and consider the extent to which these principles and procedures apply where there is no intention that the Trust Deed should become protected.

Principles

6. The insolvency practitioner should differentiate clearly to the debtor his role in providing initial advice from his responsibilities as Trustee. The debtor should be advised of the insolvency practitioner's requirement to maintain independence. The insolvency practitioner should make it clear to the debtor that his duties as Trustee, once the Trust Deed is signed, cannot be influenced by the wishes of the debtor.

7. An insolvency practitioner should ensure that the advice, information and explanations provided to a debtor about the options available are such that the debtor can make an informed judgement on which process is appropriate to his circumstances. An insolvency practitioner should also explain the debtor's responsibilities and the consequences of signing a Trust Deed.

8. If a Trust Deed is proposed, an insolvency practitioner should ensure that a fair balance is struck between the interests of the debtor and those of the creditors.

9. In the initial circular to creditors the insolvency practitioner should provide clear and accurate information to enable creditors to decide whether or not to object to the Trust Deed becoming protected and he should advise of the procedure for objections. At all times an insolvency practitioner should report accurately and in a manner that aims to be clear and useful.

Initial Considerations and Requirements

10. The practice of insolvency is principally governed by statute and secondary legislation and is subject ultimately to the control of the Court. Where requirements are set out in statute or secondary legislation, an insolvency practitioner must comply with such provisions.

11. The special nature of insolvency appointments makes the payment for, or offer of any commission for, or the furnishing of any valuable consideration towards, the introduction of insolvency appointments inappropriate.

12. An office holder should provide details and the cost of any work that has been carried out in relation to the Trust Deed other than by the office

holder or his or her staff whether chargeable to the estate or not. There should be no additional cost to the estate. Any such payment should reflect the value of the work undertaken, comply with the Code of Ethics of the Authorising Body, comply with guidance issued by the Accountant in Bankruptcy, and be approved in line with the provisions of SIP9 (Scotland).

13. In addition to the statutory requirements to provide documentation to creditors and the Accountant in Bankruptcy, the Trustee in the first written communication to all known creditors should provide details of the following matters:

    (a) where a payment has been made or is due to be made to a third party (whether by the insolvency practitioner or any other party) for work done in relation to the Trust Deed:

        • the name and address of the party carrying out the work;

        • the name and address of the party making the payment; and

        • the amount of the payment.

    (b) Where the insolvency practitioner or his firm or any associate of either (as defined in section 229[2] of the Act or section 435 of the Insolvency Act 1986) has an interest in the business of the party being paid, that interest should be detailed.

    (c) Where the Trustee's fee is not a fixed fee in accordance with section 183[3] the anticipated cost to the estate of the Trustee's fee for the period of the Trust Deed together with a statement of the assumptions made in producing the estimate, Trustees are reminded that all fees and outlays must be approved in accordance with SIP9 (Scotland).

14. Where the insolvency practitioner is consulted by two individuals who are married, in a civil partnership, cohabiting or otherwise have a relationship which could give rise to a conflict of interest, the practitioner should ensure that each is assessed individually and offer advice based on each individual's own circumstances. Where the insolvency practitioner has

---

[2] See footnote 1 above.

[3] See footnote 1 above.

been consulted by two or more parties and considers that there is a conflict of interest in the insolvency practitioner advising both or all parties, the insolvency practitioner should consider which appointment, if any, it is appropriate to accept.

Key Compliance Standards

15. Certain key compliance standards are of general application, but others will depend on whether the insolvency practitioner is acting as adviser or Trustee.

Standards of General Application

Advice to the debtor

16. In all cases the insolvency practitioner is responsible for ensuring that the debtor has been given appropriate advice.

17. The insolvency practitioner should have procedures in place to satisfy himself that appropriate information and explanations are provided to the debtor at each stage of the Trust Deed process. He should set out clearly:

    (a) the key stages of the Trust Deed process (i.e. assessing the options available, signing and witnessing the Trust Deed, asset realisations, contributions, fee approval, discharge of the debtor and Trustee, and concluding the Trust Deed);

    (b) the roles of the insolvency practitioner as adviser and as Trustee;

    (c) the intended duration of the Trust Deed, any potential delays or complications, and the possibility and likelihood of extending the period of the Trust Deed;

    (d) what is required of the debtor at each stage of the process;

    (e) the consequences of signing a Trust Deed including apparent insolvency, and the responsibilities of the debtor;

    (f) the insolvency practitioner's assessment of the likelihood of the Trust Deed becoming protected, the consequences of it not becoming protected and the consequences of the debtor failing to comply with its terms.

Assessment

18. The insolvency practitioner should have procedures in place to ensure that an assessment is made at an appropriate stage of:

    (a) whether the debtor is being honest and open and sufficiently co-operative;

    (b) the debtor's understanding of the process, and commitment to it;

    (c) the attitude of any key creditors and of the general body of creditors;

    (d) whether a Trust Deed is an appropriate solution;

    (e) whether the Trust Deed will have a reasonable prospect of becoming protected;

    (f) whether the EC Regulation on Insolvency Proceedings applies to the Trust Deed and, if so, whether the Trust Deed constitutes main or territorial proceedings.

Meeting the debtor

19. Regular assessment should be made as to whether a meeting in person with the debtor is required, which will be dependent on the debtor's attitude and the circumstances and complexity of the case.

Documentation

20. The insolvency practitioner should be able to demonstrate that appropriate steps have been taken at all stages of the Trust Deed, by maintaining records of:

    (a) discussions with the debtor, the information and explanations provided, and options outlined and the advantages and disadvantages to the debtor of each option;

    (b) comments made by the debtor, and the debtor's preferred option;

    (c) any discussions with creditors or their representatives;

    (d) the way in which any issues raised have been resolved.

    Summaries of the records maintained under (i) and (ii) above where material should be sent to the debtor.

Dealing with Assets and Contributions

21.   The Trustee should follow the Accountant in Bankruptcy's guidance notes on Trust Deeds and sequestrations when dealing with assets. The Trustee should satisfy himself that a comprehensive schedule of non-exempt assets in which the debtor has an interest has been prepared, together with explanatory notes. The Trustee should take steps to satisfy himself as to the value of the assets conveyed to the Trustee.

22.   If any asset is not going to be realised, or not realised in full, the reasons for this must be clearly explained in writing to creditors when the Trust Deed is presented to them for consideration for protection, or at any other time that such a decision is taken.

23.   The Trustee should be aware that in order to achieve protected status, the Trust Deed must convey to the Trustee the debtor's whole estate with the exception of property which would be excluded from vesting in a sequestration, except that the Trust Deed may still become protected where the debtor's dwelling house is excluded in accordance with paragraph (b) of the definition of "trust deed" set out in section 228(1) of the Act.

Standards of Specific Application

24.   The insolvency practitioner or a suitably experienced member of his staff should interview the debtor prior to the Trust Deed being signed. A meeting in person should always be offered to the debtor but a telephone interview may be conducted. It is recommended that the debtor be interviewed using a similar style of questionnaire as is used in sequestration proceedings under the Act. The questionnaire and appendices should be signed and dated by the debtor.

25.   An assessment should be made as to whether a meeting in person with the debtor is required, depending on the debtor's attitude and the circumstances and complexity of the case.

26.   If the debtor is carrying on a business the insolvency practitioner, or a suitably experienced member of staff, must assess whether it is necessary to visit the business premises as part of the information gathering and planning exercise.

27.   Whether the debtor is interviewed in person or by telephone, the insolvency practitioner must satisfy himself that appropriate client

identification and money laundering procedures have been completed and that relevant copy documentation is retained on the case file.

28. The debtor should be advised that it is an offence to make false representations or to conceal assets or to commit any other fraud for the purpose of obtaining creditor approval to the Trust Deed.

29. An insolvency practitioner may be approached to give advice on a debtor's financial difficulties, and the way in which those difficulties might be resolved. The insolvency practitioner should have procedures in place to ensure, taking account of the personal circumstances of the debtor, that:

   (a) the role of adviser is explained to the debtor and that at this stage the insolvency practitioner is advising the debtor and acting in the debtor's interests but in the context of finding a workable solution to the debtor's financial difficulties;

   (b) sufficient information is obtained to make a preliminary assessment of the solutions available and their viability;

   (c) it is explained that the debtor will need to co-operate and provide full disclosure. The insolvency practitioner should be able to form a view of whether the debtor has a sufficient understanding of the situation and the consequences, and whether there will be full co-operation in seeking a solution;

   (d) when considering possible solutions, account is taken of the impact of each solution on the debtor and on any third parties that may be affected;

   (e) the debtor is provided with an explanation of the options available, so that the solution best suited to the debtor's circumstances can be identified. This information should be confirmed to the debtor in writing.

30. Where a Statement of Affairs and Statement of Income and Expenditure are prepared by a third party, these must be checked by the insolvency practitioner. These statements must be agreed by the debtor who should be asked to sign the statements confirming such agreement.

31. The insolvency practitioner must ensure that the debtor is advised the dwelling house (the debtor's sole or main residence over which there is a secured loan) may be excluded from the Trust Deed and the Trust Deed

may still qualify for protection. The insolvency practitioner must also ensure that the debtor is advised of the risks involved in excluding the dwelling house from the Trust Deed. In particular, if there is equity in the dwelling house and the debtor chooses to exclude the property the unsecured creditors may not agree to the Trust Deed becoming protected, and the implications thereof.

32. Where heritable property is to be included in the Trust Deed the insolvency practitioner must ensure that the debtor is clearly advised that all such heritable property, including the debtor's home unless excluded, is covered by the Trust Deed. The debtor must also be advised that equity in the property requires to be realised for the benefit of the creditors.

33. The debtor should be asked to sign a separate statement confirming his understanding of the implications of and their decision in respect of heritable property being included or excluded from the Trust Deed. A copy of the statement should be sent to the debtor and one held on the case file.

34. The insolvency practitioner should be satisfied that a debtor has had adequate time to think about the consequences and alternatives before signing a Trust Deed. Insolvency practitioners are reminded that once signed, a Trust Deed is a binding obligation between debtor and Trustee and cannot be revoked.

Dealing with Heritable Property & other Assets

35. The Trustee should obtain evidence of the ownership of any heritable property. If the debtor advises that he owns the property, either in whole or in part, a property search should be obtained to confirm the position. If the property is rented, evidence should be obtained e.g. production of a rent book or written confirmation from the landlord.

36. If the debtor owns any heritable property, in whole or in part, the Trustee should obtain a professional valuation.

37. The Trustee's attention is drawn to the provisions in the Accountant in Bankruptcy's guidance notes relating to heritable property.

38. A Trustee should try to reach agreement, as soon as possible, as to how the equity in heritable property will be realised. In realising the equity the Trustee should aim to achieve the best return to creditors in the circumstances of the case. The Trustee should record on the case file the reasons for his decisions in relation to the heritable property.

39. The Trustee should consider seeking legal advice when dealing with an unequal split of a jointly owned heritable property.

40. If the Trustee disposes of or abandons his interest in heritable property, and a formal disposition or other conveyance has not been executed, he should issue a letter to the debtor stating the position and confirming that the property has been abandoned to the debtor.

Contributions

41. The insolvency practitioner should verify the debtor's income and major outlays, and agree in writing with the debtor the amount and frequency of any income contributions.

Third Party Payments

42. Where any third party payments are to be paid the insolvency practitioner should try to enter into an enforceable written agreement with the third party for payment. The Trustee should recommend that the third party obtains independent legal advice.

43. The Trustee should advise the creditors that all or part of the payments are to be paid by a third party. He should advise whether an enforceable agreement has been entered into with the third party. He should also advise that if there is no enforceable agreement and the third party fails to make payment, the third party cannot be forced to pay.

Trading

44. If the debtor owns or has an interest in a business, the Trustee should consider the manner in which he will deal with that business. The Trustee should consider whether trading should continue and if so, on what terms.

45. Where the Trustee decides to continue trading the debtor's business, such a decision should be supported by cash flow and trading forecasts. The Trustee must be able to demonstrate the matters considered and that his actions are in the best interests of creditors. The Trustee will be responsible for any ongoing trading of the debtor's business, and must introduce appropriate controls. The Trustee should be aware that he may be personally liable for loss incurred where he continues trading after the Trust Deed has been signed and as a result the value of the estate is diminished.

Meeting of creditors

46. There is no statutory requirement to call a meeting of creditors. If however the Trustee considers that it is in the interests of creditors such a meeting can be called.

47. The Trustee should record in the Sederunt Book all requests by creditors to hold a creditors' meeting. If the Trustee considers a meeting would be in the interest of creditors, a meeting should be convened. If a meeting is not convened the Trustee must record in writing in the Sederunt Book the reason for his decision.

Accounting, reporting and remuneration

48. The Trust Deed should set out the basis on which the Trustee will be remunerated.

49. Where the Trustee's fee is not fixed as per section 183 of the Act the Trustee should set out the basis and procedure for approval of remuneration and outlays and the rights of creditors to appeal.

50. Where the Trustee's fees have not been fixed the Trustee should advise creditors of their right to have the accounts audited and fees fixed by the Accountant in Bankruptcy. The Trustee should delay payment of his fee until 14 days after the issue of the report to creditors.

51. Where there is a fixed fee (including a percentage of contributions and/or realisations) approval of the Trust Deed is deemed to be approval of the fees. In fixed fee cases fees should not be taken until 14 days have elapsed since the issue of the relevant circular and in any event not before the expiry of the 5 week period for objections to the Trust Deed becoming protected. In all other cases the Trustee is reminded that the notification to creditors of the Trustee's estimated fee as referred to in paragraph 13(c) above does not amount to approval of the fee and that all fees must be properly approved in the course of the Trust Deed and in advance of being paid.

52. Where creditors were informed that the debtor had undertaken to pay regular contributions from income and payments equivalent to three consecutive months' contributions have not been received, without a formal payment break being agreed, the creditors must be informed of this

in the next annual report. The creditors should be advised of the reasons for non-payment, what action the Trustee has taken in respect of the missed contributions and the impact on the expected final return to creditors.

53. Copies of all written communications to creditors must be sent to the debtor.

54. At the conclusion of a Trust Deed which is not protected a final statement of intromissions must be sent to creditors and the debtor.

55. The acceptance of commissions from a third party by a Trustee during a Trust Deed represents a significant threat to objectivity. Such commissions should only be accepted for the benefit of the Trust Deed estate and not for the benefit of the insolvency practitioner, his firm or any associate of either (as defined in section 229 of the Act or section 435 of the Insolvency Act 1986). Such payments should be reflected in the case accounts.

Trust deeds for entities

56. In addition to Trust Deeds for individuals, insolvency practitioners should be aware that partnerships, trusts and corporate and unincorporated bodies may enter into Trust Deeds.

Partnership Trust Deeds

57. Although there should be little difference in the approach of Trustees, it must be borne in mind that a partnership Trust Deed is not a joint and several version of an individual Trust Deed entered into by an individual.

58. The Trust Deed is entered into by the partnership and requires the consent of all the existing partners for the Trust Deed to be granted. As such, the estate conveyed to the Trustee is that of the partnership, not the estate of the partners as individual debtors, and does not extend to the partners' personal assets. Similarly, only the partnership's liabilities are included.

59. The granting of a partnership Trust Deed allows a Trustee to take swift control of the partnership's assets and provides the opportunity to pre-serve the business and perhaps achieve a going-concern solution.

60. It is open, in appropriate circumstances, for some or all of the partners of the partnership to sign individual Trust Deeds. If the insolvency practitioner

considers that there is a possible conflict of interest, the insolvency practitioner should consider whether it is appropriate to accept appointment to all or any of the individual partners.

Ending of the trust deed

Protected Trust Deed achieving its purpose

61. Where the Trust Deed contains provisions on bringing the Trust Deed to a close these should be followed in so far as they do not conflict with statutory provisions.

Protected Trust Deed not achieving its purpose

62. If the Trustee considers the Trust Deed is not achieving its purpose the Trustee must consider appropriate alternatives given the circumstances of the case and bearing in mind the interests of creditors.

Trust Deed failing to become protected

63. If the Trust Deed has failed to become protected, the Trustee should immediately inform the debtor in writing and advise the debtor of his options. The Trustee should also notify creditors of the position.

64. If the debtor's estate is subsequently sequestrated, the Trustee should conclude the Trust Deed and seek his discharge from creditors. If he is appointed Trustee in the subsequent sequestration he should take steps to ensure that the Trust is terminated (see 66 and 67).

65. In a Trust Deed which has not become protected, there is no statutory procedure for bringing the Trust Deed to a close. It is normal practice for a receipt for the final dividend to incorporate a discharge of the Trustee and a discharge of the debtor. Creditors who have not acceded to the Trust Deed have no requirement to grant a discharge to the debtor.

Ending of the Trust, and subsequent sequestration

66. The granting of a Trust Deed creates a Trust. The Trustee should ensure that all assets are distributed in terms of the Trust Deed. It is generally accepted where there is a subsequent procedure such as sequestration that the Trust Deed is suspended and may revive on completion of the other procedure. The Trustee should therefore ensure that the style of Trust Deed used contains provisions for termination of the Trust in appropriate circumstances and he should adhere to those provisions.

67. In view of the possibility of the Trust reviving after the sequestration process has been completed the Trustee must have processes in place to deal with such an eventuality.

Trust Deed not completed but no further process.

68. If the Trustee concludes that the terms of the Trust Deed will not be met

    (a) he should seek his own discharge and bring the Trust Deed to a conclusion;

    (b) in the case of an unprotected Trust Deed the Trustee should also consider whether to discharge the debtor.

Trust Deed contains provisions on termination

69. It is generally accepted that where the Trust Deed contains provisions on termination, such provisions if complied with will be effective in terminating the Trust Deed. Trustees should ensure that the style of Trust Deed used contains provisions for ending the Trust on sequestration and on final distribution.

Effective Date: This SIP applies to trust deeds signed on or after **1 July 2014**

(updated on 30 November 2016 to include references to Bankruptcy (Scotland) Act 2016)

4.2 STATEMENT OF INSOLVENCY PRACTICE 8 (SCOTLAND) SUMMONING AND HOLDING MEETINGS OF CREDITORS CONVENED PURSUANT TO SECTION 98 OF THE INSOLVENCY ACT 1986

1. Introduction

1.1 *[Not reproduced. Superseded by SIP 1 with effect from 02 May 2011]*

1.2 This statement has been prepared for the sole use of members in connection with liquidations of companies registered in Scotland. The statement concentrates on creditors' meetings held under section 98 of the Insolvency Act 1986 (IA 1986), and does not purport to cover the practice to be adopted in respect of all creditors' meetings. Throughout this statement the member who has received instructions from the company's directors to advise in relation to the convening of the creditors' meeting will be referred to as the "advising member". An advising member is reminded that he must have regard to the relevant primary and secondary legislation; and that if he intends seeking nomination as liquidator he must be qualified to act as an insolvency practitioner in relation to the company.

1.3 All members and their staff should conduct themselves in a professional manner at all meetings of creditors.

2. Instructions to Convene Meeting

2.1 It is the responsibility of the company's directors to convene the creditors' meeting and to ensure that arrangements are made for the meeting to be held in accordance with current legislation. The advising member must therefore satisfy himself that the directors are aware of their responsibilities. He should also obtain written instructions from the board of directors which clearly define the matters on which he is to advise.

2.2 If the advising member receives instructions which would require him to act in a manner materially contrary to the Statements of Insolvency Practice, he should only accept those instructions after careful consideration of the implications of acceptance in that particular case. Where the directors act contrary to the guidance contained in this statement the advising member may be called upon to show that the directors' actions were undertaken either without his knowledge or against his advice.

2.3 A member who is unable to accept an appointment as liquidator of a company because he or his firm has had a material professional relationship with the company during the preceding three years may act as an advising member. However, he should only do so after careful consideration of the implications of so acting in the light of his professional body's most recent guide to professional ethics.

2.4 A member who is asked to act as advising member in relation to any company should not agree to act unless he is satisfied that he is competent to provide the level of advice needed by the company in question, or is able to recommend where to obtain the appropriate level of advice if he himself is not able to provide it.

2.5 It is most undesirable that shareholders should pass a resolution for the winding up of a company unless a liquidator is also appointed and accordingly no member should accept instructions to act as advising member unless he has good grounds for believing that such appointment will be made.

3. Venue and Time of Meeting

3.1 When choosing the venue for the meeting, the advising member should not only fulfil the legal requirement to choose a place which is convenient for persons who are invited to attend, but he should also ensure that the accommodation is adequate for the number of persons likely to attend. Subject thereto, there is no objection to an advising member arranging for the meeting to be held at his own offices.

3.2 The date and time of the meeting must be fixed with the convenience of creditors in mind and having regard to their geographical location. As an example, notices of a meeting should not normally be despatched shortly before the commencement of a known holiday period with the meeting taking place immediately after the holiday.

3.3 It is for advising member to advise the directors whether, in all the circumstances of a particular case, it would be preferable for the members' and the creditors' meeting to be held on the same or different days.

4. Notice of the Meeting

4.1 The notice convening the meeting should, where possible, be sent simultaneously to all classes of known creditors (including employees and secured creditors). The advising member should take all reasonable steps to ensure that the list of creditors provided by the directors is complete. Thus, for example, he should advise the company to identify and send notices to such creditors as hire purchase companies, landlords and public utilities.

4.2 Although the legal requirement is that notice of the meeting must be sent not less than seven days before the day on which the meeting is to be held, this is often insufficient time to enable creditors to arrange representation. For the convenience of creditors, the advising member should ensure that notices of the meeting are despatched as early as possible having regard to the circumstances of the case. This should be no later than the date when the notices are despatched to shareholders. Note that the reference to seven days means seven clear days, i.e. it excludes the day on which notices are sent and the day on which the meeting is held.

4.3 The notice advertised in the Gazette and local newspapers should appear as soon as possible and should not be deferred until shortly before the meeting. Also the advertised notice should meet the requirements of section 98(2) IA 1986.

4.4 Copies of the notice convening the shareholders' meeting should not be circulated to creditors.

4.5 When dealing with the issues of notices of the meeting, members should have regard to the provisions of Statement of Insolvency Practice 9 (Scotland) and ensure that explanatory notes setting out the manner by which the remuneration of liquidators is fixed, are sent with the notice to creditors.

4.6 Where the name of the company has been changed sufficiently recently for there to be any risk that creditors might not be aware of the new name, it is advisable to include reference to the former name or names both in the notices sent to creditors and in those inserted in the Gazette and local newspapers.

4.7 Section 98 IA 1986 requires that at least seven days' notice of the creditors meeting shall be given. Occasions may arise when for the general benefit of creditors, a liquidator can be appointed before the day fixed for the creditors' meeting. Where the company is to be placed in liquidation and the creditors' meeting is held later, the advising member should, if possible, ensure that the secretary or a director of the company signs the notices of the creditors' meeting before the resolution to wind up is passed by the shareholders.

5. Provision of Information Prior to Creditors' Meeting

5.1 Where the directors have decided to arrange for an authorised insolvency practitioner to provide information to creditors under section 98(2)(a) IA 1986, the creditors are to be given "such information concerning the company's affairs as they may reasonably require". The information which it is reasonable to request will normally include information contained in the statement of affairs and the list of creditors, when available. In addition, if the member has been appointed Liquidator by the members prior to the meeting of creditors, in terms of Rule 7.26(2) of the Insolvency (Scotland) Rules 1986, he is required to provide details of the amounts due to creditors. Requests for information need not be made in writing. However, oral requests should be treated with caution and information should not be supplied unless the caller can show that he is a creditor or a representative of a creditor. The advising member may decline to comply with a particular request for information if

(a) it is unreasonable to expect him to be in a position to supply such information within the time remaining before the meeting; or

(b) the information requested ought to remain confidential on the grounds that its release would be prejudicial to the company or its creditors.

5.2 If the directors have decided to make a list of creditors available for inspection under section 98(2)(b) IA 1986, the advising member should take steps to ensure that:

(a) the list provides details of the names and addresses of all known creditors but not necessarily the amounts due to them;

(b) the names are arranged in alphabetical order;

(c) it is available at least between the hours of 10 a.m. and 4 p.m. on the two business days before the date of the meeting;

(d) sufficient copies are available for inspection to avoid undue delays to creditors' representatives; and

(e) the place where the list is to be made available is, in all the circumstances, reasonably convenient for creditors.

6. Proxies

6.1 The forms of proxy accompanying the notice should conform to the Rules and should incorporate the name of the company and the date of the meeting before despatch in order to reduce the possibility of errors by creditors in completing the forms. The proxy must not be sent out with the name or description of any other person inserted on it.

6.2 Faxed Proxies should not be treated as invalid solely on the basis that they have been transmitted by fax.

6.3 Proxies which are lodged out of time should be treated as invalid. Proxies which are incorrectly completed in a material way will be invalid. There is a requirement for proxies to be signed by the principal or by a person authorised by him, in which case the nature of the authority must be stated.

Proxies which are unsigned or which do not explain the authority under which they are signed will therefore, be invalid. However, proxies should not be rejected simply because of a minor error in their completion provided:

(i) the form or proxy sent with the notice of the meeting (or a substantially similar form) has been used;

(ii) the identity of the creditor and the proxy holder, the nature of the proxy holder's authority and any instructions given to the proxy holder are clear.

The Chairman should satisfy himself that the person signing a form of proxy on behalf of a creditor (where the creditor is not an individual signing in person) has the necessary authority to do so. This may be assumed to be the case

(a) where the creditor is a partnership and the proxy is signed either with the firm name or by one of its partners.

(b) where the creditor is a company where the form is signed by a director or the secretary or

(c) where the creditor is a company where the form is signed by a person whose position in that company is such that he would be presumed to have ostensible authority to sign a form of proxy or

(d) where the creditor is a limited liability partnership (incorporated under The Limited Liability Partnership Act 2000) if the form is signed by a member of that partnership.

This is not an exhaustive list of those persons with authority to sign on behalf of a creditor, and in a doubtful case the Chairman should not accept or reject a proxy without further enquiry into the authority of the person signing it and, if necessary, obtaining legal advice. If necessary, he should consider using his power to adjourn the creditors' meeting to enable him to obtain advice and reach a decision.

6.4 When advising the chairman of the meeting on the validity of proxies, a member should bear in mind that he has a personal interest if he has been appointed liquidator at the shareholders' meeting and seeks to retain office following the creditors' meeting or intends to seek appointment as liquidator at that meeting. Where circumstances so demand, he should suggest prior to the meeting that the chairman takes advice on the validity of proxies from an independent source, for example the company's solicitors.

6.5 There is no requirement for proxies which are considered invalid to be returned to the creditors who have lodged them.

6.6 A creditor who is not an individual may arrange for a representative to attend a meeting on its behalf. The Chairman should satisfy himself that the individual attending the meeting is entitled to represent that creditor. The Chairman should permit a director of a company which is a creditor to attend the meeting as its representative, and likewise a partner in a partnership which is a creditor or a member of a limited liability partnership.

The Companies Act 1985 Section 375 provides that a company may by a resolution of its directors appoint a person to act as its representative at meetings, but this section is discretionary and not exhaustive of the possibilities. Any such representative is required to produce a copy of the resolution from which he derives his authority. If the copy resolution is certified as correct by the company secretary or a director, that should be taken as sufficient evidence of the representative's appointment.

If the Chairman has any doubt whether the person purporting to represent a creditor at the meeting is entitled to do so he should consider using his powers to adjourn the meeting to enable him to verify the authority of the representative and to take such legal advice as may be necessary.

Where H M Customs and Excise is represented at a meeting by a Customs Officer attending in person, the Officer's Commission constitutes sufficient authority for him to act on Customs' behalf.

A duly authorised representative of a creditor is entitled to speak and vote on behalf of the creditor as if the creditor were attending the meeting in person. If the same creditor has appointed a proxy who is present at the meeting as well as the representative, the Chairman should accept the vote of the representative to the exclusion of any vote tendered by the creditor's proxy.

7. Claims

7.1 Creditors may submit claims at any time before voting, even during the course of the meeting itself. The admission or rejection of claims for voting purposes is the responsibility of the chairman of the meeting. A claim should be accepted as valid for voting purposes, provided it identifies both the creditor and the amount claimed by him with sufficient clarity. A secured creditor should deduct the value of any security in calculating the amount of his claim. The amount for which the chairman should be advised to admit the claim for voting purposes should normally be the lower of:

(a) the amount stated in the claim; and

(b) the amount considered by the company to be due to the creditor. The advising member may assist the chairman to decide the amounts for which claims should be admitted but if he intends to seek appointment as liquidator he should bear in mind that his own personal interests might create a conflict, in which case the chairman should be advised independently.

8. Availability of Proxies and Claims for Inspection

8.1   Any person entitled to attend the meeting may inspect the proxies and claims, either immediately before or during the meeting. Notwithstanding that a form of proxy submitted is ruled by the chairman to be invalid or a claim is rejected in whole or in part these documents should be made available for inspection.

9. Attendance at the Creditors' Meeting

9.1   A liquidator appointed by the shareholders before the creditors' meeting takes place is required to attend the meeting of creditors personally. He must report to the meeting on any exercise of his powers under sections 112, 165 or 166 IA 1986. Such attendance is required even if the shareholders' appointment was made only shortly before the creditors' meeting. He must also attend any adjourned meeting. He is liable to a fine if he fails to comply without reasonable excuse. He should in such a case document at the time the reason for non-attendance and ensure that a suitably experienced colleague attends in his place.

9.2   One of the directors of the company will have been nominated to act as chairman of the meeting and he must attend. In addition, the advising member should consider whether any other director or employee of the company will be able to provide information which is relevant to the meeting and if so, he should advise that that person be invited to attend the meeting.

9.3   Creditors and their authorised representatives are entitled to attend. In addition, a person who holds himself out as representing a creditor should, in the absence of evidence to the contrary, be allowed admittance and to raise questions, but he may be unable to vote.

9.4   The chairman of the meeting should be advised that he must decide whether to allow any third parties, such as shareholders, the press or the police, to attend, after taking into account the views of the creditors present.

10. Information to be Provided to the Meeting

10.1 The advising member should ensure that a summary or a copy of the directors' sworn statement of affairs is handed to all those attending the meeting. This summary will normally be expected to include a list of the names of the major creditors and of the amounts owing to them. Sufficient copies of the full list of creditors should be available to facilitate its inspection by those attending the meeting. The meeting should be told that the sworn statement of affairs is available for inspection at the meeting.

10.2 Information to be given to the meeting should include:

(a) details of any prior involvement with the company or its directors by the advising member, or if a different person, the proposed liquidator;

(b) a report of the previously held shareholders' meeting, stating the date the notice of the meeting was issued, the date and time that the meeting was held and, if it was held at short notice, the reasons therefore and the fact that the required consents were received. The resolutions passed at the meeting should be reported and if the liquidator has not yet consented to act, that fact should be stated. If the shareholders' meeting was adjourned without a resolution for voluntary winding up being passed, there should be reported;

(i) the date and time to which the meeting had been adjourned; and

(ii) the fact that any resolutions passed at the section 98 meeting will come into effect if and when the winding-up resolution is passed.

(c) the date on which the directors gave instructions for the meeting of creditors to be convened and the date on which the notices were despatched;

(d) the details of the costs paid by the company in connection with the preparation of the statement of affairs. The details should include the amount of the payment and the identity of the person to whom it was made.

If no payments have been made in respect of these costs prior to the meeting, then the liquidator appointed under S100 may make such a payment but if there is a liquidation committee, he must give the committee at least 7 days notice of his intention to make it.

Such a payment shall not be made by the liquidator to himself or to any associate of his, otherwise than with the approval of the liquidation committee, the creditors, or the court.

(e) A report on the company's relevant trading history which should include:

(i)   date of incorporation and registered number;

(ii) names of all persons who have acted as directors of the company or as its company secretary at any time during the three years preceding the meeting;

(iii) names of major shareholders together with the details of their shareholdings;

(iv) details of all classes of shares issued;

(v)   nature of the business conducted by the company;

(vi) location of the business and the address of the registered office;

(vii) details of parent, subsidiary, and associated companies;

(viii) the directors' reasons for the failure of the company;

(ix) extracts from any formal or, if none, draft accounts produced for periods covering the previous three years or for any earlier period which is relevant to the failure of the company. The extracts should include details of turnover, net result, directors' remuneration, shareholders' funds, dividends paid, reserves carried forward at year end and the date of the auditors' report. Creditors should also be advised if the accounts have been qualified by the auditors.

(x)   a deficiency account reconciling the position shown by the most recent balance sheet to the deficiency in the statement of affairs.

(xi) the names and professional qualifications of any valuers whose valuations have been relied upon for the purpose of the statement of affairs, together with the basis or bases of valuation.

(xii) such other information as the advising member considers necessary to give the creditors a proper appreciation of the company's affairs.

(f) if a receiver has been appointed over any assets of the company, the meeting should be provided with a report on the conduct of the receivership to date, including a summary of the receiver's receipts and payments, unless disclosure would be in breach of the receiver's duty to his appointer, for example where market sensitive information was involved. In such circumstances, a receipts and payments account only should be provided, together with an explanation of the circumstances which prevent further information being given. Where any member is an authorised practitioner and is receiver of a company whose shareholders pass a resolution for voluntary winding up, that member should assist the advising member by providing this information;

(g) an explanation of the contents of the statement of affairs.

10.3 There should also be provided to the meeting details of any transactions (other than in the ordinary course of business) between the company, any of its subsidiaries or any other company in which it has or had an interest (together "the company") and any one or more of its directors of an associate of him or them (as defined in section 435 of the Insolvency Act 1986) during the period of one year prior to the resolution of the directors that the company be wound up specifying:

- The assets acquired and the consideration therefore together with the date(s) of the acquisition(s) and the date(s) the consideration for their acquisition was paid;
- The names and qualifications of any person who advised independently on the value of any assets the subject of such transactions;
- The dates on which any resolutions of the company authorising any such transactions were passed.

There shall also be reported to the creditors whether (or not) the advising member or the proposed liquidator or any partner or employee of either of them acted in any capacity either for the company (as defined above) or any other party to any transaction subject to the disclosure requirements set out above.

10.4 The advising member should take all practicable steps to ensure that there are available to hand to those attending the meeting a written summary of the more important statistical information which is contained in a report given orally to the meeting.

10.5 In assisting in the preparation of a report to be presented to the meeting, the advising member may rely upon information contained in the company's accounts and records and also upon information provided by directors and employees. He is not expected to conduct an investigation to ensure that the information is accurate, but should provide the creditors with any material conflicting information of which he is aware.

11. Conduct of the Meeting

11.1 Although the chairman of the meeting must be a director of the company and his identity must be made clear at the outset, there is no reason why the meeting should not be conducted by the advising member or some other professional adviser. It should be explained to the meeting that although this is being done on behalf of the directors, the report is their responsibility and is based upon information supplied by them. The chairman is the arbiter on all procedural matters but may seek advice from the advising member.

11.2 The Chairman should bear in mind that the purpose of the meeting is to ascertain the wishes of the creditors. Technical objections to proxies and representatives attending the meeting should be regarded as subordinate to this principle.

11.3 Creditors and their representatives attending the meeting are required to sign an attendance list. This list should be made available for inspection to anyone attending the meeting. In addition, any creditor or creditor's representative wishing to speak, ask questions, or make a nomination, should be asked to identify himself and the creditor he represents.

11.4 Creditors and their representatives should be given the opportunity to ask questions. Whilst every effort should be made to give a reasonable answer to such questions within the context of the meeting, the chairman may be advised to refuse a question to be put if, for example:

- The questioner refuses to give the name of the creditor he represents and his own name or that of his firm;

- The questioner does not claim to be or to represent a creditor;

or may decline to answer it if, for example;

- the answer could prejudice the successful outcome of the liquidation or creditors' interests;

- the answer could lead to potential court action if subsequently proved incorrect.

The chairman should be advised to state the grounds on which he refuses to allow a question. Creditors are entitled to information on the causes of the company's failure but it is not appropriate for a detailed investigation of the company's affairs to be undertaken at a meeting of creditors.

11.5 Nominations for the appointment of a liquidator should be requested before any vote is taken. The holder of a proxy requiring him to vote for the appointment of a particular liquidator is required to nominate that person, and it is therefore possible that the chairman or any other holder of such proxies may need to make more than one nomination.

11.6 The chairman must accept all nominations and put them to the meeting, unless he has good grounds for supposing that the person nominated is not qualified or is unwilling to act as an insolvency practitioner in relation to the company.

11.7 The procedure to be followed when voting for the appointment of a liquidator should be explained to the meeting. It is acceptable in the first instance for a vote to be taken on an informal show of hands and if the result is accepted by all interested parties, the chairman of the meeting may conclude that a resolution has been passed. If a formal vote becomes necessary it should be conducted by stating the names of all those nominated and by the issue of voting papers on which those wishing to vote will be required to show their name, the name of the creditor they are representing, the amount of the creditor's claim and the name of the nominated person for whom they wish to vote. It is the advising member's responsibility to ensure that voting papers are available.

11.8 When all votes have been counted, the chairman should announce the result to the meeting, giving details of the total value of votes cast in favour of each nomination. He should also give details of votes which have been rejected, either in whole or in part, and should also state which nomination those creditors supported and the reasons for rejection.

11.9 An absolute majority is required and if the first poll is not conclusive, the nominee receiving the least value of votes is excluded on the next poll where no other nominee has withdrawn. In the event of the withdrawal of at least one nominee, then the nominee with the least value of votes remains in the next poll. The same procedure should be followed in all successive polls.

11.10 If a proxy-holder has been instructed to vote for a particular person as liquidator and that person is eliminated or withdraws, then, if the second set of words in square brackets on the proxy form (Form 4.29) allowing him to vote or abstain at his discretion has not been deleted, the proxy-holder will be able to vote for such other person as he thinks fit. If the second set of words in square brackets has been deleted, the proxy-holder will have to abstain on any further ballot.

11.11   The meeting should be told of its right to appoint a liquidation committee and of the nature of the committee's functions, including its rights in relation to the liquidator's remuneration. The committee must consist of not less than three and not more than five creditors (not being fully secured) who have lodged claims which have not been wholly disallowed for voting purposes or rejected. The voting procedure should be explained. When the constitution of the committee is not contentious, a resolution may be passed on a show of hands and may also appoint a committee en bloc. If there are more than five nominations for appointment to the liquidation committee, it is recommended that voting papers should be issued on which each person voting should enter his own name, the name of the creditor he represents and the amount of the claim. Each such person should be allowed to vote for up to five members of the committee and in doing so may vote for his own appointment (if he is a creditor) or that of the creditor he represents. The provision of voting papers is the responsibility of the advising member.

11.12   When declaring the result the chairman should follow the same procedures as those outlined in paragraph 11.8 above. The five creditors receiving the greatest value of votes will form the committee.

11.13   Voting papers should be made available for inspection by any creditor or creditor's representative whose claim has been admitted for voting purposes at any time during the meeting or during normal business hours on the business day following the meeting.

11.14   Apart from the appointment of a liquidator and the establishment of a liquidation committee, the only other resolutions which may be passed by the meeting are:

- (unless it has been resolved to establish a liquidation committee) a resolution specifying that the terms on which the liquidator is to be remunerated will be determined by the Court;

- in the event of two or more persons being appointed to act jointly as liquidators, a resolution specifying whether acts are to be done by both or all of them, or by only one;

- a resolution to adjourn the meeting for not more than three weeks;

- any other resolution which the chairman thinks it right to allow for special reasons.

11.15 A record of the meeting should be prepared in accordance with Statement of Insolvency Practice 12 (Scotland).

12. Provision of Information to Liquidator

12.1 In instances where the advising member has not been appointed to be the liquidator of the company, he must provide reasonable assistance to the liquidator. This will include handing over such of the company's books and papers as are held by him, together with documents he has received in relation to the meeting of creditors (eg. claims, proxies, statement of affairs, shareholders' resolutions, attendance lists and record of the creditors' meeting). It is expected that this information will be handed over as quickly as possible and, in any event, within seven days of the conclusion of the creditors' meeting. Likewise, all sums received by the advising member from the company or on its behalf, less any proper disbursements which he has made, duly vouched, should also be handed over.

13. Report to Creditors Following the Meeting

13.1 The liquidator shall send to creditors and contributors a report of the proceedings at the meeting, together with a copy or summary of the statement of affairs. The report to creditors should include the name and address of the liquidator and of the creditors appointed to the liquidation committee. Details of other resolutions passed at the meeting should also be supplied. It is not necessary to supply a details report on all that transpired at the meeting, but matters of particular relevance should be mentioned. Creditors should be asked to bring the liquidator's attention to any matter of which they consider he should be aware.

14. Solicitation to Obtain Nomination

14.1 Members are reminded of the provisions of section 164 IA 1986 (corrupt inducement), Rule 4.39 of the Insolvency(Scotland) Rules 1986, (solicitation), and their professional body's most recent guide to professional ethics.

Effective Date: 1 February 2002

4.3 STATEMENT OF INSOLVENCY PRACTICE 9 (SCOTLAND) PAYMENTS TO INSOLVENCY OFFICE HOLDERS AND THEIR ASSOCIATES

Introduction

1. The particular nature of an insolvency office holder's position renders transparency and fairness in their dealings of primary importance. Creditors and other interested parties with a financial interest in the level of payments from an insolvent estate should be confident that the rules relating to charging have been properly complied with.

Principles

2. Payments to an office holder or his or her associates should be appropriate, reasonable and commensurate reflections of the work necessarily and properly undertaken.

3. Those responsible for approving payments to an office holder or the basis upon which the payments are to be calculated should be provided with sufficient information to make an informed judgement about the reasonableness of the office holder's requests.

4. Requests for additional information about payments to an office holder or his or her associates should be viewed upon their individual merits and treated by an office holder in a fair and reasonable way. The provision of additional information should be proportionate to the circumstances of the case.

Key Compliance Standards

Provisions of General Application

5. The information provided and the way in which the approval of payments to insolvency office holders and their associates for remuneration is sought should enable creditors and other interested parties[1] to exercise properly their rights under the insolvency legislation.

---

[1] "other interested parties" means those parties with rights pursuant to the prevailing insolvency legislation to information about the office holders' receipts and payments. This may include the

6.   An office holder should disclose:

   (a)   payments, remuneration and expenses arising from an insolvency appointment to the office holder or his or her associates;

   (b)   any business or personal relationships with parties responsible for approving his or her remuneration or who provide services to the office holder in respect of the insolvency appointment where the relationship could give rise to a conflict of interest.

7.   An office holder should inform creditors and other interested parties of their rights under insolvency legislation. Information on how to find a suitable explanatory note setting out the rights of creditors should be given in the first communication with creditors following appointment and in each subsequent report to creditors.

Suggested Format

8.   A suggested format for the provision of information is in the Appendix, including the suggested levels at which the provision of further information may be appropriate.

Provision of Information When Fixing the Basis of Remuneration

9.   When seeking approval for the basis of remuneration, an office holder should provide sufficient supporting information to enable the approving body, having regard to all the circumstances of the case, to make an informed judgement as to whether the basis sought is appropriate. The nature and extent of the information provided will depend on the stage during the conduct of the case at which approval is being sought.

10.   If the remuneration is sought on a time costs basis, an office holder should provide details of the minimum time units used and current charge-out rates, split by grades of staff, of those people who have been or who are likely to be involved in the time costs aspects of the case.

11.   An office holder should also provide details and the cost of any work that has been or is intended to be sub-contracted out and that could otherwise be carried out by the office holder or his or her staff.

creditors' committee, the members (shareholders) of a company, or in personal insolvency, the debtor.

Provision of Information When Seeking Approval of Remuneration

12. The requirements in this section are in addition to reporting requirements under insolvency legislation.

13. When seeking approval for his or her remuneration, an office holder should provide sufficient supporting information to enable the approving body, having regard to all the circumstances of the case, to make an informed judgement as to whether the remuneration sought is reasonable. The nature and extent of the information provided will depend on the stage during the conduct of the case at which approval is being sought.

14. An office holder should state the proposed charge for the period to date and provide an explanation of what has been achieved in the period and how it was achieved, sufficient to enable the progress of the case to be assessed. Where the remuneration is on a time costs basis, an office holder should disclose the charge in respect of the period, the time spent and the average charge-out rates, in larger cases split by grades of staff and analysed by appropriate activity. If there have been any changes to charge-out rates during the period under review, rates should be disclosed by grades of staff, split by the periods applicable.

15. An office holder should also provide details and the cost of any work that has been sub-contracted out and that could otherwise be carried out by the office holder or his or her staff.

Provision of Information When Reporting Approval of Remuneration

16. When advising creditors of the quantum of the remuneration and disbursements which have been approved and advising of the rights of appeal, the office holder should provide an explanation of what has been achieved in the period and how it was achieved, sufficient to enable the progress of the case to be assessed. Creditors should be able to understand whether the remuneration charged is reasonable in the circumstances of the case (whilst recognising that the office holder must fulfil certain statutory obligations and regulatory requirements that might be perceived as bringing no added value for the estate).

17. Where the remuneration is on a time costs basis, an office holder should disclose the charge in respect of the period, the time spent and the average charge-out rates, in larger cases split by grades of staff and analysed by

appropriate activity. If there have been any changes to charge-out rates during the period under review, rates should be disclosed by grades of staff, split by the periods applicable. An office holder should also provide details and the cost of any work that has been sub-contracted out and that could otherwise be carried out by the office holder or his or her staff.

Disbursements

18. Costs met by and reimbursed to an office holder in connection with an insolvency appointment should be appropriate and reasonable. Such costs will fall into two categories:

    (a) Category 1 disbursements: These are costs where there is specific expenditure directly referable both to the appointment in question and a payment to an independent third party. These may include, for example, advertising, room hire, storage, postage, telephone charges, travel expenses, and equivalent costs reimbursed to the office holder or his or her staff.

    (b) Category 2 disbursements: These are costs that are directly referable to the appointment in question but not to a payment to an independent third party. They may include shared or allocated costs that can be allocated to the appointment on a proper and reasonable basis, for example, business mileage.

19. Category 1 disbursements can be drawn without prior approval, although an office holder should be prepared to disclose information about them in the same way as any other expenses.

20. Category 2 disbursements may be drawn if they have been approved in the same manner as an office holder's remuneration. When seeking approval, an office holder should explain, for each category of expense, the basis on which the charge is being made.

21. The following are not permissible:

    (a) A charge calculated as a percentage of remuneration;

    (b) An administration fee or charge additional to an office holder's remuneration;

    (c) Recovery of basic overhead costs such as office and equipment rental, depreciation and finance charges.

22. If an office holder has obtained approval for the basis on which a charge for Category 2 disbursements is made, that basis may continue to be used where he takes a sequential appointment for which further approval of the basis of remuneration is not required, or where he is replaced.

Pre-Appointment Costs

23. When approval is sought for the payment of outstanding costs incurred prior to an office holder's appointment, disclosure should follow the principles and standards contained in this statement.

Payments to Associates

24. Where services are provided from within the practice or by a party with whom the practice, or an individual within the practice, has a business or personal relationship, an office holder should take particular care to ensure that the best value and service is being provided. An office holder should also have regard to relationships where the practice is held out to be part of a national or international association.

25. Payments that could reasonably be perceived as presenting a threat to the office holder's objectivity by virtue of a professional or personal relationship should not be made unless approved in the same manner as an office holder's remuneration or category 2 disbursements.

Provision of Information to Successive Office Holders

26. When an office holder's appointment is followed by the appointment of another insolvency practitioner, whether or not in the same proceedings, the prior office holder should provide the successor with information in accordance with the principles and standards contained in this statement.

Provision of Information to Interested Parties

27. Where realisations are sufficient for payment of creditors in full with interest, the creditors will not have the principal financial interest in the level of remuneration. An office holder should provide the beneficiaries of the anticipated surplus, on request, with information in accordance with the principles and standards contained in this statement.

Effective Date:

This SIP applies to insolvency appointments starting on or after 1 June 2012. However, insolvency practitioners are encouraged to apply the SIP to all cases regardless of the starting date where to do so would not be onerous or give rise to excessive costs.

Date of issue: 1 May 2012

APPENDIX

SUGGESTED FORMAT FOR PROVISION OF INFORMATION

Introduction

1. Information provided by an office holder should be presented in a manner that is transparent, consistent and useful to the recipient, whilst being proportionate to the circumstances of the case. The level of disclosure suggested below may not be appropriate in all instances and the office holder may take account of proportionality considerations. In larger or more complex cases the circumstances of each case may dictate the information provided and its format.

2. It is a matter for each office holder to decide what detailed information and explanations are required, having regard to the circumstances of the case. However, the importance of consistency and clarity should be recognised, and this Appendix sets out suggestions in relation to the presentation of information in a standard way. Those receiving the information ought to be able to make an informed judgement about the reasonableness of the office holder's request. The information provided should facilitate comparisons between cases.

A Narrative Overview of the Case

3. In all cases, reports on remuneration should provide a narrative overview of the case. Matters relevant to an overview are:

    (a) the complexity of the case,

    (b) any exceptional responsibility falling on the office holder,

    (c) the office holder's effectiveness, and

(d) the value and nature of the property in question.

4. The information provided will depend upon the stage at which it is being provided. An overview might include:

(a) An explanation of the nature, and the office holder's own assessment, of the assignment (including the anticipated return to creditors) and the outcome (if known).

(b) A commentary on how the assignment has been handled, including decisions on staffing or subcontracting and the appointment of advisers.

(c) Any significant aspects of the case, particularly those that affect the remuneration and cost expended.

(d) The reasons for subsequent changes in strategy.

(e) The steps taken to establish the views of creditors, particularly in relation to agreeing the strategy for the assignment, budgeting, and fee drawing.

(f) Any existing agreement about remuneration.

(g) Details of how other professionals, including subcontractors, were chosen, how they were contracted to be paid, and what steps have been taken to review their fees.

(h) In a larger case, particularly if it involved trading, considerations about staffing and managing the assignment and how strategy was set and reviewed.

(i) Details of work undertaken during the period.

(j) Any additional value brought to the estate during the period, for which the office holder wishes to claim increased remuneration.

Time Cost Basis

5. Where the remuneration is or is proposed to be calculated on a time costs basis, requests for and reports on remuneration should provide:

(a) An explanation of the office holder's time charging policy

A statement of the office holder's charging policy in relation to time, clearly stating the units of time that have been used, the grades of staff and rates that have been charged to the assignment, and the policy for recovering the cost of support staff. There is an expectation that time will be recorded in units of not greater than 6 minutes.

(b) A description of work carried out, which might include:

- Details of work undertaken during the period, related to the table of time spent for the period.
- An explanation of the grades of staff used to undertake the different tasks carried out and the reasons why it was appropriate for those grades to be used.
- Any comments on any figures in the summary of time spent accompanying the request the office holder wishes to make.

(c) Time spent and charge-out summaries, in an appropriate format.

6. It is useful to provide time spent and charge-out value information in a tabular form for each of the time periods reported upon, with work classified (and sub-divided) in a way relevant to the circumstances of the case, in particular to facilitate comparisons between cases:

Hours						Time Cost £	Average hourly rate £
Classification of work function	Partner	Manager	Other Senior Professionals	Assistants & Support Staff	Total Hours		
Administration and planning							
Investigations							
Realisation of assets							
Trading							
Creditors							
Case specific matters (Specify the matters)							
Total hours							

Hours					Time Cost £	Average hourly rate £
Total fees claimed (£)						

7.   The level of disclosure suggested by the standard format will not be appropriate in all instances and the office holder should take account of proportionality considerations:

   (a)   where the cumulative time costs are, and are expected to be, less than £10,000, the office holder should, as a minimum, state the number of hours and average rate per hour and explain any unusual features of the case;

   (b)   where cumulative time costs are, or are expected to be, between £10,000 and £50,000, a time and charge-out summary similar to that shown above will usually provide the appropriate level of detail (subject to the explanation of any unusual features);

   (c)   where cumulative time costs exceed, or are expected to exceed, £50,000, further and more detailed analysis or explanation will be warranted.

4.4 STATEMENT OF INSOLVENCY PRACTICE 10 (SCOTLAND) PROXY FORMS

1. This statement of Insolvency Practice is to be read in conjunction with the Explanatory Foreword.

2. This statement applies to Scotland only.

Corporate Insolvency - Proxies

3.1 Rule 7.15(2) of the Insolvency (Scotland) Rules 1986 ("the Rules") stipulates that, when notice is given of a meeting to be held in corporate insolvency proceedings and forms of proxy are sent out with the notice, no form so sent out shall have inserted in it the name or description of any person. No proxy form, therefore, should have inserted in it the name or description of any person for appointment as an insolvency office holder, either solely or jointly, or for appointment as a member of a committee, or as proxy holder.

3.2 Members who send out proxy forms should ensure that no part of the form is pre-completed with the name or description of any person (except for the title of the proceedings, which may be inserted for the convenience of the person completing the form).

3.3 When a member advises on the sending out of proxy forms he is required to take all reasonable steps to ensure that no part of the form is pre-completed with the name or description of any person. If the person whom a member is advising refuses to accept the member's advice in this regard the member should ensure that he has put his advice in writing so that he can demonstrate that he has given advice consistent with the law.

3.4 Rule 7.16(2) of the Rules stipulates that a proxy may be lodged at or before the meeting at which it is to be used.

Individual Insolvency - Mandates

4.1 Paragraph 11 of Schedule 6 to the Bankruptcy (Scotland) Act 1985 provides that a creditor may authorise in writing any person to represent him at a meeting and such authorisation must be lodged with the Interim Trustee or, as the case may be, the Permanent Trustee before the commencement of the meeting. There is no form of mandate prescribed by legislation. It should be noted that although the prescribed form of statement of claim provides for the insertion of the name and address of the authorised person, this does not amount to a mandate. There is no legal requirement for members to send mandate forms to creditors (or, indeed, statement of claim forms except where obliged to do so in agency cases by the contract entered into with the Accountant in Bankruptcy).

4.2   Members who chose to send out mandate forms should ensure that no part of the form is pre-completed with the name or description of any person (except for the title of the proceedings, which may be inserted for the convenience of the person completing the form).

4.3   When a member advises on the sending out of mandate forms, he should take all reasonable steps to ensure that no part of the form is pre-completed with the name or description of any person. If the person whom a member is advising refuses to accept the member's advice in this regard, the member should ensure that he has put his advice in writing.

4.4   Although the statutory provision referred to in paragraph 4.1 does not apply to trust deeds, the statements of practice set out in paragraphs 4.2 and 4.3 should be followed in trust deed cases.

Effective 1 May 1997

4.5 STATEMENT OF INSOLVENCY PRACTICE 11 (SCOTLAND) THE HANDLING OF FUNDS IN FORMAL INSOLVENCY APPOINTMENTS

1. Introduction

1.1 This Statement of Insolvency Practice (SIP) is one of a series of guidance notes issued to licensed insolvency practitioners with a view to maintaining standards by setting out required practice and harmonising practitioners' approach to particular aspects of insolvency.

SIP11 is issued under procedures agreed between the insolvency regulatory authorities acting through the Joint Insolvency Committee (JIC). It was commissioned by the JIC, produced by the Association of Business Recovery Professionals, and has been approved by the JIC and adopted by each of the regulatory authorities listed below:

Recognised Professional Bodies:

- The Association of Chartered Certified Accountants
- The Insolvency Practitioners Association
- The Institute of Chartered Accountants in England and Wales
- The Institute of Chartered Accountants in Ireland
- The Institute of Chartered Accountants of Scotland
- The Law Society
- The Law Society of Scotland

Competent Authority:

- The Insolvency Service (for the Secretary of State for Trade and Industry)

The purpose of SIPs is to set out basic principles and essential procedures with which insolvency practitioners are required to comply. Departure from the standard(s) set out in the SIP(s) is a matter that may be considered by a practitioner's regulatory authority for the purposes of possible disciplinary or regulatory action.

SIPs should not be relied upon as definitive statements of the law. No liability attaches to any body or person involved in the preparation or promulgation of SIPs.

2. Statement of Insolvency Practice

2.1 This statement of insolvency practice concerns the handling of funds by insolvency office holders in the administration of insolvency cases. It applies to Scotland only.

2.2 Members should ensure that records are maintained to identify the funds (including any interest earned thereon) and other assets of each case for which they have responsibility as insolvency office holder. Such funds and assets must be maintained separately from those of the office holder or his firm. Subject to the rules relating to the payment of monies into the Insolvency Services Account, which are set out in Insolvency Technical Reminder 1 (English Registered Companies only), case funds should be held in a bank account(s) which meet the following criteria to ensure that these principles are adhered to:

- all money standing to the credit of the account(s) is held by the office holder as case money and the bank is not entitled to combine the account with any other account (including any global, omnibus, master, hub, nominee, sub accounts or similar) or exercise any right to set off or counterclaim against money in that account in respect of any money owed to it on any other account (including any global, omnibus, master, hub, nominee, sub accounts or similar) of the office holder or his firm;

- interest payable on the money in the account(s) must be credited to that account(s);

- the bank must describe the account(s) in its records to make it clear that the money in the account does not belong to office holder or his firm;

- no individual case funds/account(s) can be set off against any overdrawn case funds/accounts (including any global, omnibus, master, hub, nominee, sub accounts or similar).

2.3 Where funds relating to a case are received by cheque payable to the office holder or his firm which cannot be endorsed to the insolvent estate, such cheques may be cleared through an account maintained in the name of the office holder or his firm. Such accounts should be operated on a trust basis and should be maintained separately from the practitioner's office accounts. Funds paid into such accounts should be paid out to the case to which they relate as soon as possible.

2.4 Monies coming into the hands of practitioners which are the property of individuals or companies for which they are acting otherwise than in the capacity of insolvency office holder must be held in an account operated on trust principles and subject to any applicable client money rules.

Effective date: 1 June 2007

Issued: May 2007

This Statement of Insolvency Practice is currently being revised and is likely to be withdrawn and re-issued during 2017. Please check www.insolvency-practitioners.org.uk for further details.

4.6 STATEMENT OF INSOLVENCY PRACTICE 12 (SCOTLAND) RECORDS OF MEETINGS IN FORMAL INSOLVENCY PROCEEDINGS

1. Introduction

1.1　This statement of Insolvency Practice is to be read in conjunction with the Explanatory Foreword.

1.2　This statement of insolvency practice concerns the keeping of records of meetings of creditors, committees of creditors, and members or contributories of companies in formal insolvency proceedings. The statement is in two parts. The first summarises the statutory provisions regarding the keeping of such records in the various types of insolvency appointment. The second sets out the minimum standards which should be observed with regard to such records in all cases as a matter of best practice.

1.3　The statement applies to Scotland only. References to the Insolvency Act are to the Insolvency Act 1986, references to the Bankruptcy Act are to the Bankruptcy (Scotland) Act 1985 and references to the Rules are to the Insolvency (Scotland) Rules 1986.

2. The Statutory Provisions

2.1　**Meetings of Creditors - All Corporate Insolvencies**

Chapter 1 of Part 7 of the Rules apply to all meetings held in corporate insolvency proceedings, other than creditor committees in liquidations, receiverships or administrations (Rule 7.1) and the comments in paragraph 2.2 to 2.8 apply only to corporate insolvency procedures.

2.2　**Report of Meetings - All Insolvencies**

The chairman at any meeting shall cause a report to be made of the proceedings at the meeting which shall be signed by him. The report shall include:

(a)　a list of the creditors or contributories who attended the meeting, either in person or by proxy;

(b)　a copy of every resolution passed; and

(c) if the meeting established a creditors' committee or a liquidation committee, a list of the names and addresses of those elected to be members of the committee.

The chairman shall keep a copy of the report of the meeting as part of the sederunt book in the insolvency proceedings. (Rule 7.13)

2.3 Chairman of Meetings

Rule 7.5 states that the Chairman of any meeting of creditors or contributories in insolvency proceedings other than at a meeting of creditors summoned under Section 98 shall be the responsible insolvency practitioner, or, except at a meeting of creditors summoned under Section 95, a person nominated by him in writing who must either be a qualified insolvency practitioner or an experienced employee of the responsible insolvency practitioner.

2.4 Meeting of Creditors - Administrations

In addition to the requirements in 2.2 above the administrator is required to annex to the report of the meeting details of the proposals which were considered by the meeting and of any revisions and modifications which were also considered. (Rule 2.13)

2.5 Meeting of Creditors - Creditors Voluntary Liquidation

The chairman of the meeting summoned under Section 98 shall be one of the directors of the company. (Section 99(1)) Insolvency Act.

2.6 Meeting of Creditors - Court Liquidation

At the first meeting of creditors or contributories in a court liquidation, the interim liquidator shall be the chairman except that, where a resolution is proposed to appoint the interim liquidator to be the liquidator, another person may be elected to act as chairman for the purpose of choosing the liquidator.

2.7 Meeting of Creditors and Members - Company Voluntary Arrangement

In addition to the requirement of 2.2 above the report of the meetings summoned under Section 3 of the Insolvency Act shall state:

(a) whether the proposal for a voluntary arrangement was approved or rejected and, if approved, with what (if any) modifications;

(b) set out the resolutions which were taken at each meeting, and the decision on each one;

(c) list the creditors and members of the company (with their respective values) who were present or represented at the meeting, and how they voted on each resolution; and

(d) include such further information (if any) as the chairman thinks it appropriate to make known to the court. Rule 1.17.

2.8 **Report as Evidence of Proceedings at Meetings**

A report of proceedings at a meeting of the company or of the company's creditors or contributories in any insolvency proceedings, which is signed by a person describing himself as the chairman of that meeting, shall be deemed, unless the contrary is shown, to be sufficient evidence of the matters contained in that report (Rule 7.25).

2.9 **Meeting of Creditors - Sequestrations**

The provisions of the insolvency rules do not extend to sequestrations. The only requirement laid out in Section 23 of the Bankruptcy Act is for the chairman to arrange for a record to be made of the proceedings at the meeting.

It is suggested that this should include similar information to that prescribed for corporate insolvency proceedings.

2.10 **Meeting of Creditors - Trust Deeds**

There is no statutory requirement for a meeting to be held in a Trust Deed, but if one is held then the comments in 2.9 above should be applied.

3. Best Practice

3.1 Records should be kept of all meetings of creditors, committees of creditors, or members or contributories of companies, held in any insolvency proceedings. The record should include, as a minimum, the following information:

- The title of the proceedings
- The date, time and venue of the meeting
- The name and description of the chairman and any other person involved in the conduct of the meeting

- A list, either incorporated into the report or appended to it, of the creditors, members or contributories attending or represented at the meeting
- The name of any officer or former officer of the company attending the meeting if not attending in one of the above capacities
- The exercise of any discretion by the chairman in relation to the admissibility or value of any claim for voting purposes
- The resolutions taken and the decision on each one and, in the event of a poll being taken, the value or number (as appropriate) of votes for and against each resolution
- Where a committee is established, the names and addresses of the members
- Such other matters as are required by the statutory provisions applicable to the relevant insolvency procedure as set out in section 2 above or, in the case of a voluntary arrangement, by the terms of the proposal.

Where a meeting has been asked to approve an office holder's remuneration, the information provided to the meeting in support of that request should form part of, or be retained with, the record of the proceedings.

3.2 The record should be signed by the chairman and be inserted into the sederunt book.

In the case of committee meetings a copy of the record should be sent to every person who attended, or was entitled to attend, the meeting.

3.3 Forms of proxy retained under Rule 7.17 should be inserted in the sederunt book.

3.4 Where a member is the office holder or is appointed office holder as a result of the proceedings at the meeting and has not himself acted as chairman of the meeting, he should endeavour to ensure that the record is signed by the chairman and complies with the above principles. If the member is not satisfied that the record signed by the chairman is an accurate record of the proceedings, he should either prepare his own record for his files or prepare a note for his files explaining in what respects he disagrees with the chairman's records.

Effective date: 1 May 1997

4.7 STATEMENT OF INSOLVENCY PRACTICE 14 (SCOTLAND) A RECEIVER'S RESPONSIBILITY TO PREFERENTIAL CREDITORS

1. Introduction

1.1 This statement of insolvency practice is to be read in conjunction with the Explanatory Forward.

1.2 This statement has been prepared to summarise what is considered to be the best practice to be adopted by receivers of the assets of companies where any of those assets are subject to a floating charge so that the office holder has legal obligations to creditors whose debts are preferential. Its purpose is to:

- Ensure that insolvency practitioners are familiar with the statutory provisions;

- Set out best practice with regard to the application of statutory provisions;

- Set out best practice with regard to the provision of information to creditors whose debts are preferential and to responses to enquiries by such creditors.

Whilst this statement does not specifically address the treatment of preferential claims in liquidations, insolvency practitioners acting as liquidators (or in any other relevant capacity) should have due regard to the principles which it contains.

1.3 The statement is divided into the following sections:

- The statutory provisions
- Categorisation of Assets and Allocation of Proceeds
- Apportionment of Costs
- Determination of preferential debts
- Payment of preferential debts
- Disclosure to creditors with preferential debts
- Other matters

2. The Statutory Provisions

2.1 The rights of creditors whose debts are preferential in a receivership derive from section 59 of the Insolvency Act 1986 ('the Act').

Where a receiver is appointed on behalf of the holders of a floating charge and the company is not at the time in the course of being wound up, its preferential debts shall be paid out of the assets coming into the hands of the receiver in priority to any claims for principal or interest in respect of the floating charge by virtue of which the receiver was appointed.

Preferential debts are defined in section 386 of the Act and are set out in Schedule 6 to the Act (as amended from time to time), which is to be read in conjunction with Schedule 4 to the Pensions Schemes Act 1993 and are those which by the end of a period of 6 months after advertisement by the receiver for claims in the Edinburgh Gazette and in a newspaper circulating in the district where the company carries on business either

(a) have been intimated to him or

(b) have become known to him.

The date at which they are to be ascertained is the date of the appointment of the receiver (Section 387(4) of the Act).

2.2 Receivers should note that the statutory provisions give a right to creditors whose debts are preferential to be paid those debts in priority to the claims of floating charge holders, and the corollary of this right is the obligation of the receiver to pay them. Failure by a receiver to pay preferential debts out of available assets is a breach of statutory duty. However it is recognised that circumstances may arise when it is administratively convenient or cost-effective to co-operate with a company's liquidator and arrange for him to pay the receivership preferential debts, and guidance on such arrangements is given in paragraph 6.2 below. It should be noted that such arrangements do not exonerate the receiver from his obligations.

3. Categorisation of Assets and Allocation of Proceeds

3.1 In order to ascertain which assets are subject to the statutory rights of preferential creditors it is necessary to confirm which assets are subject to a standard or other fixed security and which are subject to the floating charge.

3.2 The rights of statutory preferential creditors to a distribution from the assets require the receiver to identify the rights of other creditors in terms of Section 60(1) of the Insolvency Act (1986) and their order of priority.

3.3 It is not of itself sufficient for the charges to state that an asset is subject to a fixed charge or standard security for it to be subject to such a charge.

3.4 Receivers are reminded that it is the type of charge at the time of its creation which determines whether the assets are available to meet preferential debts. Crystallisation of a floating charge upon the appointment of a receiver does not affect the rights of creditors with preferential debts to be paid out of assets subject to a crystallised floating charge;

3.5 Section 59 of the Act requires that the preferential debts 'shall be paid out of the [floating charge] assets coming to the hands of the receiver in priority to' any claim for principal or interest by the floating charge holder. The effect is that a receiver is under a duty of care to the preferential creditors if, having had available assets in hand, he fails to apply them in terms of the order of priority set out in Section 60(1) including payment of the preferential debts. Where any action which he proposes to take could result in a diminution in the amount available to meet preferential debts the receiver should give the most serious consideration to the risks of such action.

3.6 When assets are sold as part of a going concern (or otherwise in parcels comprising both standard security and floating charge assets) the apportionment of the total consideration suggested by the purchaser (for example for his own financial reasons) may not properly reflect the financial interests of the different classes of creditors in the individual assets or categories of assets. In these circumstances the receiver should ensure that he will be able properly to discharge his obligations to account to holders of standard securities or other fixed security on the one hand and creditors interested in assets subject to floating charges on the other.

4. Apportionment of Costs

4.1 The amount available to meet preferential debts is the funds realised from the disposal of assets subject to a floating charge net of the costs of realisation and subject to the order of priority set out in Section 60(1). It is dependent, therefore, not only on the correct categorisation of the assets but also on the appropriate allocation of costs in effecting realisations.

4.2 These costs will normally fall into one of three categories:

- Liabilities incurred by the company (the receiver having acted as agent) and costs incurred by the receiver and recoverable by him out of the company's assets under his statutory indemnity (other than those referred to below);
- The costs of the receiver in discharging his statutory duties;
- The remuneration and disbursements of the receiver.

4.3 The receiver's reasonable costs are sometimes readily identifiable as applicable to either the standard security or other fixed security or floating charge assets, but in other cases may not be so easily allocated between the two categories of assets.

Where costs are clearly identifiable as having been incurred in the realisation or collecting in of one or other of the two categories they should be recorded as such in the receiver's records so that they can be deducted from realisation proceeds in ascertaining the amount available for each class of creditors.

4.4 If costs cannot be clearly identified as referring to the realisation of assets in each category, or refer to assets in both categories, the Receiver will require to carry out an apportionment and, so far as possible, record his reasons for doing so.

A receiver has a duty to allocate costs appropriately but that allocation will involve the exercise of professional judgement undertaken with a full appreciation that it must be made with independence of mind and with integrity.

4.5 The key principles for a receiver in his consideration of the allocation of costs are:

- The statutory rights of preferential creditors as set out in the Insolvency Act 1986 and the decisions of the courts in cases under that Act and predecessor legislation;
- The provisions of the charges
- The maintenance of a proper balance as between the classes of creditors with whose interests he is required to deal in the light of their legal rights.

In order to enable a receiver to allocate costs on an appropriate basis, contemporaneous records of the dominant reasons for incurring costs should be maintained. These will also assist him in providing explanations as to how he arrived at what he considers to be an appropriate allocation and provide evidence should that allocation be challenged by any of the parties involved.

4.6   In allocating costs a receiver should have regard to:

- The objectives for which costs were incurred, it being recognised that certain types of costs may, properly, be allocated to the standard security or other fixed charge assets in one case and to the floating charge assets in another[1]. In another case such costs may enhance realisations in both categories.

- The benefits actually obtained for those financially interested in one or other category of asset in terms of protection of those assets or their value and any augmentation of that value.

- Whether the benefits to those interested in assets subject to a standard security or other fixed security have been enhanced by action which proves to be detrimental to those interested in floating charge assets (for example where trading losses are incurred to protect or enhance the value of property subject to a standard security).

- Whether the realisation of the undertaking and assets by means of a going concern sale has resulted in a reduction in the quantum of debts which are preferential due to the transfer of employment contracts.

4.7   A receivership arises only when there is a floating charge. A receiver whose appointment extends only to part of the property (rather than to the whole or substantially the whole of the property of the Company) has the same responsibilities with respect to the allocation of costs and payment of preferential debts as discussed in this SIP but with reference only to that property which has been attached.

In apportioning the costs of fulfilling their statutory duties and in the absence of any guidance from the courts, receivers should have regard to the general principle referred to in paragraph 4.5 above of maintaining a proper balance.

---

[1]   For example the payment of rent on a leasehold property may be to preserve the value of the lease or to enable manufacturing to continue and work in progress to be completed.

4.8 The allocation of a receiver's remuneration and disbursements should be undertaken adopting the same principles as those applicable to costs and he should ensure that he maintains contemporaneous records which will enable him to make an appropriate division of his remuneration and disbursements between the different categories of assets.

5. Determination of Preferential Debts

5.1 As stated in paragraphs 2.1 and 2.2 of this statement it is a receiver's obligation to pay preferential debts out of assets available for that purpose.

5.2 Following advertisement and initial notification to potential preferential creditors of his appointment and before beginning the process of determining preferential debts, a receiver should assess whether there are likely to be sufficient floating charge realisations to pay a distribution Where no payment will be made, it is not necessary to agree preferentia claims. However, in such circumstances the receiver should write to creditors whose claims are preferential explaining why he is unable to make a payment to them.

5.3 Where there will be a distribution to preferential creditors, the receive should assist those creditors, where possible, by providing adequate information to enable them to calculate their claims. In the case of al preferential creditors other than employees, the receiver is entitled to assume they have full knowledge of their legal entitlements under the Insolvency Act and should invite them to submit their claims. The receive should then check those claims, and accept or reject them as appropriate

5.4 In determining the preferential claims of employees, the receiver is no entitled to regard an individual employee as having full knowledge of his rights and entitlements. Accordingly, the receiver should obtai information from either the company's records or from the employee before calculating the claim (other than one which is payable to the Secretary of State by way of subrogation). The employee should be provided with details of the calculation of his claim and any further explanation that he may reasonably require.

5.5 Receivers are reminded that Schedule 6 (paragraph 11) of the Act provides that anyone who has advanced money for the purpose of paying wages, salaries or accrued holiday remuneration of any employee is a preferential creditor to the extent that the preferential claim of the employee is reduced by such advance.

5.6 When an employee's preferential debt has been paid out of the National Insurance Fund under the provisions of the Employment Rights Act 1995, the Secretary of State is entitled, by virtue of section 189 of that Act to the benefit of the employee's preferential debt, in priority to any residual claim of the employee himself. A receiver is not obliged to accept the preferential claim of the Secretary of State without satisfying himself that it is correct. If a receiver is not able to accept the Secretary of State's claim he should contact the Redundancy Payments Service to explain why and attempt to reach agreement on the amount to be admitted.

6. Payment of Preferential Debts

6.1 As soon as practicable after funds become available and the amount of the preferential debts has been ascertained, receivers should take steps to pay them. Under the statutory provisions preferential debts do not attract interest (unless all creditors (except postponed debts) are being paid in full) and payments to creditors should not be unnecessarily delayed. A receiver who does not comply timeously with his obligations under Section 59 and against whom decree is obtained may find himself ordered to pay interest by the court. While insolvency practitioners cannot be expected to bear any financial risk by paying some preferential debts before all such debts are agreed, there are often circumstances when it is possible to make payment either in full or on account before all claims have been agreed and this course of action should be adopted whenever it is practicable to do so.

6.2 Situations may arise where, notwithstanding a receiver's statutory duty to pay preferential debts, it may (exceptionally) be administratively convenient or cost-effective for a receiver to make arrangements for the liquidator to make payment of the preferential debts arising in the receivership. Such arrangements are made at the receiver's risk, and should not be on any basis which could result in payment of an amount less than that which would have been available to meet those debts if the receiver had himself paid them – or which would cause delay in paying them.

6.3   The receiver should provide preferential creditors with details of any such arrangement and the reason for making them.

7. Disclosure to Creditors With Preferential Debts

7.1   When the funds realised from assets subject to a floating charge are inadequate to pay the preferential debts in full, the receiver should send those creditors a statement setting out the costs charged against the proceeds of realisation of assets

7.2   Any further information which a creditor with a preferential debt reasonably requires should be provided promptly.

8. Other Matters

8.1   Difficulties may arise in determining the rights of creditors to have debts paid preferentially in priority to a prior floating charge holder when the receiver has been appointed under a second or subsequent charge. The law in this area is complex and insolvency practitioners should seek legal advice (and if necessary apply to the court for directions) when appointed under such a charge.

8.2   Situations will arise where payments sent out are not encashed and the payee cannot readily be located. The insolvency legislation does not make provision for this eventuality and there have been no reported cases where the courts have decided the matter. A schedule of unclaimed dividends should be prepared and a special deposit account for these should be opened with the Accountant of Court's designated bank, the Royal Bank of Scotland PLC at North Bridge, Edinburgh branch with notification to the Accountant of Court including a schedule of unclaimed dividends.

Effective Date: 1 January 2001

4.8 STATEMENT OF INSOLVENCY PRACTICE 17 (SCOTLAND) A RECEIVER'S RESPONSIBILITY FOR THE COMPANY'S RECORDS

This document was issued as SIP 1 (Scotland) in February 1998. It was re-numbered as SIP 17 (without updating of the text) with effect from 2 May 2011.

1. Introduction

1.1 This statement of Insolvency Practice is to be read in conjunction with the Explanatory Foreword.

1.2 This statement has been prepared to summarise what is considered to be the best practice in circumstances where receivers are approached by liquidators or directors seeking access to or custody of a company's books and records. The best practice is considered below both with regard to company records maintained prior to the appointment of a receiver and with regard to those records prepared after the receiver's appointment.

2. Company Records Maintained Prior to Appointment of a Receiver

2.1 The records which a company maintains prior to the appointment of a receiver may be classified under two main headings.

2.2 The first comprises the non-accounting records which the directors are required to maintain by the Companies Act 1985 (as amended) (the statutory records). These consist of various registers (e.g. of members) and minute books (e.g. of directors' meetings).

2.3 The second category of records maintained by a company prior to the appointment of a receiver includes accounting records required by statute and all other non-statutory records of the company (statutory accounting and other non-statutory records). Taking each in turn:-

3. Statutory Records

3.1 The company's statutory records should be kept at its registered office or other permitted place (see paragraph 3.6 below) having regard to the provisions of the Companies Act 1985, Sections 288, 353, 383 and 411 (registers of directors, members, minute books and charges).

3.2 Directors' powers to cause entries to be made in these statutory records do not cease on the appointment of a receiver. Indeed, the directors' statutory duties to maintain them are unaffected by his appointment.

3.3 A receiver would have the power to inspect the statutory records as part of his right to take possession of, collect and get in the property of the company (cf. schedule 2, paragraph 1 of the Insolvency Act 1986). He is not, however, placed under an obligation to maintain those records after his appointment and should not normally do so.

3.4 The abolition by Section 130 of the Companies Act 1989 of the requirement for a company formed under the Companies Acts to have a common seal means that in many cases the company in receivership will have no common seal. Provided that an appropriately worded attestation clause is used, deeds can be executed without the use of the common seal. Given that the common seal may still be used for the execution of deeds by the company, however, it is considered best practice for the receiver to take possession of it.

3.5 On appointment, a receiver has two possible options:-

   (i) To leave the statutory records in the custody of the directors so that they are in a position to continue to carry out their statutory duties to maintain them.

   (ii) To take possession of the statutory records for safe keeping. In such circumstances, the receiver should remind the directors of their statutory responsibilities to maintain the records and allow them free access for this purpose. It would also be advisable for the receiver to prepare a detailed receipt for all the records taken into his possession. This should be signed by a director or other responsible official of the company in receivership.

3.6 The receiver may change the company's registered office to that of his own firm, in which case, the statutory records should also be transferred to the new registered office and the procedure outlined in paragraph 3.5. (ii) above followed.

3.7 Any statutory records (and if applicable any seals) taken into a receiver's possession (see paragraphs 3.3 and 3.4) should be returned to the directors (or liquidator) on the receiver's ceasing to act.

4. Statutory Accounting and Non-Statutory Records

4.1 All such records as are necessary for the purposes of a receivership should be taken into the receiver's possession and/or control and any which he will definitely not require may be left with the directors. If the receiver encounters difficulty in obtaining possession of the records, the provisions of Sections 234 - 236 of the Insolvency Act 1986 may be of assistance. These are the provisions allowing a receiver to apply to the court for an order for property in the control of any party to be handed to him, placing officers and others under a statutory obligation to co-operate with the receiver and allowing him to apply to the court for an order summoning officers of the company in receivership and others before it for questioning.

4.2 A receiver is under no statutory duty to bring these records up to date to the date of his appointment although for practical purposes (such as to give prospective purchasers some indication of the financial state of the business) it may be necessary for him to do so.

4.3 If a receiver does not take possession of all the records it would be advisable for him to make a list of all those not taken into his custody with a note of their whereabouts.

4.4 When making sales of certain assets (e.g. book debts or plant and machinery) it may be necessary for the receiver to hand over to the purchaser company records (e.g. debtors' ledger or plant registers) relating to those assets. In such circumstances, the receiver should ensure that the relevant asset sale agreement specifies the need for these records to be made available to the company on request. Although this will invariably be a matter of negotiation between the receiver and his purchaser, it would be preferable for him to retain the originals of such records. He may make copies available to the purchaser or allow the purchaser to retain them for a short time for the purpose of making copies. Once again, appropriate provision should be made in the asset sale agreement as to the particular circumstances and as to whom is to bear the costs.

4.5 If a receiver transfers the business of the company to a third party as a going concern, Section 49 and paragraph 6 of Schedule 11 to the Value Added Tax Act 1994 place the obligation of preserving any records relating to the business upon the transferee. This applies unless the Commissioners of Customs & Excise, at the request of the transferor, otherwise direct.

4.6 This is a wide-ranging obligation. It applies regardless of whether the VAT registration is itself transferred or whether the transfer is treated as supply of neither goods nor services.

4.7 The categories of records covered by Schedule 11 paragraph 6 are wide-ranging. They include orders and delivery notes, purchase and sale records, annual accounts, VAT accounts and credit and debit notes.

5. Entitlement of Liquidator to Records

5.1 The case of *Engel v South Metropolitan Brewing & Bottling Company [1892] 1 Ch 442* is authority under English law to the effect that a liquidator becomes entitled to possession of all books and records relating to the "management and business" of the company which are not necessary to support the title of the chargeholder as against a court-appointed receiver. The court held that a court- appointed receiver can be compelled to deliver such documents to the liquidator against the liquidator's undertaking to produce them to the receiver on request. While there is no equivalent authority with respect to a receiver appointed by the holder of a floating charge, general practice supports the proposition that delivery up of records in return for an undertaking and subsequent production on request should occur (*Lightman & Moss, Law of Receivers of Companies, 2nd Edition* paragraph 11 - 17).

5.2 A receiver has no statutory authority to destroy pre-appointment records and in due course these must be returned to the company's directors or, if the company is in liquidation, to its liquidator.

6. Post Appointment Records

6.1 Statutory Accounting Records

Relating to the period prior to the appointment of a liquidator

6.1.1 The receiver should establish appropriate accounting records as from the date of his appointment. The English case of *Smiths Limited v Middleton [1979] 3 A11 ER 842* shows that he has a duty to render full and proper records to the company in order that the company (and its directors) may comply with the duties imposed by Sections 221, 226, 227 and 241 Companies Act 1985 (preparation and approval of accounts).

6.1.2   A receiver is also under obligation to make returns of his receipts and payments pursuant to Rule 3.9 of the Insolvency (Scotland) Rules 1986. The statutory requirements and the best practice to be followed in the preparation of insolvency practice entitled "Preparation of Insolvency Office Holders' Receipts and Payments Accounts", to which members are referred to further information.

6.1.3   When a liquidator is appointed, the Engel case would seem to apply so that the liquidator becomes entitled to possession of records (see paragraph 5.1. above).

6.1.4   Receivers have no statutory authority to destroy such records and on ceasing to act must hand these over to the company's directors or, if it is in liquidation, to the liquidator.

Relating to the period after the appointment of a liquidator

6.1.5   The receiver's obligation to make returns of receipts and payments and to maintain accounting records (paragraph 6.1.2. above) remains in force after the appointment of a liquidator.

6.1.6   Section 69 Insolvency Act 1986 allows any member, creditor, the Registrar of Companies or the liquidator to enforce these duties.

7. Other Records

7.1   The remaining records, books and papers relating to a receivership may be subdivided between "company records", "chargeholder's records" and "receiver's personal records".

7.2   **Company Records**

7.2.1   Company records will include as a minimum all those records which exist as a result of carrying on the company's business and dealing with the assets. These records fall in the same category as the non-statutory records mentioned in paragraphs 4.1 to 5.2 above. They should be treated in the same way, being returned to the company's directors or if it is in liquidation, to its liquidator when the receiver ceases to act.

7.2.2   In the English case of *Gomba Holdings UK Limited v Minories Finance Limited [1989] 5BCC 27* consideration was given to precisely which records fall within the definition of "company records". It was held that an administrative receiver acts in several capacities during the course of a receivership. In addition to being agent of the company, he owes fiduciary obligations to his appointor and to the company. It is only documents generated or received pursuant to his duty to manage the company's business or dispose of its assets which belong to the company.

7.3 Chargeholder's Records

7.3.1 As explained above, in the Gomba case quoted in paragraph 7.2.2. above it was held that documents containing advice and information to the appointor and "notes, calculations and memoranda" prepared to enable the receiver to discharge his professional duty to his appointor or to the company belong either to the appointor (if he wishes to claim them) or to the receiver. They do not belong to the company.

7.4 Receiver's Personal Records

7.4.1 A receiver's personal records are those prepared by him for the purpose of better enabling him to discharge his professional duties. They will include, for instance, his statutory record which he is required to maintain by Regulation 17 of the Insolvency Practitioners' Regulations 1990 ("the Regulations"). The record must take the form set out in Schedule 3 to the Regulations.

8. Best Practice

8.1 It is considered best practice that all records mentioned above, with the exception of the chargeholder's records (paragraph 7.3. above) and a receiver's personal records (paragraph 7.4. above) should be made available on request to the company acting by its directors or, if it is in liquidation, its liquidator, unless the receiver is of the opinion that disclosure at that time would be contrary to the interests of the appointor, for instance because of current negotiations for the sale of assets (*Gomba Holdings UK Limited v Homan [1986] 3 All ER 94*). Subject to the interests of the chargeholder, it appears from this case that directors are entitled to such information as they need to enable them to exercise their residual powers and to perform their residual statutory duties considered above.

8.2 Disclosure of the receiver's personal records is a matter for his discretion, although in any legal action brought against him productions may be ordered by the Court.

8.3 Where there is no liquidator and the directors cannot be traced (or the receiver has reason to suppose that they are not reliable) he will need to consider whether he feels it necessary to present a petition for the company to be wound up using his powers under Schedule 2 to the Insolvency Act 1986. Whether or not a liquidator is appointed, the receiver has no statutory power to destroy a company's records even after the expiry of the statutory period for which the company would need to retain them (usually 6 years). Thus, if he does so without the authority of the company or the liquidator, he does so at his peril. Note also that the record a receiver is required to keep by the Regulations must be preserved for a period of 10 years from the later of the date upon which the receiver ceases to hold office or any security or caution maintained in respect of the company ceases to have effect (Regulation 20).

Issued February 1998

Re-issued 2 May 2011

Section 5

Insolvency Guidance
Papers

CONTENTS

INTRODUCTION

Insolvency Guidance Papers (IGPs) are issued to insolvency practitioners to provide guidance on matters that may require consideration in the conduct of insolvency work or in an Insolvency Practitioner's practice. Unlike Statements of Insolvency Practice, which set out required practice, IGPs are purely guidance and practitioners may develop different approaches to the areas covered by the IGPs. IGPs are developed and approved by the Joint Insolvency Committee, and adopted by each of the insolvency authorising bodies:

AUTHORISING BODIES

Recognised professional bodies

The Association of Chartered Certified Accountants

Insolvency Practitioners Association

The Institute of Chartered Accountants in England and Wales

Chartered Accountants Regulatory Board for the Institute of Chartered Accountants in Ireland

The Institute of Chartered Accountants of Scotland

Competent authorities

Department of Enterprise, Trade and Investment (for Northern Ireland)

5.1 INSOLVENCY GUIDANCE PAPER
CONTROL OF CASES

Approved by the Joint Insolvency Committee and Issued by the RPBs and The Insolvency Service

1. INTRODUCTION

Insolvency appointments are personal to an individual insolvency practitioner, who has an obligation to ensure that cases are properly controlled and administered at all times. However, issues can arise when an Insolvency Practitioner delegates work to others, or takes appointments jointly with other practitioners. In such circumstances, a practitioner's planning and administrative arrangements will need to consider how best to ensure that cases are properly controlled at all times, and that proper regard is paid to the interests of creditors and other affected parties

2. DELEGATION

2.1 Given the wide variation in the size of firms dealing with insolvency work, each practitioner will have different case loads and resources and thus a different requirement to delegate work. Delegation can take on a number of forms, including:

- delegation of work to staff in the practitioner's own office, or to sub-contractors;

- delegation of work to staff within a firm but in another location;

- taking a reduced role on an appointment taken jointly with an insolvency practitioner in the practitioner's office;

- taking a reduced role on an appointment taken jointly with an insolvency practitioner within the same firm but in another location;

- allowing a specialist insolvency practitioner within a firm to take responsibility for all work of a specific type;

- allowing a specialist within a firm to handle work of a specific type (e.g. tax);

- sharing work on an agreed basis on an appointment taken jointly with a practitioner from another firm;

- employing another firm to give specialist advice (e.g. tax), or to undertake specific work (e.g. an investigation); and

- allowing a practitioner in a former firm (following either the practitioner's move to another firm or retirement) to take responsibility for appointments for a short time pending the transfer of cases.

2.2 For each of the above examples (and in other circumstances where delegation takes place), the practitioner must be satisfied at all times that work is being carried out in a proper and efficient manner, appropriate to the case.

3. CONTROL

3.1 In determining the procedures to be put in place to ensure that an appropriate level of control can be established in relation to delegated work, it is recommended that a practitioner have regard to the following matters:

- the structure within a firm, and the qualifications and experience of staff;
- the need for the practitioner to be involved in setting case strategy at the outset, depending on the nature, size and complexity of the case;
- the procedures within a firm to ensure consultation by joint appointees, other practitioners, and staff;
- the extent to which levels of responsibility are defined, and the circumstances in which a reference to, or approval by, the practitioner is required;
- whether there are clear guidelines within a firm to deal with the administration of cases at locations remote from the practitioner;
- the ways in which compliance and case progress are monitored, and then reported to the practitioner;
- the frequency of case reviews, and who carries them out;
- the systems for dealing with correspondence received and, in particular, complaints;
- the process by which work is allocated on a joint appointment with a practitioner from another firm, the rationale for that split, and the controls to be put in place, subject always to statutory requirements; and

- the way in which specialist advisers (including agents and solicitors) and sub-contractors are chosen and engaged, and how their work is monitored.

3.2 Insolvency Practitioners are aware that they may be required to justify their decisions and demonstrate that appropriate levels of control have been established. It is recommended that for firm wide procedures, guidance is set out in writing, and that on a case by case basis, contemporaneous working papers or file notes are prepared.

4. FIRMS

In this Paper, reference to 'firm' includes, as appropriate, a company, a partnership, a sole practitioner, and a practitioner working in association with other 'firms' or practitioners in other 'firms'.

IPA July 2005

5.2 INSOLVENCY GUIDANCE PAPERS
SUCCESSION PLANNING

Approved by the Joint Insolvency Committee and Issued by the RPBs and The Insolvency Service

1. INTRODUCTION

Insolvency appointments are personal to an insolvency practitioner, who has an obligation to ensure that cases are properly managed at all times, and to have appropriate contingency arrangements in place to cover a change in the Insolvency Practitioner's circumstances. The over-riding principle is that the interests of creditors and other stakeholders should not be prejudiced.

2. CONTINUITY

It is important for insolvency practitioners to consider on a regular basis the arrangements in place to ensure continuity in the event of death, incapacity to act, retirement from practice, or the practitioner otherwise retiring from a firm

3. SOLE PRACTITIONERS

3.1   A sole practitioner should consider the steps necessary to put a workable continuity agreement in place, although there may well be considerations as to whether a sole practitioner's cases would be accepted by another insolvency practitioner. The full consequences, both practical and financial, of the relationship with another Insolvency Practitioner have to be recognised by both the office holder and the nominated successor, so that continuity can be achieved and the interests of creditors and other stakeholders safeguarded. In particular, the nominated successor would have to consider whether the obligations arising from a successor arrangement can be discharged properly and expeditiously, having regard to the number and nature of the cases to be taken over.

3.2   A retiring office holder should normally make arrangements for the transfer of cases (including, where appropriate, an application to Court) in sufficient time to ensure that the cases are transferred before the retirement takes place.

3.3   The nominated successor may need to make an application to Court for the transfer of cases as soon as possible after the other office holder's death, incapacity or, if no other arrangements have been made, retirement.

3.4 The arrangements with the nominated successor will need to be reviewed as circumstances dictate, but preferably at least annually.

3.5 The principal matters that might routinely be dealt with in a continuity agreement are set out in the Appendix.

4. FIRMS

4.1 Every insolvency practitioner in a firm (whether a principal or an employee) should consider the comments made above regarding sole practitioners, and should discuss with the firm the arrangements for succession planning, to cover death, incapacity to act, retirement, or leaving the firm. It is recommended that this is reflected in the partnership agreement or in a separate insolvency practice agreement.

4.2 In a firm with other insolvency practitioners, it is likely that the arrangements would include, at the least, an understanding that another Insolvency Practitioner will take over open cases, and make an application to court for the transfer of those cases, if the office holder is unable to do so. It will be the professional responsibility of the remaining partners (as insolvency practitioners) to take prompt action to safeguard the interests of creditors and other stakeholders.

4.3 When an office holder retires from a firm, it may be acceptable for the office holder to remain in office for a short period, with an insolvency practitioner in the firm dealing with the administration of cases. However, where the office holder needs to receive appropriate information on the progress of cases, and be consulted when decisions are to be made; the office holder is likely to require unrestricted access to case files. Such an arrangement, however, is unlikely to be appropriate other than for cases that are clearly in their closing stages. In normal circumstances, the retiring office holder should be replaced within a reasonable period, likely to be within 12 months of retirement.

4.4 Where there are no other insolvency practitioners in a firm, and in the absence of any contractual arrangements to deal with death, incapacity to act, or retirement, the remaining partners (presumably themselves members of professional bodies) should consider their own professional obligations to ensure the proper management of their practice, including making arrangements for another insolvency practitioner to step in as office holder. The firm may have to procure an application to court for the transfer of cases as soon as possible after the office holder's death, incapacity or retirement.

4.5 The principal matters that might routinely be dealt with in an insolvency practice agreement (or a partnership agreement) are set out in the Appendix.

5. DISPUTES

5.1 There can be disputes between firms and partners (and employees who are office holders) who leave the firm, principally arising from the personal nature of insolvency appointments. However, commercial disputes should not be allowed to obscure the over-riding principle set out at the beginning of this paper – that the interests of creditors and other stakeholders should not be prejudiced.

5.2 It is important, therefore, that the contractual arrangements referred to above should provide for the (essentially) mechanistic and financial consequences of an office holder leaving the firm (or upon incapacity to act). There will be similar considerations when an office holder (either partner or employee) is suspended by a firm, or is otherwise excluded from the firm's offices.

5.3 Where there are no contractual arrangements, or where a dispute arises, both parties should consider their professional obligations, and the standard of conduct required by their professional bodies. Further, an office holder must have regard to the statutory obligations of the office held.

5.4 If there is a dispute, it is for the office holder to decide how best to ensure that the obligations of office can be discharged; an application to court may be the only means of finding a solution. It is always open to an office holder to consult with his or her authorising body.

5.5 As noted above, there may be professional obligations on remaining partners to arrange for the proper management of their practice, and so ensure that they do not bring their own professional bodies into disrepute.

IPA July 2005

APPENDIX

Principal matters that might be dealt with in a continuity agreement

1   A clear statement of the circumstances upon which the agreement would become operative, and also the circumstances in which the nominated successor can decline to act.

2   The extent and frequency of disclosure to the nominated successor of case details and financial information.

3   Detailed provisions to provide for:
   - the steps to be taken by the nominated successor when the agreement becomes operative;
   - ownership of, or access to, case working papers;
   - access to practice records; and
   - financial arrangements.

Principal matters that might be dealt with in an insolvency practice agreement (or in a partnership agreement)

1   Clear statements of what happens in the event of an Insolvency Practitioner (whether partner or employee):
   - dying, or being otherwise incapable of acting as an Insolvency Practitioner;
   - retiring from practice;
   - being suspended or otherwise excluded from the firm's offices; or
   - leaving the firm.

2   Where the agreement provides for another Insolvency Practitioner (whether in the firm or in another firm) to take over appointments:
   - the time within which transfer of cases will take place, and the arrangements for the interim period, including provisions for access to information and files;
   - the obligations placed on the practitioner, the firm and the successor practitioner, both in the interim period and thereafter;
   - professional indemnity insurance arrangements; and
   - financial arrangements.

3   Where the Insolvency Practitioner is to remain as office holder following retirement or leaving the firm:

- ownership of, or access to, case working papers;
- access to practice records;
- professional indemnity insurance arrangements; and
- financial arrangements.

5.3 INSOLVENCY GUIDANCE PAPERS
BANKRUPTCY – THE FAMILY HOME

Approved by the Joint Insolvency Committee and Issued by the RPBs, The Insolvency Service and The Insolvency Service for Northern Ireland

1. INTRODUCTION

It is in the interests of the debtor and the creditors, and in the wider public interest, that a family home, and any other residential property available for use by the debtor or the debtor's immediate family, are dealt with fairly and expeditiously in a bankruptcy. This can happen only if the debtor and others who may have an interest in the properties have sufficient information to understand how the bankruptcy affects them, and the options available to them. Failure by a trustee to provide information and explanations can prolong the realisation process, cause unnecessary distress to those involved, and also give rise to complaints.

2. AFFECTED PARTIES

2.1 Where the debtor has an interest in a property falling within the estate, the trustee should consider at an early stage whether the property is or has been the home of any person other than the debtor, and if that person could be affected by the bankruptcy and the sale of the property.

2.2 Those potentially affected include:
- the debtor's spouse, former spouse, or unmarried partner;
- members of the debtor's immediate family;
- a joint legal owner;
- anyone who has contributed towards the purchase of a property (including making mortgage payments);
- anyone in occupation of the property other than under a formal tenancy agreement; and
- a trustee under a previous bankruptcy.

2.3 A trustee will make enquiries of the debtor to establish the properties within the estate and whether any other persons may have an interest in them. It is recommended that a trustee should write to the debtor and any other affected parties as soon as possible, after the appointment or of becoming aware of the property or the third party interest. An initial communication may give a broad explanation of the process and timescales to be followed in the proceedings with further, more specific information provided as it becomes available. This is in addition to the trustee's statutory obligations.

3. INFORMATION TO BE PROVIDED

3.1 A trustee should provide the debtor and any other affected parties with sufficient information at appropriate times to enable them to understand the possible consequences of the bankruptcy, so that they can make an informed decision or seek advice. The information to be provided might include (as appropriate to the circumstances):

- an explanation of the trustee's interest, and why that interest may continue after discharge from bankruptcy;
- the circumstances in which the property will revert to the debtor, and why it may not revert;
- an explanation of why the trustee needs to realise the property;
- the way in which the property and the trustee's interest would be valued;
- an explanation of how any changes in the value of the property, and payments under a mortgage, may be treated;
- how any mortgage, or other security for the repayment of any loan, may be treated;
- details of the steps that the trustee can take, and any timetable, for realising the property; and
- a copy of the Insolvency Service leaflet "What will happen to my home".

3.2 It is also recommended that a trustee:

- seeks offers from affected parties as appropriate, giving sufficient time for responses and explaining any deadlines;
- be prepared, in appropriate circumstances, to meet the debtor and other affected parties to discuss any problems that may arise; and
- advises that affected parties should take independent advice.

4. TIMING OF COMMUNICATIONS

After the initial communications outlined above, it is recommended that a trustee writes regularly to the debtor and other affected parties pending realisation of the property. Whilst such communications should be as circumstances dictate, it is recommended that this should be normally every 12 months. The matters to be dealt with might include (as appropriate to the circumstances):

- whether the trustee's intentions have changed, and the effect on the likely timetable for realisation;

- any changes in the value of the property and the trustee's interest;

- any changes to the positions of the affected parties; and

- whether the trustee is seeking offers for the estate's interest in the property.

5. DEALING WITH OFFERS

5.1 A trustee has a duty to obtain a proper price for the benefit of the estate, but the bankruptcy should not be unnecessarily protracted and account should be taken of the effect of future costs. It is recommended that the consequences of any action, or delay, in respect of a property should be explained to affected parties and where appropriate, to creditors.

5.2 If an affected party makes an offer to purchase the trustee's interest in the property the trustee should deal expeditiously with the offer. If the offer is rejected, the trustee should normally provide an explanation of why the offer was regarded as inadequate.

6. GUIDANCE FOR AFFECTED PARTIES

As noted above, it is recommend that a trustee advises the debtor and other affected parties to take independent advice in relation to the property. It may be appropriate for the trustee to recommend, in the first instance, contact with a solicitor or Citizens' Advice Bureau. The Insolvency Service leaflet "What will happen to my home" is available via www.insolvency.gov.uk

7. DUTY OF CARE

Nothing in this Paper imposes or implies any duty of care by an insolvency practitioner to a debtor, or any person with an interest in a property, over and above what may be imposed by legislation or case law.

IPA October 2005

5.4 INSOLVENCY GUIDANCE PAPERS
SYSTEMS FOR CONTROL OF ACCOUNTING AND OTHER BUSINESS RECORDS

Approved by the Joint Insolvency Committee and Issued by the RPBs, The Insolvency Service and The Insolvency Service Northern Ireland

1. INTRODUCTION

1.1 The existence and accuracy of an insolvent's accounting and other business records will affect the efficient realisation and distribution of an insolvent's assets; and may also be relevant in other circumstances, for example in disqualification proceedings or the prosecution of criminal offences. An insolvency practitioner will also need to take account of the various statutory requirements for businesses to retain certain categories of records.

1.2 Insolvency practitioners should have satisfactory systems in place to record the receipt of, and to control access to, movement of and eventual disposal of, records. This Guidance looks at the parameters of these systems: each case will need to be considered on its own merit: some cases may need significantly more detail than is suggested here.

1.3 Formal recording systems can also assist an insolvency practitioner in the effective management of storage costs.

2. CONTROL OF RECORDS

2.1 It is likely that any system implemented by an insolvency practitioner would record:
- the practitioner's initial enquiries to establish the nature and location of records;
- the steps taken to safeguard records;
- requests made of directors and others to deliver up records;
- what records have been taken under the practitioner's control, and when and how this was done;
- the location of the records;

- whether third parties have had access to the records, and for what purpose; and

- the eventual disposal of the records, and when and how this was done.

2.2 It will be particularly important in cases where the insolvent's records are referred to in legal proceedings (whether for the purpose of civil asset recovery or in other circumstances) that a formal recording process has been followed. Accordingly, an insolvency practitioner should be able to show that any system is applied consistently and that staff are trained in its use.

3. RECORDS IN ELECTRONIC FORM

An insolvency practitioner will need to consider how to deal with information held in electronic form. Retrieval and storage of such information may include, as appropriate, securing servers and personal computers (or hard drives), copying information from those sources, or obtaining hard copies. The system of control is likely to follow the principles set out above.

4. JOINT APPOINTMENTS

Where an insolvency practitioner is appointed jointly with a practitioner from a different firm, responsibility for records should be included within the agreed division of duties. Where both practitioners receive records, each should implement a system of control.

IPA 14 March 2006

5.5 INSOLVENCY GUIDANCE PAPER
DEALING WITH COMPLAINTS

Approved by the Joint Insolvency Committee and Issued by the RPBs, The Insolvency Service and The Insolvency Service Northern Ireland

INTRODUCTION

It is in the interest of complainants and insolvency practitioners, and in the wider public interest, that complaints directed at practitioners are dealt with professionally and expeditiously. Failures to do so can only exacerbate any problem, prolong any sense of grievance felt by a complainant, and undermine confidence in the insolvency profession. As a result, practitioners, their firms and the profession may be brought into disrepute.

This paper is intended to remind insolvency practitioners of their duty to deal properly with complaints, and to suggest some matters that insolvency practitioners might usefully consider. The rules of some authorising bodies (and the rules which apply to the holders of standard consumer credit licences) impose requirements additional to, and which override, the suggestions in this guidance paper,

STEPS TO BE TAKEN

It is likely that the following steps will be appropriate:

- A complaint should be acknowledged promptly.

- The insolvency practitioner should ascertain the background facts as quickly as possible and seek additional information from the complainant as required.

- If the insolvency practitioner concludes that a complaint is unjustified, the complainant should be provided with a full and clear explanation of the reasons for that conclusion.

- If an error has been made, the insolvency practitioner should rectify the error promptly and offer an apology.

- The complainant should always be notified that a complaint can be referred to the insolvency practitioner's authorising body at any time.

The complainant should be kept aware of the steps that are being taken by the insolvency practitioner to review and respond to the complaint, the likely timetable for the response, and the reasons for any delay.

THE DUTIES OF INSOLVENCY OFFICE HOLDERS

It is a feature of the work of insolvency practitioners that complaints may arise because of an incomplete understanding of the legislation under which insolvency office holders are required to act. In many cases, actions or outcomes that are obvious to insolvency practitioners may be seen as wrong or unfair by complainants, as the duties of the office holder may be misunderstood.

When responding to a complaint, an insolvency practitioner should provide where appropriate a clear explanation of the matters affecting the duties of an office holder, including the relevant legislation.

OTHER MATTERS TO CONSIDER

The matters that an insolvency practitioner should consider in relation to complaints include:

- The desirability of establishing a formal complaints procedure within the firm, set out in writing, which can be communicated to complainants.

- Whether complaints should be reviewed by another principal in the firm (where possible) or by an independent practitioner.

- Early resolution of complaints by telephone conversations and meetings. Guidance on what constitutes a good complaints procedure is issued by certain of the authorising bodies.

PROFESSIONAL INDEMNITY INSURANCE

A complaint may, in some circumstances, have to be notified to an insolvency practitioner's professional indemnity insurer. In such cases, any action or response by the practitioner will necessarily be subject to any conditions imposed by the insurer.

IPA October 2009

5.6 INSOLVENCY GUIDANCE PAPER
RETENTION OF TITLE

RETENTION OF TITLE ("ROT") CLAIMS

This guidance can be applied to all ROT claims within any insolvency procedure.

PRE-APPOINTMENT

At this stage, a formal appointment will not have been made. However, it remains the IP's responsibility to advise their clients or potential clients appropriately with regard to ROT. If there are the possibility of ROT claims in future, the responsible IP will have procedures in place to document their strategy for dealing with them if appointed.

If a sale of the business or its assets is envisaged post-appointment, the IP should consider making reference in the contract of sale to the way in which goods potentially subject to ROT are to be treated. Where appropriate, the IP should also agree in advance with any purchaser how any ROT claims might be dealt with.

POST-APPOINTMENT

The IP should contact creditors at the earliest opportunity if the IP believes that there may be ROT claims. The IP should deal with such claims promptly and take any reasonable steps to allow or facilitate the identification by the claimant of any such goods.

The IP should secure any items that may be subject to any such claims if it is reasonable to do so.

GENERAL

The IP should be prepared to communicate and cooperate within reason with any ROT claimant so long as it does not cause the IP to turn aside from the general conduct of the insolvency procedure.

Any claimant must be prepared to communicate expeditiously and cooperate within reason with the IP, make known its claim and provide sufficient evidence of the validity of any such claim and be able to demonstrate that the goods subject to the claim can be identified. Any claimant that fails do to do so should not be surprised that its claim is dismissed.

Issue date: 10 November 2014

Section 6

Other Professional
Guidance

CONTENTS

6.1 A GUIDE TO THE INSOLVENCY PRACTITIONERS ASSOCIATION ETHICS CODE

Foreword

The Joint Insolvency Committee (JIC) is undertaking an on-going review of the Code of Ethics for Insolvency Practitioners. To date, that work has comprised of a number of work strands, including the revision of Statement of Insolvency Practice 1 (SIP 1), which came into effect on 1 October 2015.

The review process identified that increased awareness amongst stakeholders of the existing Code of Ethics to which practitioners work would aid stakeholders' understanding of an insolvency practitioner's work, and potentially promote transparency and trust within the profession.

SIP 1 was revised accordingly to include a provision that an insolvency practitioner should inform creditors at the earliest opportunity that they are bound by the Insolvency Code of Ethics when carrying out all professional work relating to an insolvency appointment.

Additionally, an insolvency practitioner should, if requested, provide details of any threats identified to compliance with the fundamental principles and the safeguards applied. If it is not appropriate to provide such details, the insolvency practitioner should provide an explanation why.

To assist members in fulfilling these new requirements, the IPA has produced a Guide to the Ethics Code, which its members are at liberty to use. It is intended as a useful summary which may be provided by members to interested parties, such as creditors and other stakeholders, or more junior staff. It may, for instance, be provided alongside any case-specific response to a SIP 1 enquiry, provided as part of a staff training or induction programme, or as part of an internal complaints handling procedure.

For the avoidance of doubt, there is no regulatory expectation that this Guide be supplied to any particular group of third parties; it is merely intended to assist members in explaining the complex framework within which they are expected to work in instances when **they** consider it would be useful to do so. Similarly, this Guide is not intended for use by members themselves, who should continue to refer to the full text of the Code.

The Guide is available in PDF from our website and members may reproduce the guide upon their own websites without further permission from the IPA.

The broader review of the Code is ongoing and is likely to take some time to complete. Any change to the existing Code will be subject to a full consultation with members, as and when an appropriate stage in the review process has been reached.

1. Introduction

1.1 Insolvency Practitioners ("IPs") are in a position of trust in their dealing with the affairs of an insolvent company or individual. The professional bodies that regulate insolvency practitioners recognise this and operate under an agreement with the government whereby each body has agreed to apply an ethical code to its members, and will seek to ensure that those members work to common professional standards, to enable creditors and others to receive an efficient service at fair cost.

1.2 The regulators have, therefore, agreed an Ethics Code to ensure that all insolvency practitioners are held to high professional standards, and regulators will have regard to those standards as a benchmark when considering the conduct of IPs when undertaking their regulatory work or in relation to complaints made against IPs.

1.3 The Code gives five Fundamental Principles which should govern all of an IP's actions, the headings of which are as follow, with details in the code:

- Integrity
- Objectivity
- Professional competence and due care
- Confidentiality
- Professional behaviour

2. Threats to the Fundamental Principles

2.1 The Code acknowledges that an IP's actual or perceived adherence with the Fundamental Principles may be threatened in certain circumstances. It identities that these threats typically fall under five main categories:

- Self-interest threats – will the proposed action unfairly directly benefit the IP, his/her firm, a close or immediate family member or an individual within the IP's firm?

- Self-review threats – will the IP find themselves reviewing the work or judgements of an individual connected with his/her firm (or their own work)?

- Advocacy threats – is a position or opinion being promoted to the point where the IP's objectivity is subsequently compromised?

- Familiarity threat – is an individual within the firm becoming too antagonistic or sympathetic to the interests of others as a result of a close relationship?

- Intimidation threats – these may occur where an IP is deterred from acting objectively by threats either actual or perceived

3. The Framework Approach

Identify > Evaluate > Respond

3.1 Rather than endeavouring to anticipate every circumstance that may present a threat to the Fundamental Principles, the Code sets out a method (a "Framework Approach") which should be adopted by an IP to ensure their compliance with the Fundamental Principles.

3.2 An IP should consider the Fundamental Principles and threats to them in all of his / her activities, both before they accept an insolvency appointment and during the process of that appointment. Once an IP has identified any actual or potential threats to their compliance with the Fundamental Principles, s/he should then evaluate the severity of the threats that have been identified and respond appropriately. That response may in some circumstances be to decline an appointment, and in others of lesser severity, to take steps that will reduce the threat to an acceptable level.

3.3 A commonly encountered threat to accepting an insolvency appointment is a potential "conflict of interest" situation. This is most likely to be encountered where there have been some previous dealings between the parties.

3.4 Therefore, before accepting an insolvency appointment an IP should undertake thorough assessment to ensure that there is no prior relationship that would make it inappropriate to accept the appointment. The IP should also evaluate what s/he will be expected to do during the appointment and on whose behalf it will be done to ensure that not only will s/he be acting with independence and objectivity, but will be seen to be doing so by people with no specialist knowledge or understanding.

3.5 The Code itself provides a number of specific instances where accepting an appointment is absolutely prohibited. Outside of these prohibitions and in all other instances, the Code requires practitioners to identify any threats presented (including conflicts of interest) and evaluate their severity. It may be possible for some threats to be managed by the IP to an acceptable level and the Code provides a number of practical suggestions about how this might be achieved.

3.6 In instances where there is uncertainty on the IP's part whether or how to take an action or accept an appointment s/he may consult others to reduce the threat, or share the responsibility for those aspects of the work. S/he may, for example consult a creditors' committee, obtain legal advice or involve another IP to perform a part of the work undertaken (for example, an investigation into the directors' conduct).

3.7 The IP should document the steps they have taken to identify, evaluate and respond to any threats and the strategy behind their decisions. This process should be repeated if further information comes to light that would (for example) have made acceptance of the appointment inappropriate (had it been known at the time). In such circumstances, the IP may need to consider whether they should resign.

3.8 Since 01 October 2015, an IP should, if requested, provide details of any threats identified to compliance with the fundamental principles and the safeguards applied. If it is not appropriate to provide such details, the insolvency practitioner should provide an explanation why.

Financial incentives

4.1 It is never acceptable for an IP to offer an inducement to obtain an insolvency appointment, although it is acceptable for an IP to pay an employee partly or wholly on the basis of introductions obtained by the efforts of the employee.

The purpose of the Guide is to assist stakeholders in understanding the ethical standards expected of Insolvency Practitioners and is not a definitive statement of expected professional standards. Nothing in this summary seeks to fetter the authority of the IPA's regulatory and disciplinary committees to make determinations about a Member's conduct. Members should refer to the full text of the Ethics Code and it remains encumbent upon them to be satisfied that his/her conduct meets the legal and professional requirements placed upon Office-Holders/Members.

The full text of the Ethics Code may be found here:

http://www.insolvency-practitioners.org.uk/regulation-and-guidance/ethics-code

This Guide may be reproduced by IPA members without express prior permission.

© Insolvency Practitioners Association 2016

6.2 APPROACH TO SIP9 REPORTING AND FEE ESTIMATES – R3 GUIDANCE

The IPA is pleased to support and endorse the following R3 guidance note and hopes it will provide the assistance that practitioners have requested when preparing fee estimates and reporting to creditors.

This guidance does not constitute legal advice nor does it seek to instruct or direct practitioners to take, or avoid taking, any action. Practitioners should be aware that any guidance endorsed by the IPA cannot fetter the authority of its regulatory and disciplinary committees to make determinations about a practitioner's conduct.

The IPA accepts no liability in respect of actions that practitioners may take in accordance with this guidance, as it must be for each practitioner to be satisfied that his/her conduct meets the legal and professional requirements placed upon Office Holders. Therefore, practitioners may consider it appropriate to seek independent professional advice in respect of the subject of the guidance, in appropriate cases.

R3 GUIDANCE TO MEMBERS – APPROACH TO SIP 9 REPORTING AND FEE ESTIMATES ENGLAND AND WALES

A. Overview – the Need for Narrative

1. The following guidance is intended to provide members with some ideas and examples of matters which might be relevant to include as part of a meaningful narrative explanation to stakeholders in relation to the time spent by members and their staff in dealing with an appointment. It is anticipated that the narrative will precede the time and charge-out summary and, whilst some aspects may be generic in nature, the broader narrative would need to be tailored and be proportionate to the specific circumstances of each case.

2. The interests of the recipient of the report are paramount. The provision of large volumes of generic information, particularly where the information provided is not or is unlikely to be relevant to the specific case should be avoided as it will not assist the readers understanding of what work has or is proposed to be undertaken and may confuse or cause misunderstanding. Whilst a number of potentially useful and computational tools exist, practitioners should consider whether the

provision of these to creditors is helpful, or whether they are ostensibly for internal use within their practice. Provision of a higher level of detail may be helpful when responding to a request for additional information.

3. The suggestions below are intended to show how a member might support and explain the numerical information provided in any table of time spent. Suggested categories of activity are attached; again, these will need tailoring to the nature of the engagement.

4. Population of a numerical table (or tables) alone will not be sufficient to comply with the legislative and best practice requirements in relation to disclosure of the member's fees, where these are based on time costs. A case specific narrative, in terms of scope and disclosure, will be required.

5. It is of paramount importance, and a fundamental principle of the narrative disclosure, that it clearly distinguishes between the following:

   - work that has been performed solely to comply with statutory requirements (e.g. statutory reporting on directors' conduct and statutory returns),

   - that which adds value, or is necessary to realise assets and distribute funds, and

   - work that has been necessarily been performed but ultimately did not add monetary value to the insolvent estate (e.g. an investigation that did not identify any transactions to pursue) although there may be value in creditors being satisfied that proper investigations have been carried out even if no successful claims or realisations resulted.

6. It should be clear to recipients what has been undertaken in the period being reported upon.

7. There are a number of differing points in the conduct of a case in which narrative will be required. These are:

   - Resolutions to support all fees bases – These will require narrative explaining the work that will be undertaken

   - The fees estimate, where fees are to be based on time costs – These will require both narrative and figures

   - Progress reports – These will require narrative explaining the work undertaken in the period, supported by figures if fees are being taken on a time cost basis

This guidance is intended to cover all of the above areas.

B. General

8. Members should be aware that where fees are based on a fixed amount or percentage calculation, there will also be a need to provide some form of narrative explanation of the work done. It should be sufficiently detailed to ensure that creditors understand why the basis requested is expected to produce a fair and reasonable reflection of the work done by the Office Holder and his or her staff, and should cover the same or similar matters as those outlined below. Whilst it is not necessary to directly compare the fee proposed or charged to that which would have been charged had an alternative basis been used, it remains necessary to provide sufficient information to facilitate the making of informed judgements about the reasonableness of the office holder's requests. This might be achieved, for instance, by referring to prevailing market rates for collection activities or specific tasks or types of work.

9. When mixed bases for the calculation of remuneration are being used (or are proposed to be used), it will be particularly important to provide clear information about the tasks comprised in each of the categories, and the remuneration basis applicable to it. Reference can also usefully be made by Office Holders to the provisions of SIP 14 with regard to the apportionment of costs between fixed and floating charge realisations.

10. The narrative should provide an explanation if work has now been done that was not originally anticipated, for example, if a creditors' committee was appointed after the fee estimate had been prepared. The impact and implications of any variances from the fee estimate should be explained in the narrative statement.

11. Where significant amounts of time in a category are allocated to a particular grade of staff, the narrative should contain an explanation as to why, for example, the complexity of the work requires the involvement of that particular grade of staff (and, where the grade of staff might appear higher than might ordinarily be expected for the task, and explanation of the rationale for the more senior person doing that work), and the reason for the time spent. Similarly, it may be helpful to explain where any particular cost savings have been made in the grade of staff ultimately used, when compared to that previously anticipated.

12. Members should ensure that the narrative reports on matters arising during the period of the review and avoids repetition, save where it is required for contextual purposes. Where material is repeated, it will be helpful to note that the information was previously reported and when.

C. Suggested categories of activity

13. The following are examples of typical workstreams that may be highlighted in a time and charge-out summary (these are not prescriptive or exhaustive). The numbered paragraphs below refer to the categories of activity set out in the illustrative time and charge-out summary below.

C.1 Case Administration and Planning

14. This category of activity is likely to encompass work undertaken for both statutory and case strategy purposes. The narrative will provide an opportunity to explain the value to creditors of the work undertaken, bearing in mind that efficient case administration and planning adds value in terms of the time taken to carry out a job, the costs involved and ensuring, for example, a coherent planned process with as little duplication of effort as possible.

15. The narrative might usefully set out the nature and type of work, such as dealing with appointment and closure formalities, advertising, bonding, production of the statement of affairs, preparation of receipts and payments accounts and any fee estimates, submission of tax and VAT returns, winding up of pension schemes, non- statutory creditors' or shareholders' reports and/or meetings (unless there is a separate reporting category), liaising with creditors' committees, as well time spent determining or revising case strategy and general case management, including case reviews.

16. It may be helpful to set out the number and frequency of returns in relation to, say, the filing of receipts and payments accounts. Where assistance has been provided by any third party, say in relation to the preparation of the Statement of Affairs, or the winding up of the pension scheme, this should be explained in the narrative and the reasons why it was considered desirable and necessary to instruct a third party.

17. The narrative might also explain the reasons for any unanticipated costs being incurred, for example as a consequence of the company records being incomplete or inaccurate, a pension scheme being identified that was not known to exist at the date of appointment, or tax returns being brought up to date. Any revision in case strategy should be explained, together with the associated costs and the benefit to stakeholders in adopting the revised strategy.

18. Where appropriate, the narrative should explain the reasons for the production of any additional, non-statutory, reports (unless there is a separate reporting category), and the benefit derived as a consequence. Time spent liaising with a creditors' committee should be explained and it may be helpful to set out a brief explanation of the matters being considered by the committee in addition to the frequency of agreed reporting.

19. Consideration should be given to stating the anticipated duration of the case, and the impact this may have on the extent of work required.

C.2 Reporting

20. Members may wish to include a narrative explanation setting out to whom they are reporting and the frequency. An office holder may have obligations to report to secured creditors, committees, creditors and shareholders, for both statutory and case management purposes. Reports may include administrators' proposals, progress reports and SIP 16 statements. Members may also wish to explain, in relation to any non-statutory reports, the reason for these being produced and the benefit to the estate, or recipient, in so doing.

C.3 Enquiries and Investigations

21. The extent of disclosure in this section will be a matter for the discretion of the Office Holder and his or her legal advisers. Issues relating to privilege, disclosure prejudicial to the conduct of the insolvency process and 'tipping off', need to be considered when deciding what is disclosed here and in how much detail. This category will likely incorporate both the statutory obligation to review the directors' conduct as well as any necessary investigations to identify assets, and potential recovery actions in relation to antecedent transactions or voidable transactions.

22. Members should consider incorporating work done in relation to collecting and reviewing the company's accounting records, in order to identify potential assets and actions. If there has been a delay in the production of records, or they are incomplete or inaccurate, the impact on progress and costs may be commented upon within the narrative.

23. It may also be appropriate to comment on the co-operation of the directors or bankrupt in relation to any investigations.

24. Where a milestone approach has been used in relation to the fee estimate, members should set out the progress made to date, whether the milestone has been reached, and if the fee estimate has been exceeded, or is likely to be exceeded, the reasons for this.

25. If the review has identified any material antecedent transactions, or assets, that would warrant further investigation or legal action, these should be disclosed to creditors, together with a revised fee estimate if appropriate. This should help to ensure that all creditors will be satisfied that these areas have been investigated in a proportionate way even if there has been no monetary realisation as a result.

C.4 Realisation of Assets

26. The narrative should be clear as to what work has been done by the Office Holder, as well as what, if any, aspects are being outsourced to a third party (for example use of debt collection agents, or use of agents to dispose of assets). This is particularly relevant in terms of asset realisations given the many options available for asset disposals. Further analysis, or categories, may be required to assist understanding where there are numerous assets or categories of assets.

27. The narrative should set out the marketing and disposal strategy adopted in relation to each asset (or category of assets), the anticipated timescale, and progress made to date. Members should set out the reasoning and impact behind the strategy adopted, in terms of time, cost and financial benefit to creditors.

28. Where the Office Holder has deemed it necessary to change strategy, the reasons for this should be explained in the narrative along with any impact on timing and costs as a result.

29. The narrative should make it clear what, if any, legal action will be required to facilitate any realisations, both in terms of securing and disposing of the assets. Any difficulties in realising assets should be set out; for example, sitting tenants, the need to procure a possession order, whether the strategy is time dependent, and the likelihood of achieving the timescale. Creditors should be advised of any likelihood of a revision to the fee estimate if the initial strategy is not implemented.

30. The narrative should also comment upon work done in relation to identifying, securing and insuring assets as well as the actual realisation and what, if any, aspects are anticipated to be outsourced to a third party (for example, use of agents to market or auction chattel assets), or whether litigation may be required in connection with, say, realisation of book debtors or directors' loan accounts.

31. Where appropriate, details should be provided of work done to facilitate the sale of a business, including preparation of a sales pack, dealing with interested parties, and contract negotiations. Where not included within a trading scenario (see C.5 below) members may also wish to comment here on work done in dealing with ROT claims, third party assets, negotiations with landlords, and dealing with tenants and utility companies in relation to properties.

32. The narrative should also make it clear what, if any, work will be required in terms of health and safety or environmental issues, in addition to work done in relation to dealing with utilities companies and other essential suppliers (if appropriate).

C.5 Trading

33. The narrative should include the reasons for trading the business post insolvency, the duration of trading and, where trading continues at the time that the time cost summary and/or the fee estimate is provided, an estimate of any future duration. Where trading is likely to continue indefinitely to support an ongoing marketing strategy, the narrative should comment on the strategy adopted and progress made at the date of the report.

34. The narrative should explain the extent to which the Office Holder and his or her staff have been involved in the trading, both from a management control and financial perspective, as well as any statutory obligations. It

will therefore likely include information in relation to work done regarding the preparation of cash flow forecasts, profit and loss accounts, management accounts, dealing with customers, suppliers (and related ROT matters), landlords and employees. It should be clear from the table and the narrative what the cost of the involvement of the Office Holder's staff in trading has been on a weekly or monthly basis as appropriate.

C.6 Creditors

35. This category will include both statutory and non-statutory matters and members may wish to make a distinction in the narrative as well as making it clear what work has been done for the benefit of creditors (e.g. agreeing claims, paying a dividend) and to what extent this has been impacted by the quality of the books and records.

36. Members should identify any significant additional work in relation to agreeing claims, for example the need to employ lawyers or quantity surveyors to agree claims, as well as the nature of the dividend being paid (e.g. preferential, prescribed part, unsecured). The narrative should be clear as to whether any disputes, litigation or contentious matters have arisen, the extent to which members have engaged in such disputes, the reasons why and the overall benefit to creditors.

37. If not disclosed elsewhere this category may also include work done in relation to the production of statutory reports, or non-statutory reports. Where non statutory reports have been produced, the reasons for doing so, and the benefit, should be explained to the general creditor group.

38. This category might also include the general handling of communications with stakeholders such as customers and suppliers.

C.7 Employees

39. The narrative should make it clear to what extent the Office Holder anticipates communicating with employees as well as the nature of the work being done, including liaising with the RPO and Job Centre Plus, providing support to employees in terms of completion of forms, liaising with (or appointing) union representatives and payroll providers, reviewing employment contracts, in addition to the admission of claims.

40. Where appropriate, the narrative might set out the level of interaction and queries the Office Holder has dealt with both in respect of employees, the RPO and any other relevant parties as this will be likely to vary from case to case depending on the number of employees, the nature of the business and type of appointment.

41. If there are likely to be claims for unfair dismissal and protective awards and the Office Holder has attended or contributed to Tribunals, the extent of involvement of the Office Holder and his or her staff, the reasons for the involvement and/or the benefit derived, should be set out in the narrative.

C.8 Case Specific Matters

42. This will include any matters specific to the case not covered by one of the other categories of activity. These may include dealing with matters specific to the industry in which the business operates, or matters of an exceptional or time-consuming nature. Where not incorporated elsewhere, or specific to, say, investigations or asset realisations, the narrative may incorporate matters such as engagement with stakeholders generally, legal advice in relation to litigation, as well as general advice regarding validity of appointment and/or security, work done in relation to seeking an extension to an administration appointment or legal advice pertaining thereto.

Illustrative time and charge-out summary

	Hours							
Type of work	Partner	Man-ager	Other Senior Profes-sional	Assis-tants & support staff	Total hours	Time cost £	Aver-age hourly rate £	See notes on suggested scope in num-bered para-graphs in sec-tion C above
Adminis-tration & Planning								C.1.
Report-ing								C.2.

Type of work	Partner	Hours Man-ager	Other Senior Profes-sional	Assis-tants & support staff	Total hours	Time cost £	Aver-age hourly rate £	See notes on suggested scope in num-bered para-graphs in sec-tion C above
Enquiries and In-vestiga-tions								C.3.
Realisa-tion of Assets								C.4.
Trading								C.5.
Creditors								C.6.
Employ-ees								C.7.
Case specific matters (e.g. . . .)								C.8.
Total Hours								
Total An-ticipated Fees (£)								

Notes

- Population of the categories alone will not be sufficient to comply with the legislative requirements regarding a fee estimate, nor the disclosure require-ments. A case specific narrative, in terms of scope and disclosure, will be required.

- Fixed fee / percentage resolutions will also require some form of narrative regarding the scope of the work to be done, albeit it is not anticipated that this will be as detailed as that required when producing a fee estimate in support of a time cost resolution, however it should be sufficiently detailed to ensure that creditors understand why the basis requested is expected to produce a fair and reasonable reflection of the work that the Office Holder anticipates will be undertaken.

- Members may find it more useful to differentiate between work that is required by statute and work that adds value, or is necessary to both realise assets and distribute funds.

6.3 QUESTIONS AND ANSWERS ABOUT THE PRE-PACK POOL

The Pre-pack Pool is an independent body of experienced business people who will offer an opinion on the purchase of a business and/or assets from an administrator of an insolvency company, where a connected party is involved.

The Pool has been set up in response to a series of recommendations contained in the Graham report on pre-packaged administrations. Those recommendations were endorsed by Government, and an Oversight Group comprising regulators, trade bodies and other stakeholder organisations from the business community has come together to implement the recommendation for the formation of a Pre-pack Pool.

The following Questions & Answers have been prepared to assist applicants, IPs and others gain an understanding of how the Pool works. A revised Statement of Insolvency Practice 16 has been issued to coincide with the commencement of the operation of the Pool.

6.3 QUESTIONS AND ANSWERS ABOUT THE PRE-PACK POOL

CONTENTS

BACKGROUND

THE PRE-PACK POOL

MAKING A SUBMISSION TO THE POOL

THE POOL MEMBER'S OPINION

THE ROLE OF THE INSOLVENCY PRACTITIONER (IP)

November 2015

30. What is the duty of the IP or the company to provide details of valuations, marketing and interest in the business, unknown to the applicant connected party but relevant to the application?

FURTHER INFORMATION FOR APPLICANTS

31. How are cases allocated to the Pool members?

32. Are there any specific conditions attached to the application?

33. What is the purpose of a viability study?

34. Is the purchaser's application to the Pool confidential?

35. How can I be sure my submission is reviewed by someone familiar with my kind / size of business?

36. I am in England / N. Ireland / Scotland / Wales, will/can my application be reviewed by someone only from my area?

ABOUT THE POOL MEMBERS

37. What qualified the Pool members to make these decisions?

38. Who chose the Pool members?

39. How do I apply to be a Pool member?

ADMINISTRATION OF THE POOL

40. Who administers the Pool?

41. How is the Pool overseen?

42. What is the role of the IS / BIS in the Pool system?

GENERAL INFORMATION

43. What is SIP 16?

44. Why is the Pool system voluntary?

45. Why does the Pool only look at connected party pre-packs?

46. I want to see a purchaser's application to the Pool. How can I obtain a copy?

47. I am a creditor, how do I know that a higher price might not be offered by someone else?

COMPLAINTS

48. I think I have lost money as a result of the pre-pack sale. Who can I complain to?

49. I think the purchaser has acquired the company for too little. I want to complain/ seek redress. What can I do next?

50. I want to complain about the directors of the company who bought the company from the administrator. How do I do that?

Background

1. What is the Pre-pack Pool?

   The Pre-pack Pool (the Pool) is an independent body of experienced business people. It has been set up in response to a series of recommendations contained in an independent review of pre-packaged administrations (The Graham Review). A Pool member will offer an opinion on the purchase of a business and / or its assets by a party connected to a company where a pre-packaged sale is proposed. Only one member of the Pool will deal with an application.

2. What is the Graham Review?

   Teresa Graham CBE was asked to report on the pre-pack administration procedure and make recommendations for reform by the Secretary of State for Business Innovation and Skills (BIS) as part of the Government's wider 'Transparency and Trust' agenda.

   The report was issued in June 2014 and considered the full economic impact of the process. The report made six recommendations for reform. The creation of the Pre-pack Pool was a key recommendation of the Graham Review.

   - Graham Review Report into pre-pack administration – June 2014 (https://www.gov.uk/government/publications/graham-review-into -pre-pack-administration)
   - Government response to the Review Report – June 2014 (https://www.gov.uk/government/consultations/insolvency -practitioner-regulation-and-fee-structure)

3. What is a pre-packaged administration?

   Administration is a formal procedure under the Insolvency Act 1986 as amended. The administrator is a licensed insolvency practitioner (IP). Not all administrations involve a pre-packaged sale.

   While there is no legal definition of a pre-packaged sale, the term is widely accepted to mean an arrangement under which the sale of all or part of a company's business or assets is negotiated with a purchaser prior to the appointment of an administrator and the administrator effects the sale immediately on, or shortly after, appointment.

Such sales are used in circumstances where it makes commercial sense and is in the creditors' best interests, to facilitate a sale of the company's business / assets quickly.

4. What is a connected party?

There is a legal definition of a connected party. Broadly speaking, it is those with a significant prior connection to the insolvent company, and will include directors, shareholders, and close family members of those persons and also companies in the same group. The full legal definition can be found in the Insolvency Act 1986. If in doubt about whether the prospective purchaser is a connected party for this purpose, independent advice may be sought from an IP or a solicitor.

The Pre-pack Pool

5. Why does the Pool exist?

The Pool has been introduced as a result of concern being expressed in some quarters that pre-packaged sales, (which necessarily and quite legally are completed in a short period of time and without prior consultation with creditors), lack sufficient transparency. This lack of transparency is perceived as particularly acute where the purchaser has a significant prior connection to the company (i.e. is a connected party). BIS accepted the Graham Review's recommendation that for sales to connected parties, some of these concerns may be overcome by having an independent party review the proposed sale and offer an opinion on the appropriateness of the grounds for the sale. This may provide reassurance to creditors that an independent person had considered the reasonableness of the proposed transaction.

6. What does the Pool do?

The Pool, through its members, operates only to review and opine on applications made voluntarily by connected parties. It provides optional, external scrutiny of transactions, which may provide creditors with some additional reassurance that a proposed purchase by those previously connected to the insolvent company is not, in the Pool member's opinion, unreasonable. They may alternatively conclude that they have not seen sufficient evidence to be persuaded this is the case.

If the Pool member considers the sale to the connected party is not unreasonable, they will issue a response to the effect that it is not unreasonable to proceed. Alternatively they may state they have not seen sufficient evidence to be satisfied as to the grounds for the pre-pack transaction. The Pool member will not give reasons for his / her opinion. However, if the Pool member is minded to issue a not unreasonable opinion but is unable to do so due to a lack of supporting evidence in specific areas, then they may highlight this in the opinion issued.

7. What are the benefits of approaching the Pool?

Use of the Pool provides the potential for enhanced stakeholder confidence both in the transaction and in the purchasing entity. This may be valuable to a purchaser when endeavouring to preserve stakeholder relationships and mitigate potential reputational damage.

8. Who is on the Pool?

The Pool members are experienced and senior business people who have been selected following a public recruitment exercise. The names of the Pool members are published on the Pre-pack Pool website prepackpool.co.uk

9. What powers does the Pool have?

The Pool has no powers, as such. The Pool member will issue an opinion on the reasonableness of the grounds of the proposed pre-packaged sale outlined in the application. The opinion will not determine whether or not a sale to a connected party can or cannot proceed. Responsibility for a sale will rest ultimately with the administrator.

Making a submission to the Pool

10. How do I make a submission to the Pool?

    Submissions to the Pool by prospective purchasers are made via the Pool's website prepackpool.co.uk

11. What does it cost to obtain a decision from the Pool?

    £800 + VAT.

12. What does the fee cover?

    The fee covers all costs associated with the provision of the opinion by a Pool member. This includes the Pool member's time to review and consider the application and supporting evidence supplied as well as the administrative costs associated with the application.

13. When should I make a submission to the Pool?

    As early as possible and in advance of the proposed transaction with the administrator.

14. What information do I need to include in my submission?

    All documentation must be sent electronically. It is up to the applicant to decide what to submit, but it is expected to cover at least the following matters:

    - Name of purchasing entity (where known)
    - Names and addresses of beneficial owners of the old and new businesses
    - Names of directors of old and new businesses
    - Nature of any connection and nature of likely involvement in new business
    - Details of any losses suffered by the owners/directors personally
    - An outline of the proposed transaction – heads of agreement etc
    - Name and email address of proposed administrator (where known)
    - Latest financial information available re the old business
    - Value of the assets being purchased and how that reflects going concern
    - Details of any prior offers made and marketing undertaken (where known)

15. What additional information will assist my application?

Applicants are advised to think carefully about what they include. The quality rather than the quantity of documentation is important. The Pool member will consider issues such as:

- The circumstances and background to the financial difficulties.
- How well and widely the company has been marketed by the current owners in the recent past.
- How the market has otherwise been tested in the past 12 months.
- The underlying valuation of the business and assets to which the connected party has access.
- The reasons why the business needs to be sold quickly by way of a pre-pack, rather than later on in the administration process.
- Any other available evidence that the proposed purchase consideration represents fair value.

A viability review can be provided by a connected party that wishes to make a pre-packaged purchase. It must state how the purchasing entity will survive for at least 12 months from the date of the proposed purchase. The connected party should consider providing a short narrative detailing what the purchasing entity will do differently in order that the business will not fail (the viability statement). A copy of any viability review and statement prepared by the purchaser will be of assistance to the Pool member, and is particularly encouraged to be provided where any part of the purchase consideration is to be deferred.

16. Is there any additional guidance for applicants?

Yes. A list of suggested evidence/information to submit with an application is available on the website and may be found via this link: http ://www.prepackpool.co.uk/.

17. How long will I have to wait for a response from the Pool?

The Pool aims to provide a response within two business days from the time the application papers and fee have been received.

18. Can I choose the Pool member?

No. Applications are submitted to the Pool members on a strict rotational basis. If an applicant believes any of the Pool members have a conflict of interest, this should be raised at the outset. There is the ability to highlight conflicts as part of the application process. A list of Pool members is published on the Pre-pack Pool website prepackpool.co.uk

19. Where can I get help with my application?

Prospective purchasers can submit an application directly, or they may wish to obtain professional advice or assistance in relation to their application or the process.

You may wish to seek advice from an IP (but see Q.26). Alternatively, you might decide to ask your accountant, solicitor, a Business Link / Business Gateway advisor or another qualified professional with experience of business or financial matters, including but not necessarily insolvency.

20. Can the Pool staff or oversight group assist me?

No. The web portal is automated and whilst email contact can be made for the purposes of notifying any problems with the website (via info @prepackpool.co.uk) this is not an advice service nor is it designed to provide immediate responses.

The Pool member's opinion

21. What is the Pool looking for when it issues an opinion?

The Pool member will take an independent view of the reasons for a pre-packaged sale to a connected party. They will consider whether the pre-packaged sale, as described to them, is an appropriate way to proceed in all the circumstances. The Pool member will consider the grounds given by the applicant for the pre-pack transaction, specifically with regard to the impact on creditors of the company in administration, and why there is a need to acquire the business through a pre-pack administration.

22. What will the Pool member base their opinion on?

The Pool member will base their opinion on whether there appears to be any grounds to question the merits of the proposed transaction in the context of the absence of creditor scrutiny. They will consider whether;

- a case is made for the necessity of a pre-pack,

- the creditors' position is adversely affected, and
- the Pool member is satisfied (on the evidence presented) that the proposed pre-packaged sale represents a reasonable method of disposal of the old company's business/assets.

23. What does the Pool member's opinion mean?

The Pool member will issue one of three opinions.

Nothing found to suggest that the grounds for the proposed pre-packaged sale are unreasonable

This means the Pool member has been provided with sufficient information and nothing within the information suggests the proposed pre-packaged sale to the connected party is unreasonable.

Evidence provided has been limited in some areas, but otherwise nothing has been found to suggest that the grounds for the proposed pre-packaged sale are unreasonable

This means the Pool member has been provided with information and there is nothing within that information to suggest the proposed pre-packaged sale is unreasonable. However some elements of the evidence presented or arguments made by the connected party (mostly likely to be considered by the Pool member as not being of major significance) were limited and not sufficiently made out.

There is a lack of evidence to support a statement that the grounds for the proposed pre-packaged sale are reasonable

This means the Pool member was not persuaded the grounds for proceeding through a pre-pack transaction were sufficiently made out, on the basis of the evidence presented or arguments made by the connected party.

24. Can a sale to a connected party proceed via a pre-pack if the Pool has not been satisfied with the evidence provided?

Yes. If the administrator decides to accept an offer from a connected party and proceed with the sale, they will have to explain to the creditors why they felt the sale was appropriate.

An administrator is obliged to provide a clear explanation and justification for the sale in accordance with Statement of Insolvency Practice 16 (SIP 16).

25. Why won't the Pool give reasons for its decision?

The Pool has been set up to provide quick responses to applications. Providing detailed reasons for the Pool's decision would add to the delay and the costs.

26. Can I appeal an opinion of a Pool member?

No. Cost and speed are key factors here, and neither the Pool member nor the Pool directors will enter into correspondence on the opinion given. There is no appeal mechanism.

27. When will I know the identity of the Pool member?

The Pool member's identity will become known to the applicant only when the Pool member's opinion is received. The Pool member's opinion will also be provided to creditors in the administrator's SIP 16 statement where the connected party has provided this to the administrator. The administrator's SIP 16 statement is also filed at Companies House.

If the administrator has requested a copy of the opinion and this has not been provided by the connected party this will be stated in their SIP 16 statement also.

The role of the insolvency practitioner (IP)

28. Can the IP acting (or likely to be acting) as administrator for the company advise the connected parties on the approach to the Pool?

As IPs work within a Code of Ethics, the proposed administrator is unlikely to be able to provide advice and assistance in connection with the application. However, the IP may be able to offer general information regarding the Pool and their reporting obligations.

29. What is the regulatory consequence of an IP proceeding with a sale to a connected party if the Pool member has issued an opinion that there is insufficient evidence that the grounds for the pre-packaged sale is reasonable?

An opinion that there is insufficient evidence that the grounds for the pre-packaged sale is reasonable doesn't prohibit the sale. It is for the IP to decide whether to proceed with such a sale or not.

IPs are subject to regulation and authorised to act as IPs by recognised professional bodies. The insolvency regulators look at practitioners' conduct through complaints received and proactive monitoring. Where systemic problems are identified, the regulators have the ability to take appropriate action.

A complaint would not be well founded solely on the basis that a pre-packaged sale transaction was entered into when an opinion had been issued that the evidence was insufficient to support the grounds for a pre-packaged sale.

30. What is the duty of the IP or the company to provide details of valuations, marketing and interest in the business, unknown to the applicant connected party but relevant to the application?

    The IP has no such duty. The IP has no relationship with the Pool and the Pool will not be seeking any third party verification of facts or presumed intentions of relevant parties engaged in the sale. However, where an applicant is closely connected, some elements of this information may be available to them and they may be able to obtain the appropriate permissions to use it in support of their application.

Further information for applicants

31. How are cases allocated to the Pool members?

    Cases are allocated by rota, excluding those with a known conflict of interest.

32. Are there any specific conditions attached to the application?

    All applications are submitted to the Pool on the basis of terms and conditions. Applicants must accept these terms and conditions. If an applicant is in any doubt about the effect of the terms and conditions they may wish to seek legal advice prior to submitting an application.

33. What is the purpose of a viability study?

The viability of the purchaser, while of interest to its future trading partners, would not ordinarily be a major consideration for the Pool member, as its focus is on addressing concerns of creditors of the insolvent. However, the provision of a viability review may be of considerable benefit to the Pool member, especially where the payment of the purchase consideration is deferred and therefore is dependent upon the success of the new company. The viability review should cover the greater of 12 months or the period over which any consideration is to be deferred. It should be noted that in providing their opinion, the Pool member is not warranting the viability of the new business, they are merely considering the prospects for the purchase consideration being fully discharged.

34. Is the purchaser's application to the Pool confidential?

Yes. The Pool website is appropriately secure and data is held in accordance with prevailing data protection requirements.

As part of the application, the applicant will be asked to give consent to the Pool member's opinion that is sent to the administrator or intended administrator. Where no proposed administrator is identified in the application, the subsequently appointed administrator will approach the connected party to request a copy of the opinion from the applicant.

The administrator will not see the application, but the opinion will list the documents provided with the application.

The purchaser's application to the Pool is not a public document as the information it contains is likely to be market sensitive.

35. How can I be sure my submission is reviewed by someone familiar with my kind / size of business?

Industry specialism will not be a part of the Pool member allocation process. Applications are submitted to the Pool members on a rota basis. All Pool members are experienced business people with the appropriate skills to consider applications from any sector or size of business. The opinion is based on the documents provided. Should there be any industry specific information which will assist the Pool member in considering the application this should be provided as part of the supporting evidence submitted.

36. I am in England / N. Ireland / Scotland / Wales, will/can my application be reviewed by someone only from my area?

No. It is not considered that decisions will or should be influenced by regional or national considerations. If there are any specific regional or national considerations the applicant considers relevant, these should be included within the evidence submitted as part of the application.

About the Pool members

37. What qualified the Pool members to make these decisions?

The Pool members are experienced business people. Many will be chartered directors (of the Institute of Directors), others will be accountants or lawyers, and they can be former-IPs. They will adopt a commercial approach and use their business experience and acumen to form their opinion.

38. Who chose the Pool members?

The Pool members were selected following a public recruitment process. Applications were considered by a group of representatives from creditor bodies, the business community, government and the insolvency profession. A copy of the public advertisement can be viewed here [link].

39. How do I apply to be a Pool member?

Applications may be sent to the administrative address of the Pool, info@prepackpool.co.uk, in response to announced invitations for new or replacement members, or at any time if you wish to register your interest. There are no current vacancies, as a full complement has been recruited.

Administration of the Pool

40. Who administers the Pool?

Pre-pack Pool Ltd (PPP), company number 09471155 which operates under the terms of a service agreement with the Oversight Group.

41. How is the Pool overseen?

The performance of the Pool will be monitored by an Oversight Group established to coordinate and oversee the creation, development and operation of the Pool. The Oversight Group shall report to the Insolvency Service (IS) and BIS.

The Oversight Group is made up of representatives from creditor organisations, business groups, government, the insolvency profession and insolvency regulators.

42. What is the role of the IS / BIS in the Pool system?

The IS / BIS as oversight department for business generally and the insolvency profession (and its regulation) is concerned to ensure that there is an effective system for administrations and specifically the use of sales to connected parties via a pre-pack where appropriate. It is not, however, directly involved in the Pre-pack Pool, but has encouraged and endorsed its creation. The IS is part of the Oversight Group established to coordinate and oversee the creation, development and operation of the Pool.

General information

43. What is SIP 16?

SIP 16 is the Statement of Insolvency Practice 16. It sets out the principles and compliance standards with which an IP must comply when dealing with a pre-packaged sale of a company's business when he has been appointed administrator.

44. Why is the Pool system voluntary?

At the current time the government wishes to see if a low cost, non-statutory approach can satisfactorily address concerns.

45. Why does the Pool only look at connected party pre-packs?

The Graham Review found it was sales to connected parties that caused most concern to creditors. It highlighted a need for additional transparency where a business is to be sold with little or no notice being given to its creditors.

46. I want to see a purchaser's application to the Pool. How can I obtain a copy?

The application is not a public document. It is therefore not available to third parties. However, the documents provided to the Pool will be listed in the opinion statement provided by the Pool member and circulated by the IP with the SIP 16 disclosure statement.

47. I am a creditor, how do I know that a higher price might not be offered by someone else?

The underlying aim of the Pool is to ensure unsecured creditors feel reassured that a proposed sale to a connected party, on the terms offered, was not an unreasonable course of action in the circumstances.

It is not a function of the Pool to assess the likelihood of the connected party bid being the highest made to the administrator, nor prevent a situation where the administrator sells to the connected party at a price below a higher unconnected bid. Nor can it guarantee the connected party will not buy the assets of the old business at a price that someone subsequently might say they would have bettered. Those are considerations for the administrator to consider. The administrator must inform creditors, via the SIP 16 disclosure, why they considered the pre-packaged sale was appropriate.

Complaints

48. I think I have lost money as a result of the pre-pack sale. Who can I complain to?

The existence of the Pool does not preclude the use of any of the existing avenues of query, challenge or complaint about the administrator's actions, which may include challenge through the courts, complaint to the administrator and / or their firm, or through the Insolvency Service Complaints Gateway (https://www.gov.uk/complain-about-insolvency-practitioner) (or in Northern Ireland to the administrator's authorising body).

49. I think the purchaser has acquired the company for too little. I want to complain/ seek redress. What can I do next?

If you believe the company was sold at below value, in the first instance, you should raise this with the administrator. If you are unsatisfied with their explanations, you can make a complaint through the Insolvency Service Complaints Gateway (https://www.gov.uk/complain-about-insolvency-practitioner) (or in Northern Ireland to the administrator's authorising body). Concerns about the new company and its management may be directed to Investigations and Enforcement Services at the IS (https://www.gov.uk/complain-about-a-limited-company).

50.   I want to complain about the directors of the company who bought the company from the administrator. How do I do that?

If your complaint is about the directors' conduct before the administration then you should raise this. One option is to contact the administrator or the Director Disqualification Unit at BIS directly. If your complaint is about the directors' conduct after the acquisition of the company then you should complain to Investigations and Enforcement Services at the IS (https ://www.gov.uk/complain-about-a-limited-company).

Section 7

IPA Regulations and
Guidance

SECTION 7 — IPA REGULATIONS AND GUIDANCE

CONTENTS

7.1 IPA PROFESSIONAL INDEMNITY INSURANCE REGULATIONS

(Adopted by Council on 14th July 2016 pursuant to Article 62.1 of the Association's Articles of Association)

1. Definitions

1.1 In these definitions the following expressions shall have the following respective meanings:-

Gross Fee Income	the aggregate of all fees and income for professional services rendered, (net of VAT and disbursements and excluding for the avoidance of doubt interest dividends and rents received by the Professional Practice, income and capital profits from investments made by the Professional Practice and bad debts written off), attributable to the Member and his staff agents or locums (whether working under a contract of service or for services) from insolvency or insolvency related work, including both formal and informal appointments and advisory work where insolvency considerations apply including for the avoidance of doubt, fees received in respect of work subcontracted to others unless it is clearly demonstrated to the Individual Member's satisfaction that the subcontractor is taking professional responsibility for his work and has appropriate PII cover
PII	Professional Indemnity Insurance which is underwritten in accordance with the minimum requirements of these Regulations
Principal	a sole practitioner, partner, director or other person held out as a principal of a Professional Practice who is engaged in Insolvency Administration

| Professional Practice | A Firm including one whose business or practice is not confined to Insolvency Administration |

1.2 The following words shall have the same meaning as defined in the Articles of Association of the Association:-

> Association, Firm, Individual Members, Insolvency Act, Insolvency Administration, Insolvency Appointment, Insolvency Authorisation, Insolvency Practitioner.

2. Introduction

2.1 PII is compulsory for each Individual Member who holds one or more Insolvency Appointments.

2.2 These Regulations set out the requirements for the minimum level of cover which must be obtained.

2.3 Individual Members are required to provide a certificate from their insurer setting out the principal terms of their PII cover to be submitted to the Association with each Insolvency Authorisation application or upon request.

3. MINIMUM TERMS OF COVER

3.1 Each Individual Member is required to have a minimum PII cover for any one claim of whichever is the greater of:-

3.1.1 £250,000; or

3.1.2 2.5 times his Gross Fee Income, subject to clause 3.3 below.

3.2 Where an Individual Member is in partnership or association with other Insolvency Practitioners and they are covered by a single PII policy, the minimum PII cover required shall be calculated by aggregating each Individual Member's Gross Fee Income.

3.3 The required minimum cover under the policy need not exceed £1,500,000.

3.4 PII policies must comply with any IPA approved minimum terms for PII policies, as may be published from time to time, and shall include fidelity insurance covering the dishonest acts or omissions of principals and employees of the Individual Member to the same level of cover as applies to the PII itself.

4. EXCESS

4.1 The minimum PII cover for each Individual Member can include an excess of not more than £20,000.

4.2 Where an Individual Member is in partnership or association with other Insolvency Practitioners and they are covered by a single PII policy, the excess may not exceed £20,000 (or such other figure as aforesaid) multiplied by the number of Principals.

4.3 In the case of a Firm being a corporate practice, the number of Principals shall only include those who have entered into a legally binding personal obligation in respect of the excess.

5. RUN-OFF INSURANCE

5.1 An Individual Member who retires or ceases to act as an Insolvency Practitioner, is required to satisfy the Association that adequate run-off cover is in place for a minimum of six years after ceasing to act at an indemnity level not less than that applying immediately prior to retirement or cessation.

6. TRANSFERS BETWEEN PRACTICES

6.1 An Individual Member who transfers from one professional practice to another is required to satisfy the Association that adequate PII arrangements are in place to cover any claims made in respect of work done by him whilst at his previous practice in respect of the preceding period of not less than six years.

Effective Date: 1 January 2017

7.2 IPA PROFESSIONAL INDEMNITY INSURANCE GUIDANCE

1. The Professional Indemnity Insurance ["PII"] Regulations make PII compulsory for Individual Members and set out the minimum requirements acceptable to the Insolvency Practitioners Association. **However, you are strongly advised to obtain a greater level of cover and to take advice from your insurance broker.** You should also review the extent of the cover available, since some policies will, for example, include legal costs within rather than in addition to the limit of the indemnity cover.

2. Most PII policies provide for a minimum level of risk, known as "excess", to be borne by the insured. You should consider both your firm's and your own personal resources when deciding what level of excess is appropriate for you. The maximum excess provided under these Regulations is £20,000 per Principal (as defined by the PII Regulations).

3. From discussions with underwriters, it is considered that there is currently sufficient competition in the PII market for all Members to obtain an adequate level of PII cover on relatively competitive terms. However, should you, for any reason, find it impossible to obtain minimum cover, or if insurers decline insurance or attempt to avoid your policy, you must bring this matter to the attention of the Secretary of the Association without delay. You will be obliged to give full information to the Membership and Authorisation Committee, who will then consider the consequences.

4. Failure to obtain and maintain PII cover may also invalidate your Insolvency Bond and thus your ability to act as an Insolvency Practitioner.

5. Almost invariably, PII policies are written on a claims made basis, which means that the insurance will provide cover for claims first made or circumstances arising and notified to the insurers during the term of the current policy, irrespective of when the activity giving rise to the claim occurred. It is therefore important that, assuming (which is usually the case) that the policy provides such cover, the policy remains in force to provide protection against any claims which may arise in the future for work done in the past.

6. If you are an Individual Member in partnership with others, or you have an arrangement where you are covered by another Professional Practice's PII policy, you must ensure that the PII cover provided by such policy or policy or policies is adequate to cover the requirements of these Regulations as they apply to you.

7. Gross Fee Income, as defined in the Regulations, should be based on the most recently completed accounting year immediately preceding the start of the policy. If you are commencing practice, you should give your broker your best estimate of your anticipated Gross Fee Income or ensure that he is provided with such information by the person responsible for such matters within your firm.

8. You should ensure that your PII policy includes fidelity insurance to cover any dishonest acts or omissions of principals employees and subcontractors in a manner and in terms not more limited than those contained in the approved minimum wording. The minimum policy wording must also be written on the basis that former-partners, and employees and subcontractors are covered.

9. Run-off cover for retiring Insolvency Practitioners may be provided under the PII of a continuing practice or you may need to take out an individual policy. Either way, you should personally check with your broker that you would be covered if any claim were made after you have retired from practice in respect of work done while you were in practice. If your former or successor practice has agreed to include run-off cover for you in its current cover, you must provide full details to the Association, who will need to be advised of any changes during the minimum six-year period. You will be responsible for taking out a new policy in the event of any run-off cover lapsing during the six-year period.

10. If you transfer from one practice to another, you must satisfy the Association that the PII cover remains in place for the work you carried out at your former firm. This should either be by having the old practice confirm that their PII policy will cover any claims made for a period of not less than six years or that your new PII cover will accept responsibility for a similar period. It is important to ensure that, on changing firms, there is no gap in the PII cover and you may be asked to confirm to the Association the terms of any leaving agreement.

11. If your existing practice merges or breaks-up into small firms, you are required to ensure that there is no break in the existence and level of PII cover and to provide appropriate confirmations to the Association. You must ensure that, on a merger or split or any other alteration to the practice, there continues to be an adequacy of cover in accordance with the Regulations.

12. Self-certification of your PII arrangements will be requested by the Association as an item of your renewal of your Insolvency Authorisation. For the purposes of inspection, you will be asked to make your PII policy available to our inspectors. Alternatively, you may obtain from your insurer a certificate setting out the basic details of your cover including the sum insured per claim and in aggregate, the period of insurance, the names of the principals in the practice, the commencement of the insurance period, the amount of the excess and any specific instructions or conditions attaching to the cover. The Association may check with your brokers or insurers that the information is correct.

13. If you become aware of a claim or circumstances which might give rise to a claim falling under your PII policy, you are required to notify your insurers promptly since failure to do so could seriously prejudice your or your firm's rights and entitlement to indemnity under the policy. You should not wait until there have been developments or delay pending the completion of a detailed report of the matter.

14. The existence of claims or circumstances should be regarded objectively and insurers notified immediately even if the allegations are vague or unspecified and regardless of the fact that you think liability is unlikely. It is considered good practice to have a review of potential PII claims as an agenda item for partners' meetings and prior to the renewal of PII cover, a circular sent to all partners and senior staff requiring confirmation that they are not aware of any claim or circumstance which might give rise to a claim. Your broker may well be able to provide you with a claims handling / risk prevention booklet to assist in this respect, in which case it should be obtained and its advice adhered to.

15. In consultation with your broker, you may wish to think about the following issues when deciding whether a PII policy is suitable for your purposes:-

    15.1 The sum insured per claim and in the aggregate?

    15.2 The excess?

    15.3 What does the policy cover?

    15.4 Does the policy cover dishonest acts of principals and employees and former principals and employees?

    15.5 What triggers coverage - claims, notice of intention to claim, or circumstances arising?

15.6   Is there a provision in the policy covering a claim "series" i.e. claims arising from the same or a series of acts or omissions?

15.7   Are there any exclusions or conditions breach of which might entitle the insurer to avoid the whole policy?

15.8   What are the notice requirements, and consequences of late notification?

15.9   What are the complaint handling requirements?

16.   You should avoid having double insurance.

17.   It is suggested that you provide your brokers with a copy the IPA's Regulations, Guidance Notes and with any IPA approved minimum terms for PII policies, as may be published from time to time, and ask them to confirm that your PII policy meets the minimum requirements laid down by them.

7.3 IPA CLIENT MONEY REGULATIONS

1. These Regulations are made by the Council on 28th April 2000 pursuant to Article 62 of the Association's Articles of Association (adopted by Special Resolution passed 28th April 2000).

2. **COMMENCEMENT**

   These Regulations shall come into force on 1st August 2000.

3. **DEFINITIONS**

   3.1 In these Regulations the following expressions shall have the following respective meanings:-

Articles		the Articles of Association of the Association adopted by Special Resolution passed on 28th April 2000;
Bank	(a)	a branch in the United Kingdom of:

   the Bank of England;

   the Central Bank of another member State of the European Union;

   an authorised institution within the meaning of the Banking Act 1987; or

   a building society within the meaning of the Building Societies Act 1986 which has adopted the power to provide money transmission services and has not assumed any restriction on the extent of that power; and

   (b) a branch outside the United Kingdom of:

   a bank within the meaning of paragraph (a) above;

   a bank which is a subsidiary or parent company of such bank; or

   a credit institution (as defined in EEC Directive number 77/780) established in a member state of the European Union other than the United Kingdom, and duly authorised by the relevant supervisory authority in that member state; or

   a bank on the Island of Guernsey that is registered as a Deposit Taker under the Protection of Depositors (Bailiwick of Guernsey) Ordinance 1971; or

   a bank on the Island of Jersey (including a registered person under the Depositors and Investors (Prevention of Fraud) (Jersey) law 1967); or

	a bank on the Isle of Man (including a bank which is licensed under section 3 of the Banking Act 1975, as amended);
Client	a person in respect of whom there is no Insolvency Appointment at the relevant time;
Client Bank Account	an account with a Bank in the name of the Firm separate from other accounts of the Firm which may be either a general account or an account designated by the name of a specific Client or by a number or letters allocated to that account and which, in all cases, includes the word 'client' in its title;
Client Money	money of any currency held or received by a Firm from or on behalf of a Client;
Estate Account	an account with a Bank in respect of a person over which the Individual Member holds an Insolvency Appointment and shall include the Insolvency Services Account;
European Union	includes the European Economic Area where any provision relates to a matter to which the European Economic Area Agreement relates;
Principal	an Individual Member who is either a sole practitioner or a partner in a Firm which is a partnership or a director of a Firm which is a body corporate;

3.2 The following words and expressions shall have the same meaning as defined in the Articles:-

Association, Firm, Individual Member, Insolvency Appointment

3.3 References in these Regulations to any statutory provision shall include any statutory modification or re-enactment thereof

4. OPENING A CLIENT BANK ACCOUNT

On opening a Client Bank Account a Firm shall give written notice to the Bank concerned:

4.1 that all money standing to the credit of that account is held by the Firm as Client Money and that the Bank is not entitled to combine the account with any other account or to exercise any right to set-off or counterclaim against money in that account in respect of any sum owed to it on any other account of the Firm; and

4.2 that any interest payable in respect of sums credited to the account shall be credited to the account; and

4.3 requiring the Bank to acknowledge in writing that it accepts the terms of the notice.

5. PAYMENT INTO A CLIENT BANK ACCOUNT

5.1 Client Money received by a Firm as cash shall unless otherwise expressly directed by the Client be paid forthwith into a Client Bank Account.

5.2 Every other remittance received by a Firm which is drawn in favour of the Firm or of any Principal and which comprises or includes Client Money shall be paid forthwith into a Client Bank Account.

5.3 A Firm shall not pay any money into a Client Bank Account, unless

    5.3.1 the Firm is required or permitted to make such payment under these Regulations; or

    5.3.2 the money is the Firm's own money and:

        5.3.2.1 it is required to be so paid for the purpose of opening or maintaining the account and the amount is the minimum required for that purpose; or

        5.3.2.2 it is so paid in order to restore in whole or in part any money paid out of the account in contravention of these Regulations.

5.4 A Firm shall not be regarded as having breached Regulation 5.3 simply because it transpires that money which the Firm paid into a Client Bank Account in the belief that it was required so to do under these Regulations should not have been paid into such an account, provided that immediately upon discovering the error the Firm takes the necessary steps to withdraw the money which has been paid into such account in error.

5.5 Where Client Money of any one Client in excess of £10,000 is held or is expected to be held by the Firm for more than 30 days, the Client Money shall be paid into a Client Bank Account designated by the name of the client or by a number or letters allocated to that account, unless the Client directs otherwise.

5.6 Subject to Regulations 5.8 and 6.1 if the aggregate amount of Client Money held or received by a Firm in respect of any one Client at any one time is such as would, if deposited in an interest bearing account at a rate no less than that from time to time posted publicly by the relevant Bank for small deposits subject to the minimum period of notice of withdrawals, result in or be likely to result in material interest being received thereon such sum shall be placed in an interest bearing Client Bank Account.

5.7   Subject to Regulations 5.8 and 6.1 all interest accruing to the sums placed in an interest bearing account (in accordance with Regulation 5.6 or otherwise) shall be accounted for to the Client concerned.

5.8   Regulations 5.6 and 5.7 shall not apply to Client Money held by a Firm as stakeholder.

5.9   In addition to payments in permitted by Regulation 5.3, the special nature of insolvency practice requires that the following money may be paid into a general Client Bank Account of the Firm:

5.9.1   cheques and drafts accountable to Estate Accounts but where the payee is incorrectly designated;

5.9.2   money received by a Firm the legal entitlement to which is uncertain;

5.9.3   money received in respect of an Insolvency Appointment but subject to conditions which prevent its being paid into an Estate Account;

5.9.4   money received in respect of an Insolvency Appointment but where the appropriate Estate Account has been closed or has not been opened.

5.10   All money paid into a general Client Bank Account pursuant to Regulation 5.9 shall be paid out or transferred to the appropriate Estate Account as soon as practicable.

6.   PAYMENT OF INTEREST ON CLIENT MONEY

6.1   Regulations 5.6 and 5.7 shall not affect any agreement in writing, whenever made, between a Firm and a Client as to the payment of interest or money in lieu thereof on Client Money held or received by the Firm for that Client.

6.2   It shall be a breach of these Regulations if a Firm fails to comply with any of the terms of any such agreement as is referred to in Regulation 6.1.

6.3   For the purposes of Regulations 5.6 to 5.8, 6.1 and 6.2 Client Money held by a Firm for two or more clients acting together in one or more transactions shall be treated as though held for a single client.

7.   WITHDRAWALS FROM A CLIENT BANK ACCOUNT

7.1   When a remittance is paid into a Client Bank Account which includes money which is not Client Money, the money which is not Client Money shall be withdrawn from the account as soon as practicable.

7.2   Money shall not be withdrawn from a Client Bank Account except the following:

7.2.1   money, not being Client Money, paid into a Client Bank Account for the purpose of opening or maintaining the account;

7.2.2   money paid into a Client Bank Account in circumstances which amount to a contravention of these Regulations or which would have so amounted but for Regulation 5.4 or 5.9;

7.2.3   money required to be withdrawn under Regulation 7.1;

7.2.4   money which would remain in a Client Bank Account after all Clients whose money has been credited to that account received payment in full of sums due to them from that account whether under these Regulations or otherwise;

7.2.5   money which has become transferable to an Estate Account following the start of an Insolvency Appointment;

7.2.6   money properly required for a payment to or on behalf of a Client;

7.2.7   money properly required for or towards payment of a debt due to the Firm from a client otherwise than in respect of fees or commissions earned by the Firm;

7.2.8   subject to Regulation 7.4, money properly required for or towards payment of fees payable to the Firm by the Client and specified in a statement delivered to the Client showing the details of the work undertaken;

7.2.9   money withdrawn on a Client's prior authority or in conformity with any contract between the Firm and the Client;

7.2.10 money which may properly be transferred into another Client Bank Account.

7.3 Money withdrawn under Regulation 7.2.5 to 7.2.10 shall not exceed the total of the money held for the time being on account of the Client concerned.

7.4 Money shall not be withdrawn from a Client Bank Account for or towards payment of fees payable by the Client to the Firm unless:

7.4.1 the precise amount thereof has been agreed by the Client or has been finally determined by a court or arbitrator; or

7.4.2 the fees have been accurately calculated in accordance with a formula agreed in writing by the Client on the basis of which the amount thereof can be determined; or

7.4.3 thirty days have elapsed since the date of delivery to the Client of the statement referred to in Regulation 7.2.8 and the Client has not questioned the amount therein specified.

7.5 Money which may be withdrawn from a Client Bank Account in accordance with Regulation 7.2.7 or 7.2.8 by way of payment from the Client to the Firm shall be withdrawn as soon as practicable after the Firm becomes entitled to withdraw it under that Regulation.

8. RECORDS AND RECONCILIATION

8.1 A Firm shall at all times maintain records so as to show clearly all Client Money it has received and the details of any other money dealt with by it through a Client Bank Account, clearly distinguishing the money of each Client from the money of other Clients and from Firm money.

8.2 Each Client Bank Account shall be reconciled against the balances shown in each Client's ledger not less frequently than monthly and records shall be kept of such reconciliations.

8.3 Records kept in accordance with Regulations 8.1 and 8.2 shall be preserved for at least six years from the date of the last transaction recorded therein

9. THE RESPONSIBILITY OF A PRINCIPAL

9.1 A Principal shall be responsible for any breach of these Regulations on the part of his Firm, and liable to disciplinary action accordingly, unless he proves that responsibility for the breach was entirely that of another Principal or other Principals.

7.4 IPA CLIENT MONEY GUIDANCE

1. In order to harmonise regulation as much as possible, the Association has adopted Regulations based on those adopted by the Institute of Chartered Accountants in England and Wales. Those Regulations, however, cover many other areas of professional practice than insolvency practice; and the Regulations adopted by the Association have accordingly been adapted to reflect the particular needs of Insolvency Practitioners.

2. For convenience only, the Regulations have been drafted in terms of the duties imposed on Firms. Disciplinary proceedings can, however, be brought against Individual Members under Regulation 9.1. Attention is drawn to the defence in that Regulation.

3. Regulations controlling the use of Client Bank Accounts are necessary to preserve their integrity, so that third party funds are segregated from those of the Firm, readily identified and protected in the event of the Firm's financial failure.

4. Most money handled by Insolvency Practitioners will not fall into the definition of Client Money, since it will be in respect of an established Insolvency Appointment. The handling of such money is in many cases closely regulated by statute; and in addition Members are reminded of the terms of Statement of Insolvency Practice 11 "The Handling of Funds in Formal Insolvency Appointments". The Regulations deal rather with the handling of money prior to a formal Insolvency Appointment or where there is no such appointment.

5. Money held by a Firm as stakeholder is governed by the Regulations but the payment of interest provisions do not apply (Regulation 5.8).

6. Unless the Firm agrees otherwise in writing with a client (Regulation 6.1) a Client Bank Account must be an interest bearing account if 'material interest' would be likely to accrue within the meaning of Regulation 5.6. Any interest earned must in the absence of such agreement be accounted for to the Client in accordance with Regulation 5.7.

7. 'Material interest' shall be deemed to be likely to accrue if the sum of money is or is likely to be held for at least the number of weeks shown in the left hand column of the following table and the minimum balance in the Client Bank Account (or credited to the Client in the case of an account comprising the money of two or more Clients) equals or exceeds the corresponding sum in the right hand column of the Table:

Number of Weeks	Minimum Balance
8	£500
4	£1,000
2	£5,000
1	£10,000

The above is merely a guide to the interpretation of 'material interest'. The obligation of the Individual

Member is to take reasonable steps to ensure that the Client does not suffer material loss if money remains on bank accounts bearing low or no interest. There may be circumstances, for example, where money should be placed on overnight deposit.

7.5 IPA CONTINUING PROFESSIONAL EDUCATION GUIDANCE

Members are expected to take steps to ensure that they keep abreast of developments in statutory and case law, in professional practice and in the commercial environment relevant to the competent performance of insolvency administration.

CPE FOR AUTHORISATION APPLICANTS AND AUTHORISATION HOLDERS

Members applying for, or applying to renew, an authorisation to act as an insolvency practitioner (IP) are required to show that they have undertaken the minimum level of relevant structured continuing professional education (CPE) as a necessary part of becoming, and continuing to be, fit and proper to be an IP.

In addition, the Membership & Authorisation Committee may require an authorisation holder to undertake specific CPE, as part of or additional to the minimum CPE requirement.

MINIMUM LEVEL OF CPE

The minimum level of relevant structured CPE is 25 hours in the twelve months immediately preceding an application for, or to renew, an authorisation.

RELEVANCE OF CPE

CPE should be relevant to the work that the applicant undertakes or intends to undertake. Thus for example for an IP who acts or intends to act in relation to individual voluntary arrangements, the major part of CPE would be expected to cover personal insolvency including alternative non-statutory solutions in order that he/she should be able to advise debtors on all the options available to them or otherwise be able to satisfy him/herself that debtors have been so advised – that is, not limited to an IVA or bankruptcy. For an IP who specialises in liquidations and/or administrations, the major part of CPE would be expected to cover corporate insolvency; but a part would also be expected to cover personal insolvency to warrant an authorisation which enables him/her to undertake any of the insolvency procedures.

The IPA may require a member to provide further information about the relevance of particular parts of his/her CPE to the type and nature of the work which he/she undertakes or intends to undertake. For this purpose, members may find it useful to carry out their own analysis of their knowledge and skills for the work

July 2007

they undertake or intend to undertake, and what might be expected of them; and to identify CPE aimed at developing or filling gaps in that knowledge and those skills.

STRUCTURED CPE

Structured CPE will include:

- attending IPA Conferences and Members' Meetings.

Structured CPE may include:

- attending or speaking at courses, conferences, seminars and lectures
  - organised by the Association of Business Recovery Professionals (R3), other commercial course and conference providers, in-house or by other professionals or their firms
  - covering knowledge and application of technical and regulatory aspects of insolvency law and practice or
  - development of interpersonal, business and management skills and competences.

Structured CPE may also comprise where the subject matter is insolvency related:

- research and preparation of papers for courses, conferences or seminars, lectures or articles

- attendance at technical or regulatory committees

- reading material provided in advance of attendance at a structured CPE course, conference, seminar or lecture or technical or regulatory meeting.

Structured CPE may also comprise formal presentations, talks or discussions of insolvency related subjects at professional gatherings which may also be of a social nature.

Where members find it difficult, because of their geographical location, to attend sufficient courses, conferences, seminars and lectures without involving unreasonable time and cost, there may be scope to organise their own structured discussion group with fellow professionals in their locality which may count towards the minimum CPE requirement.

Members may use distance learning as readily accessed CPE also counting towards the minimum requirement: it should nevertheless be structured (by them). But given the value attached to, and achieved by, interaction and networkng with fellow professionals at courses, conferences, seminars and lectures, distance learning would be expected to account for no more than half the minimum CPE requirement; and it may be further restricted where the Membership & Authorisation Committee is of the view that the member should attend courses, conferences, lectures or seminars generally or in relation to specific aspects of insolvency.

The minimum level of relevant structured CPE is likely to need to be supplemented by for example reading professional journals, law reports and similar.

CALCULATION OF CPE HOURS

The actual time spent on CPE will usually be the appropriate amount. However, unless the circumstances are demonstrably different, the following would generally apply:

- full day course – 6 hours
- half-day course – 3 hours
- evening seminar/lecture – 1 hour

IPA One-Day Conferences are usually accredited for 6 hours CPE: IPA Members' Meetings are usually accredited for 2 hours CPE.

RECORDS OF CPE

Those applying for, or who have, an authorisation are required to maintain records of the CPE which they have undertaken; and should have available to produce to the IPA on request details and evidence of courses, conferences, seminars and lectures they have attended, including the topics covered, and of other CPE undertaken in relation to the last three years.

OTHER MEMBERS

Members who do not have or who do not intend applying for an authorisation are not required to undertake CPE. But if they are in any way involved in insolvency administration or insolvency related work, then it is very much in their own interests and those of their firm, creditors, insolvents and others who are affected by an insolvency that they should maintain a knowledge of current insolvency law and practice.

[Approved by Council: 19 July 2007]

IPA PANEL OF SOLICITORS

Requests from Members for technical/legal assistance may be referred to:

Stuart Frith, Partner, Restructuring & Insolvency
Stephenson Harwood LLP
1 Finsbury Circus, London, EC2M 7SH

Email: stuart.frith@shlegal.com
D: +44 (0)20 7809 2376
M: +44 (0)7970 686462

Kathryn Maclennan, Legal Director, Business Services Insolvency
Hill Dickinson LLP
50 Fountain Street, Manchester, M2 2AS

Email: Kathryn.Maclennan@hilldickinson.com
D: +44 (0)161 817 7213

Robert Paterson, Partner
Gowling WLG
4 More London Riverside, London, SE1 2AU

Email: Robert.paterson@wragge-law.com
D: +44 (0)20 7759 6674

Stewart Perry, Partner
Clyde & Co LLP
The St Botolph Building, 138 Houndsditch, London, EC3A 7AR

Email: stewart.perry@clydeco.com
D: +44 (0)20 7876 4338
M: +44 (0)7917 613055

Nick Pike, Partner, Restructuring & Insolvency
Pinsent Masons LLP
30 Crown Place, London, EC2A 4ES

Email: nicholas.pike@pinsentmasons.com
D: +44 (0) 20 7490 6469
M: +44 (0) 7973 176 826

Insolvency Practitioners Association

Valiant House
4-10 Heneage Lane
London
EC3A 5DQ
www.insolvency-practitioners.org.uk

Membership & Events	020 7623 5108
	membership@ipa.uk.com
Regulatory & Ethical Helpline:	020 7397 6407
Students, Examinations & Licensing:	020 7397 6400
Monitoring & Complaints:	020 7697 6430
	regulation@ipa.uk.com

The Insolvency Service

Head Office/ IP Regulation Section
The Insolvency Service
4th Floor, 4 Abbey Orchard Street
London, SW1P 2HT
www.bis.gov.uk/insolvency

0207 637 1110

IPRegulation.Section
@insolvency.gsi.gov.uk
Insolvency Enquiry Line:

Estate Accounts & Insolvency
Practitioner Services
3rd Floor, Cannon House
18 Priory Queensway
Birmingham, B4 6FD

0121 698 4000

EAIPS.EA.Enquiries
@insolvency.gsi.gov.uk
0300 678 0015
Redundancy Enquiry Line: 0330 331 0020

R3 Association of Business Recovery Professionals

8th Floor
120 Aldersgate Street
London
EC1A 4JQ
www.r3.org.uk

Switchboard:	020 7566 4200
Fax:	020 7566 4224
E-mail:	association@r3.org.uk

Insolvency forms for insolvency professionals

Lexis®Smart Forms

LexisNexis has worked with leading practitioners from the insolvency profession to produce standard forms that replace previously prescribed forms.

All insolvency forms, whether prescribed or not, are available as Smart Forms - LexisNexis's popular and time-saving, editable PDF packages.

For more information about the LexisSmart Insolvency forms
call **0330 161 1234**, and quote code **100238**
or visit **www.lexisnexis.co.uk/insolvencyforms**

The Future of Law. Since 1818.